George Sylvester Morris

British Thought and Thinkers

Introductory Studies

George Sylvester Morris

British Thought and Thinkers
Introductory Studies

ISBN/EAN: 9783337029654

Printed in Europe, USA, Canada, Australia, Japan

Cover: Foto ©Thomas Meinert / pixelio.de

More available books at **www.hansebooks.com**

BRITISH

THOUGHT AND THINKERS:

INTRODUCTORY STUDIES,

CRITICAL, BIOGRAPHICAL AND PHILOSOPHICAL.

By GEORGE S. MORRIS, A M.,

LECTURER ON PHILOSOPHY IN THE JOHNS HOPKINS UNIVERSITY, BALTIMORE;
TRANSLATOR OF UEBERWEG'S "HISTORY OF PHILOSOPHY," AND
ASSOCIATE OF THE VICTORIA INSTITUTE, LONDON.

CHICAGO:
S. C. GRIGGS AND COMPANY.
1880.

PREFACE.

THE first eleven chapters of this volume are founded, with slight changes (consisting mainly in amplification of the theoretical portions of chapters VII, IX and X), on "public lectures" recently delivered before a mixed audience of ladies and gentlemen at the Johns Hopkins University, Baltimore. Simultaneously with their delivery, another, more extended and technical, course, on the history of British speculation from Bacon to Spencer, was in progress, attended only by university students. To this course, the lectures here in substance reproduced were partly introductory, while in part they were intended to present a general summary of results reached and illustrated in more profuse detail in the special course.

From the foregoing statements the scope and purpose of this volume may be inferred. It is introductory, rather than exhaustive — an invitation to reflective and systematic study, rather than a substitute for it. At the same time, I hope, by the expression of deliberate and reasoned opinions, to have pointed the way to correct views concerning the essential nature and value of the most conspicuous current of abstract thought in the English language. I have not thought it needful to make radical changes in the style by which the material here employed was first adapted for use in the lecture-room. The large biographical element in more than half of the chapters will not be unwelcome to those who realize that a thinker's life is one of the indispensable keys to the due appreciation of his thought; and I cannot but confidently wish that some, through the allurements of biography, may be won over to the serious contemplation of the grand problems of philosophic thought and to a quickened sense, both of their dignity and of their absolute and vital import.

By the addition of a chapter on Herbert Spencer the main thought of the volume is followed out of the British past into the immediate present.

GEORGE S. MORRIS.

ANN ARBOR, MICH., September 14, 1880.

CONTENTS.

CHAPTER I.

	PAGE
INTRODUCTORY.—GENERAL PHILOSOPHICAL ATTITUDE OF THE ENGLISH MIND - - - - -	7

CHAPTER II.

MEDIÆVAL ANTICIPATIONS OF THE MODERN ENGLISH MIND.—JOHN OF SALISBURY, ROGER BACON, DUNS SCOTUS, WILLIAM OF OCCAM   -   -   -   -   30

CHAPTER III.

ENGLISHMEN OF THE RENAISSANCE.—EDMUND SPENSER, SIR JOHN DAVIES, RICHARD HOOKER   -   -   53

CHAPTER IV.

WILLIAM SHAKESPEARE — POET-PHILOSOPHER   -   -   80

CHAPTER V.

FRANCIS BACON   -   -   -   -   -   -   -   114

CHAPTER VI.
Thomas Hobbes - - - - - - - 141

CHAPTER VII.
John Locke - - - - - - - - 168

CHAPTER VIII.
George Berkeley - - - - - - 202

CHAPTER IX.
David Hume - - - - - - - 234

CHAPTER X.
Sir William Hamilton - - - - - 265

CHAPTER XI.
John Stuart Mill - - - - - - 302

CHAPTER XII.
Herbert Spencer - - - - - - 337

BRITISH THOUGHT AND THINKERS.

CHAPTER I.

INTRODUCTORY.

GENERAL PHILOSOPHICAL ATTITUDE OF THE ENGLISH MIND.

SCHOPENHAUER made a familiar thought famous by putting it in a simple but striking and epigrammatic form. *Die Welt ist meine Vorstellung,* said he. The world is for me an idea. It is a representation in my mind. To how many of us has not this thought occurred, with something of a dazing, dreamy effect, as we have mused on the complete dependence of our idea of the universe, or all that therein may be, on our own minds! I can remember how, as a mere boy, more than once, in an evening reverie, an experience somewhat in this vein came to me. All my boyish ideas of things seemed, as pure creations of my own fancy, to melt away, and there remained, as the whole sum and substance of the universe, only the abstract, but otherwise empty and uninstructive, and, by any law of sufficient reason, inexplicable, necessity of being, plus a dull, confused, and yet thoroughly unique, and for this reason indescribable, sensation, as of a chaos of shapeless elements, moving noiselessly among each other—a *plenum* of scarcely greater value than an absolute *vacuum*. Then came the return to what is termed the literal fact of experience, or, better, to the world such as, under the influence of a dawning mental activity, guided by sensitive experience and by instruction, it had actually shaped itself in my imagination — the earth, with its green fields and forest-covered mountains, the world-inhabited heavens, the changing seasons, man and his past history and unrevealed earthly destiny, not to mention the myriad little and familiar things which would necessarily crowd the foreground of such a picture in a boy's mind. The view which a moment before had demonstrated so signally its capability of dissolving, recovered its relative consistency and became again a slowly-changing panorama of *a* world, or of "*the* world," as it was for me. It was into such a conception of a world — a conception kaleidoscopic, apparently half arbitrary, half accidental — that I, following unwittingly a bent common to the universal mind of man, was more or less blindly seeking to introduce order and permanence. What must be? Why must anything be? Why must all things be? Such a rock of rational necessity as a successful answer to these questions would have furnished I was (though unconscious of the full significance of my striving) seeking, in order to arrest and fix the quicksands of a *Vorstellung*, or idea of the universe, of which I only knew (with Schopenhauer) that it was mine. I need hardly say that the immediate result of my reflections was tolerably negative. I have indicated, however, in the narration of this experience, the elements of a problem which presents itself to mankind in all climes and ages. It is, if I may so express it, to effectuate a sort of rational anatomy of existence, or, at least, of our ideas of it. The sea itself would not move in billowy motions if it had no fixed boundaries. The blood flows in tracks marked out in veins and arteries. The soft and yielding flesh adheres to a firm framework of bone. So man would find in his whole conception of things the skeleton of rational necessity, about which the multifarious or apparently fortuitous elements of that conception may group themselves, or the rather, by which the order of their grouping is determined. The "idea" which was but a changing picture in the imagination — a *representation* — must change to an idea which shall be a rational type, a self-evidencing law, an all-sufficient, all-explaining, all-necessitating reason. The varying and inexplicable element furnished in sense and sensuous imagination must crystallize in the majestic forms of eternal thought, of reason divine. It is this mental work which Goethe, in noble lines, attributes to the angels who constitute the "heavenly hosts." The gracious benediction and command which the Divine Being addresses to them runs thus:

"Das Werdende, das ewig wirkt und lebt,
Umfass' euch mit der Liebe holden Schranken,
Und was in schwankender Erscheinung schwebt,
Befestiget mit dauernden Gedanken!"
Prolog im Himmel: Faust.

Thus the world which was "my idea" (in Schopenhauer's phrase) is to be transformed, in its measure, into the image, or rather into a participation, of the divine idea of the world. The evanescent is to give way to the permanent. The passive reception of appearances is to give place to an active apprehension of realities.

I have thus stated, in outline, the grand and comprehensive motive which underlies all finite thought as such, and which therefore reveals itself, clearly or obscurely, in all the thought of man. It were easy to show, in detail, how it governs at once the systematic inquiries of philosophical speculation, the exact inquiries of physical science, and the freer intuitions of poetic fancy, as well as, also, the sober contemplations of history. Nor would it be more difficult to show that in this presupposed ideal of stable Truth — believed to be attainable for man: else why and how strive after it? — moral and æsthetic elements are intrinsically involved. But to attempt this here would be to go aside from the purpose of our present inquiry, as well as to repeat a labor already well performed by others. My object now is only to direct attention to the universally observable fact that men, finding themselves in, or in possession of, a mental world, which is at first (as regards their own *insight*) so largely, or exclusively, subjective, variable, phenomenal (and so, to use Kant's metaphor, like a restless ocean), believe in a continent of objective, stable Truth, think that they have glimpses of it, seek to approach it, and set up way-marks (in their literature and institutions) of their progress toward it, and by their notions (or knowledge) of it form their judgments as to the significance and value of human life and history, and of the physical universe itself. And it is through the different notions which the men, the thinkers, of an epoch, a race, a clime, a great nation, form and express concerning the geography of this continent, through the spiritual colors of which they profess to have caught glimpses, the maxims of hope, of conviction, or of despair, sorrowful, reckless, or even blasphemous, which they have inscribed upon the guide-posts set up by them; it is through all these, and through other signs flowing from, or otherwise necessarily connected with, these that the peculiar complexion, the special attitude or tendency of the thought of a particular epoch or nation is known and judged.

Or, to put the case otherwise, and at the same time to ward off the suggestion that this philosophical view of it is too remote from the actual state of some of the facts involved: is it not true that all literature, all art, all civil and social institutions, are, in their fundamental measure, like philosophy and science, interpretative and explanatory? Does not the epic poet, who sings of human deeds, weave all the elements of his story into one high *argument*, whether of fate, free-will, or providence? and is it not the argument, binding the isolated, transient deeds of heroes and tribes in the network of an organic, rational whole, merging the individual in the universal, the accidental in the necessary, by which both the singer and his hearers are rapt? Does not the tragic poet perform a like function on the stage? Even the lyric poet, when he bodies forth some feeling of the breast within, passes judgment upon the feeling, *i.e.* he assigns to it a definite value; he explains it by putting it into relation to something other and deeper than itself; and this he does, if not in so many formal words, yet in the very form and color of his utterance. The true artist is at once nature's critic and interpreter. The wise law-giver is the critic and interpreter of human nature. Each looks beneath the surface. Each is a diviner. Each exhibits a law or type extracted from the heart of the nature of things or of man, that nature's veriest self, its true self, at all events a standard whereby the unworthiness or inadequacy of the ideas contained in our accidental, every-day, consciousness is condemned or corrected; a light which reveals the world and life in profundities of meaning, or in a brilliancy of coloring previously unknown.

Man is mind, is spirit, and all of the products of these his characteristically spiritual, *i.e.* human activities, including his religious faiths and convictions (not previously mentioned), imply an order of explanations pointing beyond the mere or first *Vorstellung*, or impression, to a somewhat by which first impressions are corrected, to norms of truth and judgment independent of subjective or purely individual prepossessions. They all more or less completely refer the seen to the unseen, or to that which at first is not seen. They would have sight yield to insight. To the truth of this statement even materialistic explanations (so far as they are professedly systematic or philosophical) form no exception; for they all agree in finding the ultimate element or ground of reality in the invisible atom.

By all that has gone before I have simply been setting forth familiar signs and products of the idealism innate in the universal mind of man. Nay, rather, why do I not say, without qualification, the idealism which is innate in Mind, the universal source and "king of being"; of which latter, man, being in his essence an express and conscious participant, of necessity shares in the former. So putting the case, I make it more evident that the idealism of human nature is no accident, but a constituent and necessary element of human nature; nay, more, is that which essentially constitutes it. For how should Mind not have faith in itself? — and Idealism is just this faith. How should Mind not know itself? — and Idealism is just this knowledge. Further, Mind is conscious intelligence. Intelligence is an active function, not simply a passive possession; strictly passive, it were no longer intelligence, for then, inactive, it would not have intelligence of itself. Still further, intelligence is only of the intelligible. Reason apprehends only what is rational. Mind, therefore, can comprehend no world which is not permeated with its own attributes; the absolutely unintelligible, irrational, being inconceivable and hence utterly incapable of being brought into relation to mind, is for it no better than the non-existent. Mind seeks itself therefore in the universe, chiefly in forms of law, order, purpose, beauty. It must reduce its conception of the universe, given first in the form of isolated, unexplained impressions, to the order and harmony of a rational, and hence explicable, apprehensible whole. And this search, this necessity, of Mind, again, precisely is idealism. Finally, and most characteristically of all, man seeks and finds himself only in the realization of an ideal, the Idea of Man, as perfected in truth, goodness, and love. He is therefore thus, and immediately, in proportion to the perfection of his manhood, a living text and lesson of Idealism.

Such is the law, such is the universal tendency, such is the inherent necessity of Mind. The exceptions are purely apparent, phenomenal. For knowing mind all reality is ideal, either strictly and intrinsically, or at least functionally and typically. Of the whole import of this truth few are fully conscious. Some expressly deny it *in terms*. Millions ignorantly or wantonly crucify it. And yet, though the thought of brief epochs, or of certain individuals or classes of individuals, may have borne formal but false witness against it, the exception thus apparently constituted is far from sufficient to invalidate the universal law: all the great literatures of the world, the thought of every nation which has been a grand power in the history of civilization, has been deeply, and from the very necessity of the case, idealistic.

In considering the question concerning the peculiar direction of any particular nation's thought, the only question, from this point of view, can be, whether the idealistic tendency is more or less marked and intense — not whether it be present or absent.

But, as has been seen, the idealism of man crops out in different forms of intellectual activity and productivity, as in literature and religion, art and society and government. Moreover, it is characterized in different cases by unessential but interesting differences, according as it is peculiarly attracted in the several cases by various forms or signs of the ideal, such as law, fitness of adaptation, goodness, order, beauty. Thus among the Romans we find a peculiar reverence for law, among the Greeks a passionate love of the beauty of limit and proportion, and among the Hebrews a regard for moral goodness or righteousness. Or, again, the idealism of which we speak may be specially characterized by the degree and manner in which the ideal, regarded as the power and substance of reality, is conceived. It may be referred, in the consecrated language of a revealed and accepted religion, immediately to the power of God, with no attempt to understand or to render rationally intelligible how God is its author. Or its reality — the truth of the dogma that it alone has reality, and that even in the most lifeless stone the measure of reality is proportioned to the ideality typically or intrinsically present — may be perceived, admitted, enforced, without attention to the fact that the ideality is inexplicable apart from living personal mind as its cause and constant supporter. Then we have the various forms of philosophical hybridism — pantheism in its protean forms, intellectual naturalism, certain phases of mysticism, doctrines of an impersonal idea, an unconscious but ideal something, underlying or accounting for the world. These are illustrated in certain Oriental phases of thought and imagination, which also have their notable analoga in the history of European philosophy, ancient and modern. They mark a certain logical incompleteness in thought, and infect, in a measure, the speculations of some who would utterly reject the mystical pantheism to which they conduct. (I have elsewhere pointed out how this is true of Aristotle's physical conceptions, in *The Theory of Unconscious Intelligence as opposed to Theism.* London, 1876, pp. 6-8.) These views easily lend themselves to poetic treatment, and are very common in the poetic literature of ancient and modern times. Finally, the ideal, considered as present throughout the universe, the source of its intelligibility and the very essence of its reality, may be clearly and consistently grasped as itself inexplicable and absurd unless viewed as the direct expression of living, personal mind. Man has no exact conception of an *idea* apart from a mind which possesses it. He cannot conceive rationality except as the attribute and living function of a mind or spirit. The rationality found in nature is therefore an *absurdum* unless viewed as the direct or indirect effect and function of self-conscious spirit. The idealism (in theory) which holds fast to these axioms, acknowledges God, whose rational power and wisdom it detects in all things. Mind, which can only be conceived as living and conscious and, in its perfection, as rooted and acting in forms of truth and goodness, love and beauty, becomes, for this theistic idealism, the acknowledged and self-evident king of the universe. And so man, in his humble way, is brought into direct and sympathetic relation with the universal, all-pervading, all-explaining Power. The theoretical expression of *this* idealism may be in terms identical with the language of a monotheistic religion, the only difference being that he who affirms the former must do so on the ground of an explicit philosophical conviction, while the latter may be simply accepted without this conviction, but on other more or less good and sufficient grounds.

I say, then, that the question as to the peculiar complexion or tendency of a nation's thought is a question as to the peculiar stripe of its idealism. A materialistic habit of thought is not native to the human or to any other full-grown mind, for mind is simply deceived when it thinks it sees and understands in or concerning matter anything but the reflection (however dim) of its own perfections. Further, a nation's, like an individual's, thought is judged by the conceptions current in it concerning the world, life, and man. Without the interest, perennial, inexhaustible, which attaches to such conceptions, imagination itself would lose its glow, and the subtler hues of thought and feeling would become fitful, fatuous, unmeaning, or rather would sink into a dull and leaden monotone of lifeless color. Nor does it make matters any clearer — the rather it confuses them — to disguise, or seek to disguise, the fact, that the questions which revolve about these conceptions are strictly philosophical ones, and that every characteristically spiritual activity of man, in its products in literature, art, polity, social organism, civilization, strictly imply, and in their measure exhibit, a *philosophy* of human life and of the whole universe of human thought or knowledge. At the same time I scarcely need to say that the individual men, or even nations, in whose thought and works the foregoing truths are illustrated, may have no definite consciousness of the fact that they are virtually philosophizing. They may even feel and profess a decided repugnance to philosophical speculation, strictly and technically so called.

Precisely this is the case with the English mind, whose first and most prominent characteristic may perhaps be described as consisting in this, namely, that its interest is far more concentrated upon the vital and practical side of truth than upon the abstract or theoretical side. Truth, in its living, effective power, so absorbs its attention that little care is left for inquiries concerning its ultimate grounds and guarantees, or for laborious exactness in the statement of it. Possession is nine-tenths of the law. The English nation possess genuine character. Character is vitalized truth. In their national character the English possess a body of such truth, in the power and through the inspiration of which they have been enabled to work out (during a period of 1200 years) an historical destiny of the most honorable and glorious kind. Faith in this truth is faith in themselves. To relinquish it would be moral suicide — to doubt of it, moral treason. Its warrant is found in its historic power, in its present vitality. This truth the English possess, or perhaps it were truer to say that it possesses them; and possession, I repeat, is nine-tenths of the law. Under these circumstances inquiry concerning the remaining one-tenth, the validity of the title by which possession is held, may naturally appear to a "practical people" idle, and almost frivolous.

The only other nation known to Occidental history, which has possessed anything like so palpable and consistent a character as the English, namely the Romans, in like manner, and even in a more marked degree, were remarkable for their almost absolute neglect of abstract speculation. Their old-fashioned reverence for law and duty, and their self-respect, were ideal forces which wrought in them and through them, and fitted them for the rough and solid work of world-subjugation. No wonder that they felt a greater interest in the practical solution of living, flesh-and-blood problems, which the progress of events forced upon them, than in their theoretical explanation. If the ideal, which is the only essential side of human nature, has a really sustaining support and source of constant nourishment in a sterling national character, it is by no means an obviously superficial question to ask why human nature should bother itself continually about such subtilties as the ultimate constitution and ground of existence, the abstract conditions and laws of perfect humanity, the sources of moral obligation, the meaning of beauty's charms, the intrinsic value of human life. Certainly, to err through neglect of such matters, for such a reason — and not, for example, like the Spaniards of the last two centuries, by reason of mental indolence and effeminacy — is a noble error. Such error, you may say, is the sign of a peculiar *naïveté*. It marks a nature so complete in itself, a nature which finds such reason to be satisfied with itself, that it never occurs to it to ask further questions. Granted; but genuine *naïveté*, if a mark of relative childhood in understanding, is also a mark of fresh and harmonious wholeness, and that relative *naïveté*, which comes from an obstinate shutting of the eyes in certain directions, may produce a similar effect. Certain it is that this happy, unbroken wholeness (if not completeness) of the English character has naturally extorted the admiration of other nations, in whom the harmony, or harmonious correspondence, between inward thought and aspiration, and material and historical condition, is, or has been, far less perfect than in the case of the English. Heine, in a well known epigram, ascribed to the English the empire of the sea, to the French the empire of the land, and to the Germans the empire of the air. The "sea," which the English rule, we will interpret as the whole ocean of concrete existence, moral and physical. The "land," of the French rule, shall denote the clear and exact (though incomplete) analysis of ideas. (Compare Taine, *Art en Italie*, 1866, pp. 18, 19.) The "air" in which the Germans are at home will then be the region of ideal speculation, of ultimate causes and reasons. Now, if the criterion of a valuable existence be placed in its historic εὐδαιμονία, or "fortunateness," how much more fortunate has not the English people been than the French or German! The French, exercising their analytic talent, formed very definite, sharp-cut ideas of the rights of man; but sought with hopeless, unintelligent energy, through, one might almost say, dozens of revolutions, to give them practical realization. The Germans, with unsurpassed penetration and comprehension,—as of the problems of universal existence in general, so of the grounds and elements and worth of an organized political life in particular,—yet presented till recently the most lamentable spectacle of national disintegration and impotence. From this point of view one easily appreciates the force of an utterance like the following, on the part of a German, writing twenty years ago (Emil Feuerlein, *Philos. Sittenlehre, in ihren gesch. Hauptformen.* 2. Theil, p. 9, Tübingen, 1859). "Naïve in the nobler sense," says this writer, "appear to him who becomes acquainted with a man like the Englishman in his home and in his vocation, those marks of a solid, pithy, morally undissevered nature, the breath of which a stranger feels in the whole English atmosphere. Has no German in this air ever felt as though, through the vision of a moral force so in harmony with itself, he might and would gladly be healed from his own [moral and political] disunity and dismemberment, and in the enjoyment of this more natural world be restored to inward soundness?" It is no wonder that in the midst of all the aspirations and agitations and revolutions through which the continental nations of Europe, during the last century, have sought to improve their political condition, the example of England — its constitution, its vigorous, self-poised life, its *character* — has been the sometimes unacknowledged but, more frequently, openly avowed guiding-star. Such an example is a veritable inspiration, since it is the outcome of ideal forces — the only real ones and the only ones that can act upon man. These forces are, in this case, conscious self-knowledge, self-restraint and self-assertion, the first conditions of strictly human life, whether in individual or in nation.

Yet let no one, from the facts now presented, draw an

over-hasty conclusion as to the uselessness of such thorough mental work as the Germans have done and as the conception of philosophy universally contemplates. Germany, as a nation, appears to-day in quite another light than that which surrounded it twenty years ago. And he is a sorry and short-sighted seer who does not discover the first and final cause of its recent remarkable exhibition of concentrated moral and physical power in the intellectual and moral *Gedanken-arbeit*, or travail of thought, which has been going on in German climes for the last two hundred years. During all this time the Germans have been making their character. In an eminent sense this character is their creation, and hence, by an indefeasible title, their possession. It now bears its fruit, shows its power. And history has yet to show whether such a character, and the commanding power which results from it, are not more inalienable and indestructible than a character which, as in the case of the Romans and English, is, largely, simply accepted as a natural, but otherwise inexplicable, gift — in a measurable degree an accidental and unconscious, rather than a conscious, possession. Theoretically considered, there can be no doubt that it is to the former that the inheritance of the earth in the long run, by inherent rational necessity, belongs. Were it not that I perceive in the history of English thought and in the English mind the signs and elements of a far more than ordinary purely intellectual and moral vitality, I should, for one, certainly look for a far less glorious future for the empire of English thought, and consequently for English power and influence in general, than I now anticipate.

If the record of the English, namely, in the history

of philosophy proper, is not a shining one, if, indeed, they have no properly national philosophy at all which can be called either deeply and thoroughly or even brilliantly reasoned, yet they have solid endowments, which have been influential, and in some directions splendid, in their past fruit, and which are quite sufficient to justify substantial hopeful expectations for the future. The strong or marked sides of the English mind are three, the religious, the scientific and the poetic. Religion and science, in different ways, furnish problems to philosophy. The poetic faculty, the power of creative imagination, is the pledge of speculative ability.

On the religious side the English share with their Teutonic ancestors and neighbors in a certain depth and sincerity of spirit, which is opposed to all sham, is never long satisfied with mere appearance, admits no separation of substance from form, and demands, along with a formal assent to the doctrines proposed to faith, an inward experience of the power of truth, accompanied by appropriate works. In other words, the English are genuinely religious. This appears throughout their whole history. The tone of aspiration, of adoration, of deep, sometimes fierce, religious earnestness, which is struck in what Mr. Stopford Brooke terms the "first true English poem," the poem of Caedmon, reappears in all the critical epochs of the development of English life, and has thoroughly permeated English manners and literature. The key-note of the Reformation was struck in England in the fourteenth century, and no nation has been more tenacious in maintaining its fruits than the English. But, it need not be said, a genuine religious spirit is necessarily idealistic. It carries with it the habit of referring actions to moral standards of judgment, of seeing in events a providential agency, of regarding the universe as an outcome of the divine will and in some sense a constant manifestation of divine reason. Only, in the matter of religion, the intensely practical attitude of the English, their sense, perhaps, of the substance of religion as a vital element absolutely essential to individual and national life, and as something already safely in their grasp, in their possession, seems to me to render them impatient of inquiries relative to the ultimate warrant of faith. The immediate, practical warrant of religious faith may indeed be found in vital experience and in historic power. Such a faith is not to be stigmatized as absolutely blind and unreasonable. Yet it is far short of *insight*. It is not faith resting on and illuminated by intelligence. If reasonable, it is not wholly rational. It implies a childhood in understanding, against which the Apostle of Christianity to the Gentiles utters an express warning. A consequence of the religious attitude of the English mind to which I am now referring is, or has often been, a disposition to cut short inquiry and to cleave knots of difficulty with the oracular utterance, "Thus it is written,"—forgetting that, legitimate as this course may be under given circumstances, it cannot always be pursued without inducing a fatal bondage to the letter "which killeth," in distinction from the spirit, which, illuminating and giving sight, also "giveth life." This is, in its measure, precisely such a substitution of mechanism for intelligence and life as, in other fields of explanation, English science-philosophy has sought to effectuate. Another and a related consequence of the same mental attitude has been a disposition to restrict the sphere of human reason by emphasizing the existence of a sphere of mysterious and essentially unintelligible truth, somehow made known to man in terms, but for the rest only to be unquestioningly received by him as an unconditional prerequisite for the restoration and preservation of his soul's health. This is, considered *in se*, no better than the old attempts to attract or exorcise spirits, good or bad, by pronouncing a series of unmeaning syllables. But, then, here again a distinction is to be made. The body cannot flourish unless certain physiological processes are executed in it, which we may not understand, but in which, would we live, we must have sufficient faith to supply—by appropriate eating and drinking, for example—the conditions necessary to their due and normal progress. In like manner, spiritual life and moral health cannot exist without obedience from a sense of duty to laws and principles, the whole import and rationality of which we may not yet be prepared to perceive or appreciate. But, just as, in the former case, men might have had from the beginning a reasonable confidence that every fact of the physiological process was essentially, not mysterious, but explicable, so in matters pertaining to the spiritual life of man in religion it is in vain that you say to him, "This and that formula you must accept as an accurate statement of the facts, laws and principles (or some of them) concerned, but neither you nor I, nor those who come after us, can ever expect to be able to render such an account of them as shall satisfy the reason and intelligence of man." Yet this is just what the English mind, through the mouth (for instance) of such a typical and genuine representative of it as Francis

Bacon, as well as through others (to be mentioned in the following chapters), has presumed to declare as final truth. It is on spiritual and moral inquiries, according to Bacon, that God has pronounced a curse, upon which therefore man should only venture very daintily, if indeed at all, to enter. The appropriate field of knowledge for man is physical nature, *i.e.* the realm of things which "do appear" to man in sensible experience. Bacon's attitude well illustrates the manner in which English theology and English science, in their philosophical negativism, extend the hand to each other. The same thing is illustrated in a more developed form in recent phases of religious and "scientific" philosophy in England. Thus, we find, on the one hand, Dean Mansell, as the representative of the religious side, after the precedent set by Bishop Peter Browne, in the eighteenth century, and still others before him, and with philosophical weapons borrowed, through Sir William Hamilton, from Kant, proving the utter disparateness of the divine spirit and the spirit of man, and of the ways of God and man's ways, so that the former are for human reason absolutely incognoscible. And, on the scientific side, we have Mr. Herbert Spencer, as the lineal descendant of the more renowned British philosophizers and as the accredited mouth-piece of the philosophizing science of to-day, quoting Mansell with delighted approval in support of the (gratuitous) conclusions which the scientific (in distinction from the philosophical) method, applied to specifically philosophical problems, necessarily and naturally arrives at, namely, that these problems are inherently insoluble for man. The phenomenal, sensibly observable, is, it is held, (relatively) knowable; the real is absolutely unknowable. The true philosophy is to have no philosophy, to deny the possibility of philosophy, or else to term by that magnificent name the broadest generalizations and the negations of physical science.

But this *"asylum ignorantiae"* does not satisfy all Englishmen. There be those that would comprehend and explain. Only, that intellectual *naïveté*—or, shall I say, a certain insular *Bornirtheit*, or contractedness?—with which we have already met in our analysis of certain sides of the English mind, seems here again to intervene between volition and execution. Here, in the attempted explanation of God's relation to the world, data of sense are apt to be uncritically adopted as data of ultimate fact, truth, reality, and consequently to be introduced with absolutely confusing effect into the lofty problems of religious philosophy. Religious controversialists persist obstinately in not accepting practically all that is implied in a text which for them should be authoritative, and which declares explicitly that the explanation of the apparent is to be found in the non-apparent, of the sensible, in the intelligible. Hence a proneness to tarry among, and expatiate in, logical distinctions and analogies which lie on the surface, and are addressed to sense and the analytic understanding, rather than to penetrate with the power of comprehensive, synthetic, vital reason into the very heart and center of the questions involved.

On the whole, both in religion and in science, I think we may say with obvious truth that the characteristic disposition of the English mind is to lay hold upon alleged revealed or natural laws of fact, in their immediate, practical relation to the life and interests of men, and as narrowly observable in detail with the microscopic vision of sense. With this goes a tendency to neglect that more comprehensive and penetrative mental labor which traces the rational connection of all law with its birthplace in the mind and will of an Absolute Spirit. Religion and Science (by which latter I understand all results of the application of the mathematico-mechanical method, or all systematic knowledge of *phenomena*) occupy, on the whole, exclusively the theoretical interests of the English mind. Philosophy (stigmatized often as metaphysical jargon) is their common waste-basket. (I shall have more fitting occasion hereafter to examine and characterize more in detail the scientific attitude of the English mind.)

This, however, is only one, and that the least inspiring, half of our picture. Along with and in spite of this — to a philosophic mind — exasperating self-limitation and self-obfuscation of the English upon those lines of theoretical inquiry which would lead directly to philosophy, we find that this nation possesses, in the language of a German historian, "a preëminent gift for poetry, perhaps the most perfect that has ever fallen to the lot of any people." And this poetic gift is not a mere talent, it is real genius. It is not satisfied with pleasing outward forms and tones alone. It is all-penetrating. It ranges over the whole scale of the heart's emotions. It does not shrink back from any flights of intellect. For it nature is peaceful and gay, or wild and darkly significant. With it human life is an idyl, or more frequently a drama, in which invisible powers are the actors. Human life is a theater of actions heroic, comical or tragic, or the portal to an

"Undiscovered country, from whose bourn
No traveller returns,"

and from which, it is fully recognized, no just soul would fain return. "Among all the nations which participate in our modern civilization," says, further, the author above quoted, "the classical nation in poetry is the English."

Now I have spoken above of the poetic faculty of the English, their power of creative imagination, as the pledge of their speculative ability. And indeed the close relation between poetic and philosophic endowment has long been recognized — since Plato's time, for example, before whom it had been amply illustrated in notable instances. The difference between the poet and the philosopher is one of system and of systematic intelligence, rather than of inspiration. The leading interpreters, even of scientific method, among the English of to-day recognize the essential necessity of a certain poetic gift, a "scientific imagination," as it is called, for the purposes of scientific discovery. In the British poets, accordingly, we find the best British philosophy. What English moralist, for example, is equal to William Shakespeare, who is not only the real historian of the modern mind (an office which of itself implies profound philosophic insight), but also, in the language of the title-page of a recent German publication, "*der Philosoph der sittlichen Weltordnung*," "the philosopher of the moral order of the world"? What professed English philosopher has possessed so profound an appreciation of the idealistic philosophy of nature as Wordsworth? What religious philosopher in England has approached the subtlest problems of religious thought with more sympathetic and discerning insight than Coleridge? What living English thinker has fathomed in well-reasoned, systematic prose the dark questions of theodicy, and illumined them more brilliantly with the light of rational faith and insight, than Tennyson? Not to mention many others, whose poetic flights have been ballasted with solid weights of thought.

Can it be, now, that a real philosophic talent, thus attested, may not be expected sooner or later to manifest itself in the forms of thoroughly reasoned speculation? I cannot so believe. Under the influence of German precedents, I think I see developing to-day signs, and very promising ones, of a movement which may in its final developments realize our hopeful expectations for a more brilliant future of English philosophy. Yet it were perhaps wiser to leave to history the passing of judgments for which she alone is competent. For a like reason it were doubtless better to omit speculations concerning possible modifications of English thought which may result from the wide enlargement of the empire of the English tongue, although from this point of view it were not difficult to formulate grounds of hope.

CHAPTER II.

MEDIÆVAL ANTICIPATIONS OF THE MODERN ENGLISH MIND.

> "Es ist ein gross Ergötzen
> Sich in den Geist der Zeiten zu versetzen,
> Zu schauen, wie vor uns ein weiser Mann gedacht,
> Und wie wir's dann zuletzt so herrlich weit gebracht."
> Gœthe's Faust: Scene I.

> "A great delight is granted
> When, in the spirit of the ages planted,
> We mark how, ere our time, a sage has thought,
> And then, how far his work, and grandly, we have brought."
> Taylor's translation.

IN these words of the pedant, Faust's companion, taken apart from the irony and stern criticism with which Faust, in the next following lines, rebukes the spirit in which they are uttered, we may find an apt text for some of the contemplations which now lie immediately before us. The thoughts which, in this view, I would especially connect with them, concern (1) the fascination there is for us moderns, when, with fresh, humane sympathies, we are enabled to reproduce in imagination the lives and thoughts of our ancestors, appreciating the things which gave them joy and sorrow, with intelligent charity for their errors, and generous recognition of their successes, and, above all, with such a quickened sense of the oneness of their humanity with our own, that we see in them ourselves in their circumstances; and (2) the continuity of intellectual types, the fixity of national intellectual species, as established in the present case by the comparison of a few representative Englishmen of the time of the schoolmen with what we already know of the prevailing tendencies of the English mind.

We are apt to look down and back with an air of lordly contempt upon what is termed the scholastic period in the history of European thought, with about as much, or rather as little, intelligence, as if we were in the period of manhood to despise the memories of youth. A race, a civilization, must have its time of schooling as well as an individual. And during this time it will naturally exhibit the same ineptitudes, weaknesses, follies, but also the same bright prophecies of hope, which are discernible in "the growing boy." Nay, more, we shall perhaps find, on closer inspection, that, like the boy, it, too, "still is nature's priest,

> And by the vision splendid
> Is on its way attended";

the vision, namely, of realities, which we, for the very atomic dustiness of our perfected worldly wisdom, are unable to see, or, from the loss of our boyish simplicity, are ashamed to confess.

The scholastic period was the early schooltime of our Occidental christian civilization. Christendom, especially in central and northern Europe, had then but recently emerged from heathendom; and even on the ground of the ancient pagan civilizations it had, on the one hand, sprung up at an epoch when these civilizations had already decayed, or were decaying, and leaving no natural heir behind them, and when, on the other, the necessities of its own existence forced it, in the greatest measure, to break off the line of tradition, which might otherwise have preserved for it not only the elements, but the riches, of ancient culture. The Occidental mind was then like an overgrown, undisciplined boy, such as all savages are said, as a rule, to be. The first condition of its future mastership was, then, that it should itself be mastered. It could learn to rule both itself and others only by first undergoing a suitable and prolonged training in regulated obedience. Such training the church, as a central authority, through the schools, as its instruments, furnished, and it were no less irrational than ungrateful to ignore, or pretend to ignore, the service to civilization thus rendered. Yet it was with scholasticism as with all schools. Those who had (through their ancestors) received its benefits, first celebrated their release from its restraints by hurling at it their manly anathemas, very much as the boy, when the period of his youthful schooling is over, is apt to turn his back on the scene of his scholastic discipline, and on his teachers, with the exclamation "Good bye, old school! you can't rule me any longer." So, in the time of the Renaissance, when, through the restoration of ancient letters and learning, the modern mind leaped forward out of the period of youthful guardianship into the confident glow of dawning manhood, scholasticism was dismissed with contemptuous and otherwise forcible maledictions, in utter forgetfulness of the circumstance that, but for its previous scholastic discipline, the Renaissance mind would have been utterly unfitted to expatiate with such intelligent rapture in the new fields of thought and learning finally opened up to it. For this injustice some reparation has of late years, under the lead, especially, of Continental scholars, been made. Of intellectual maturity, of ripe wisdom, I suppose there is no more certain mark than a tolerant catholicity. An earlier and inferior stage of intellectual development has its inherent necessity, its relative or historic justification. It is not the part of wisdom to begin by attempting to kick it all over and to annihilate it, with a view of beginning absolutely *de novo*. No such break of continuity is possible. The past is to be corrected, if need be, and supplemented: it cannot be overthrown. On the other hand, it is not to be worshipped. Any attempt to perpetuate its dominion by holding the mind of man back to methods and points of view which have no longer any (or, at most, only a subordinate) *raison d'être*, is no less unreasonable and imbecile than is ignorant contempt.

Now if with unprejudiced minds and at least so much of sympathetic spirit as the Roman poet possessed, who could consider nothing pertaining to man as foreign to himself,—if, I say, with such mind and spirit, we look at scholasticism in itself, in its historic setting, and in the vital interests which were felt to be concerned in it, we shall surely discover about it somewhat of that imperishable charm which is never wanting where human hearts throb and human brains are active. As to its historic setting, scholasticism is a part or appurtenance of mediævalism. And what a picture does not this word suggest to the instructed and appreciative mind! Castles with dungeons and towers and lordly halls, knightly lords and ladies, esquires, pages and faithful vassals, chivalrous votaries of love, more valiant than intelligent defenders of religion, grave and yet spirited bearers of secular responsibilities; burghers and tradesmen with guilds and banners, singing-schools, and fisting-schools, and peasants, hard-pressed, no doubt, and over-worked and brutalized, yet still, in their degradation, retaining sparks of imagination kept aglow by tales of fairies and hobgoblins, quickened symbols of their hopes and joys, or of their dreads. In general, the old pagan imagination, or its lineal descendant, interfused with christian story and imperfectly regulated by christian dogma. No wonder that the European literature of the last century, in those developments to which the name "Romantic" is applied, has found a fruitful and lively source of inspiration, in distinction from classic themes and motives, in mediæval legend and story. Sense and imagination, the gayest and the darkest colors side by side, a sort of right of might, tempered more by sentiment than by reason, these make up the most obvious side of mediæval life, in which to-day the poetic fancy finds delight. In such a scene as this the scholastic doctor appears, in the gray and sombre, or, at best, neutral tints of the friar's garb. The earth is still the centre of the universe, and its surface is imagined to extend but little beyond Christendom. And of Christendom the scholastic doctor, surnamed "angelic," "irrefragable," "invincible," etc., as the case may be, is reputed to carry the brain. The professed and accredited exponent and expounder of the christian graces, he is also robed in the imperial purple of learning and of thought. The young men and strong run by thousands together to listen to his eloquent words, to wonder at his subtle distinctions, and to admire and appropriate his wisdom, or that of his master, the pagan christian, Aristotle (*precursor Christi in naturalibus*).

As at once the messenger of God, and the "tamer" and interpreter of human reason, his person and office are held sacred by all; except, indeed, in those rare cases in which he is deemed to have transgressed limits imposed by the church or his order. He is the representative of intellectual power, and as such receives the respect and reverence which are always granted to such power. By virtue of its very real authority, William of Occam could say to Ludwig of Bavaria, "Defend me with thy sword, and I will defend thee with the [no less mighty] pen." Scholasticism was in some sense the balance-wheel of mediæval life. It was the pilot, in its time, of modern civilization, storm-tossed in the ship Church, and when it had guided it to the port of modern life and thought, its office having ceased, it naturally disappeared from view.

Now scholasticism, like the church, its mistress, knew no barriers of language, of political or national separation, within its geographical boundaries. Within the embrace of the church all of European Christendom was one fold, with one language, the Latin, consecrated to religion and discussion, and with substantial homogeneity of intellectual interests. The great schools of Italy, Spain, France, England, were frequented freely, and in immense numbers, by students from all countries. The eminent scholastic doctors were equally Italian, French, English, or of any other christian nationality. England, or the British Isles, sent out its full quota of generals and soldiers into the army of scholasticism. Of the former I need only mention John Scotus Erigena, of Scotch-Irish extraction, whose place is in the very front rank of scholastic philosophers for profundity and acuteness, as he is the first important one in point of time (about 800-877); John of Salisbury; Alexander of Hales, "*Doctor Irrefragabilis,*" whose *Summa Theologiae* marks a leading turning-point in the history of scholasticism; Duns Scotus, the "subtle doctor," founder of one of the two most influential schools of later scholastic thought; Roger Bacon, according to many, the greater predecessor of his more illustrious and fortunate namesake, Francis Bacon; and William of Occam, "*Doctor Invincibilis,*" "*Inceptor venerabilis,*" the "inceptor," namely, in the early part of the fourteenth century, of a doctrine which was the death-warrant of the scholastic philosophy. And what I would urge is, that if you consider among these schoolmen those who were strictly English, you find in them already distinct evidences of that type or direction of thought which in the last two hundred and fifty years has become so pronounced a characteristic of the English mind.

The leading traits of this type may be enumerated (summing up our last chapter) as follows: (1) Subordination of theory to practice; (2) Profession of agnosticism or scepticism respecting ultimate philosophical questions; and, (3) Zealous cultivation of physical science as a thing of palpable, demonstrative, and practical certainty and utility.

Consider for a moment John of Salisbury. Living in the twelfth century, a man of scholarly tastes, he devotes himself, by preference, to the study of so much as was then known of the classic literature of antiquity, Cicero being his favorite author. The influence of these studies on his own Latin style was such that he has received frequent and high praise for his elegant diction. An earnest churchman and sincere believer, he is yet, as a practical Englishman, more concerned with the external political relations of the church than with those subtle and, in his view, comparatively nugatory discussions regarding questions of doctrine, of faith and philosophy, which were going on in the church's schools. What thoughtful student will not recognize, with some inclination to indulge in an innocent smile, the characteristic philosophical *naïveté* and practical, moral, earnestness of the British mind in the following historical statement from Ueberweg? "In opposition to the fruitless contentions of the schools, John lays great stress on the '*utile*', and on whatever furthers moral progress." A practical farmer might occupy this position, and it would excite no remark. We should recognize appreciatively the moral worth of the man, and quietly ignore any depreciatory utterances of his concerning the value or importance of matters which he was in no condition to understand or prosecute. But, on the part of a cultivated man of letters, of philosophy, and of religion! However, we must not push this line of critical observation too far. Likely enough the scholastic contentions of John of Salisbury's day did and could not but seem not only "fruitless" but tasteless enough to a person possessing a marked degree of refined taste, and not endowed with the power of speculative insight and comprehension. The important thing for us to notice about John is that, like the members of the Academic school, of whom Cicero could inform him, he, too, held that all inquiries directed to the speculative attainment of absolute truth must be, from the nature of things, unavailing. The true *utile* for man lay in faith. And, on the other hand, beyond faith we could not get through the use of our intellectual faculties; nay, we could not thus even attain to faith, but only, at best, to probable opinion.

A more striking and personally interesting figure is that of Roger Bacon. Born in the year 1214, near Ilchester, in Somersetshire, his life extends through nearly the whole of the classic century of scholasticism. And yet, though a student and teacher in the schools, wearing the dress of a Franciscan monk, and acknowledging, with the rest of his contemporaries, the supremacy of the interests of faith (as including those of religion and morality, and hence of perfected and successful manhood itself), his image stands out in picturesque and impressive contrast with the intellectual life of his time. As a student at Oxford and Paris his commanding mental qualities obtained early recognition. He was the critic of his teachers, not a merely passive recipient of their knowledge. The genuine and the palpable could alone content him. First, what do the acknowledged authorities for our faith and knowledge, the Hebrew and Greek Scriptures, the works of Aristotle, the commentaries of the Arabians (then held in the highest esteem) really teach? That this could not be known through the Latin translations then current, Bacon was convinced. These translations were the imperfect work of ignorant bunglers. Instead, therefore, of wasting long, plodding years on the technicalities of grammar and logic — which, rightly considered, are, in Roger Bacon's view (with which John Locke agrees), but different names for an innate and unstudied art which every healthy mind naturally possesses — he would have scholars devote themselves first to a careful and thorough study of Hebrew, Greek and Arabic. They must be able to read these languages with ease and correctness for themselves. Only on this condition could they expect rightly to understand the Scriptures, or Aristotle or his Arabian commentators. Accordingly Bacon, while teaching at Oxford, devoted himself earnestly to the study of these languages, and spared no expense to procure for himself the best manuscripts. No wonder that, in the simple imagination of the people, or in the ignorant imagination of illiterate ecclesiastics, the story (repeated by Bayle) could find currency that he had discovered a receipt for teaching any one "in a very few days Hebrew, Latin, Greek, and Arabic."

But all valuable and accessible knowledge is not, in Bacon's view, to be acquired through the interpretation of texts. There is another book, the book of nature, to be read, and by another method, made up of a combination of mathematics with experiment. In his appreciation of mathematics, as an instrument of scientific method, Bacon was far in advance of his age, and a herald of modern physical science, which, in the estimation of a living German historian of modern thought, first arrived at complete theoretical independence, and was ready to be separated from philosophy, when Newton formally stated, and successfully inaugurated the application of, its method, as consisting in the regulated "combination of induction with mathematical deduction" (Windelband, *Geschichte der neueren Philosophie*, I, 290). Roger Bacon, naturally, could not be expected to draw the line of distinction between philosophy and science, and their respective methods, for which the times were then not ripe. But in his *naïve* faith in the applicability of mathematics to all branches of knowledge he appears as the prototype of many English (and also Continental) enthusiasts of a later day, as Hobbes and Locke, Descartes and Spinoza, and in an important and essential sense even the author of the "Critique of Pure Reason" himself. Mathematics is for him, in his own language, the very "alphabet of philosophy." It is the "first among all sciences," not only in rank, but also as to the time of its "discovery." It is in some sense innate in man, and was known to the holy men at the beginning of the world. It is the "door and key" to all sciences, including that which we now exclude from the rank of a science, namely, magic. It alone furnishes absolutely valid demonstrations, and through its aid alone, therefore, can man arrive at the knowledge of truth without any admixture of error. We need it for the interpretation of Scripture even, and for the establishment of moral science. It is, in Bacon's words, an instrument in the hands of "the church of God for the common benefit of believers, the conversion of unbelievers, and the repression of those who cannot be converted." (See L. Schneider, *R. Bacon*, Augsburg, 1873.)

But the chief theoretical interest of Bacon lies in the knowledge of nature, in the discovery of her mechanical secrets, the consequent dispelling of the rude ignorance of which he complains as universal, and the improvement of man's present estate. Accordingly we read of his spending very large sums, perhaps the most of his large estate, in the purchase of instruments, and in making experiments. Of so great importance was this way and kind of knowledge to him, and so far did he carry his researches in this direction, that he was believed to possess magical secrets which nought but collusion with the devil could account for. Accordingly he was forbidden by his monastic superiors to "communicate to any one anything concerning his labors and the results of his investigations," and compelled to live an unwilling exile ten years in France. At last invited by a pope, who was favorable to him, to communicate to him what he knew, at the age of fifty-two he set about the composition of immense works, which he completed in a year and a half, and sent, along with certain mathematical instruments, by a trusty messenger, a pupil of his own, to Rome. "After the death of his papal patron" he became again the victim of "the envy and superstitious ignorance of his brother monks," at whose instigation he was accused of practicing the black art and teaching dangerous doctrines, and was compelled to pass ten years in a dungeon at Paris. A few years before his death the old man was at last released and permitted to return to his native England, where he died and where, at Oxford, he lies buried.

There is something deeply pathetic and even tragic in the fortunes of Roger Bacon. His fate was that which has so often, and from the very necessities of the case, befallen real greatness in the world. It stands alone, on heights unknown to its contemporaries, who look on it with ignorant contempt and reward it with sacrilegious buffetings. That is perhaps more true of him, which is alleged of Francis Bacon, that he "took a view of everything as from a high rock." His experience reminds one of Heine's saying: "Wherever a great mind utters its thoughts, there is Golgotha." Says Prof. Noack: "In view of his knowledge of languages and of the natural sciences Roger Bacon stood as a giant among his contemporaries." Many are the inventions and discoveries (as of gunpowder — though incorrectly) which have been ascribed to him, and still more startling are those which he predicted. It is reported that it was a passage stolen from Roger Bacon by some author known to Columbus that, arresting the attention of the latter, led him to the formation of his world-discovering plans. By his appreciation of mathematics, and the solidity of his own scientific work (*e.g.* in optics), Roger Bacon certainly is superior to his successor, Francis Bacon, Lord Verulam. On the other hand, the points of intellectual resemblance between the two Bacons are numerous and very striking. If Francis Bacon is by general admission an accurate representative of the English mind on one of its most striking sides, in Roger Bacon we must recognize a prophecy or evidence of the same English type shining out of the profounder darkness of the Middle Ages.

To his contemporaries Roger Bacon was a wonder. Hence the appellation which they gave him, "*Doctor Mirabilis.*"

I cannot, for obvious reasons, enter here upon a detailed examination of the speculations of the eminently "subtle doctor," Duns Scotus, born either in Northumberland, or in the north of Ireland. It is sufficient for our present purpose — which is to discover in the earlier times the moral and mental features of the Englishman as now known to us — if I show, in the most general way, what was peculiar in his position as a theologian and philosopher.

In Thomas Aquinas and Albert the Great the scholastic philosophy had reached its culmination. Revelation and Aristotelianism had been combined in a way to render theology as nearly as possible rational, while yet maintaining certain limits of reason and the necessity of faith, the latter resting on the absolute authority of the data of revelation duly delivered and interpreted by the organs of the church. With reference to this philosophy the attitude of Duns Scotus was sharply critical. He would contract still further the limits of reason's power, and attribute still more to revelation. But in particular he insisted upon reversing the relation which St. Thomas had maintained as existing between will and intellect, both in the divine and the human spirit. According to Thomas, the acts which proceeded from the divine will found their sufficient and explaining reason in the ideas of the divine mind. If God, through his creative will, was the author of good, it was not arbitrarily, but because through his intelligence he saw that it was good. Intellect determined will. Duns Scotus asserted the contrary; not absolutely, but relatively or generally, *i.e.* with reference to the majority of the subjects of human judgment. All of the profounder forms of philosophical idealism, for example, regard the world as an expression of eternal and necessary reason, and consequently of eternal and necessary goodness; imperfect, indeed, and incomplete, yet not arbitrary, for then it would be no better than a product of senseless, but irresistible fate, or of blind force, and as such would be utterly inexplicable. For philosophy the reality of the world is proportioned to its ideality, or rationality; only on this condition is it intelligible; in other words, only on this condition is a philosophy of finite existence possible. But for Duns Scotus the world is capable of no such rational explanation. It cannot be regarded as the world which either absolute reason or absolute goodness required. It is not to be regarded as intrinsically a manifestation of divine intelligence, as such, or of divine goodness. It is only to be viewed as a means, by the right use of which on man's part the only end of its existence, namely, the salvation of mankind, is attained. This, then, is the only reason or explanation of the world's existence. It is simply a means incidental to the attainment, on man's part, of eternal life. Nor can it be said to be intrinsically a necessary means, *i.e.* the only one which God could have chosen. It was, indeed, "fittingly," but still arbitrarily, chosen by God, and in so far is accidental. God's sovereign will created it, but no necessity of eternal reason and goodness determined him to create it. But, once created, and the laws of its natural and moral order being once fixed, the immortality of the divine nature makes it impossible that these should be changed. Thus, then, it is because God has with arbitrary sovereignty decreed, as a condition of salvation, that we love our neighbors, that such love is evermore right or due. The good is good because God wills it; we may not say that he willed it because it was good. Only one thing Duns Scotus admits that God could not have refrained from commanding, and that is the love of himself; all else is arbitrary.

A similar doctrine is taught by Scotus concerning the freedom of the human will, although with modifications or concessions which relieve it of somewhat of its apparent irrationality.

Duns Scotus died while still young, in 1308, at Cologne, whither he had been sent to take part in a disputation. According to the common account, he was only thirty-four years old when he died. His was no idle life. Students of his works say they miss in them the philosophic poise and calm which characterize the writings of St. Thomas, the leader of his opponents. They even profess to discover in them some signs of that literary and intellectual barbarity which was destined to mark the close of the scholastic period. However this may be, it is obvious that the defense of his doctrines was with him no mere pastime. His interest in them was profound and vital. On their practical adoption, in the spirit in which he taught them, doubtless depended, in his view, the security of the church, the welfare of society, the present moral safety, and the final salvation of men. Who does not see in them the direct reflex of that spirit of unconditional obedience, of absolute, unquestioning respect for duty, which will hear neither of reasons nor of reasonings, which distrusts them, and, with some attempt at demonstration, proclaims them necessarily fruitless, and with a certain practical sense simply and absolutely holds fast to the *things* which reason would explain — the spirit common to all nations, as the Romans and English, with whom the notion of law and its power and authority is fundamental?

A still more striking instance illustrative of the general thesis of this chapter is furnished in the character and teaching of William of Occam, county of Surrey, England. As at once a scholastic doctor, and the most influential herald of the philosophical doctrine termed Nominalism, he is a living symbol of scholasticism in the act of suicide. The scholastic philosophy, in pursuing its particular end, was also, however blindly and inefficiently, in its time the guardian and defender of the only possible positive, (by which I mean *affirmative*, the opposite of *negative*, or merely critical, agnostic,) namely, of idealistic philosophy. The particular and only conscious aim of scholasticism was the rational justification of ecclesiastical dogma. The only way in which it could accomplish this was by maintaining a doctrine then termed Realism. How the acceptance of this doctrine was deemed to render measurably intelligible, or at least conceivable, the central mystery of christian theology, the Divine Trinity, it were beside my purpose to attempt here to explain. It is enough to mention that the problem of Realism, or Nominalism, was really, by implication, the problem of all philosophy. It was the particular form, namely, which this problem assumed at the historic epoch of which we are now treating, and in the hands of men whose main and conscious interest was theological and ecclesiastical, rather than purely and properly philosophical. The form of the problem was therefore in a measure accidental and imperfect. Still, I repeat, it was practically the only form in which, during the Middle Ages, the great question of philosophy received, at least indirectly and incidentally, a hearing. This question is, whether the universe of existence, relative and absolute, is, synthetically, rationally, intrinsically comprehensible, or only analytically, superficially observable. This is tantamount to the query, whether existence is knowable *per se*, or not. For, if thus knowable, it is such only as the expression of kingly mind, of compelling reason, which

> " To the law of All each member consecrating
> Bids one majestic harmony resound."

If not knowable *per se*, it is then knowable only as it happens to strike, or to be reported by others to, each individual, only in the impressions which each or all receive, namely, in a series of isolable, but more or less orderly, phenomena, of which we only know that we experience (or, in the language of present English psychology, *feel*) them, but of which no really causal or otherwise rational and ultimate account is possible. The assertion of Realism amounted, in its way and measure, to the affirmation of the former of these alternatives; of Nominalism to the latter. For Realism the reality of the particular — the individual concrete thing — consisted in its relation to a something universal. Only in its relation to this was it conceivable, knowable, or existentially possible. The universal — the power and life of mind — might be conceived, Platonically, as that, by virtue of *their* "participation" *in which* sensible objects acquired whatever of reality they possessed, or, with Aristotle, (changing the phraseology rather than the intention,) as that which, being *in things,* constitutes their very nature. In either case the essence of all, even the most individual existence, was either directly or functionally rational. But mediæval Realism did not remain within the limits of this perfectly safe and easily defensible generality. It asked itself whether, in those general conceptions of genus and species, which must be included in every definition of a particular object, there is given us a knowledge of so many diverse, but still universal, rational substances. Are genera and species real entities? We should call this to-day a narrow and unfortunate, because utterly misleading, way of putting the fundamental problem of philosophy. For this problem turns upon the explanation of the particular and phenomenal. But if genera and species are regarded as so many distinct substances, obviously our conception of them is assimilated to our conception of the particular and phenomenal objects which they should explain. In other words, we tend to explain the particular by itself, or, what amounts to the same thing, by that which is conceived as like unto it. Or, still otherwise expressed, we seek still to carry the habit of the analytic method, whereby we *apprehend* the individually concrete, sensible and phenomenal, over into spheres of contemplation to which only the method of synthetic *comprehension* is appropriate. It is in its measure the old story of sense still encroaching on reason. It may be said that the same criticism would apply to the Platonic theory of ideas. It certainly does apply to this theory, if we regard Plato as having in good earnest meant to assert the particular, sensibly distinct, substantive existence of the ideas; but not, if this description of the theory be, as such, purely "mythical" (in Plato's language) or figurative, and intended only as a way of impressing upon the imagination the grand, underlying thought that the reality, as well as the intelligibility, of things is exactly proportioned to their ideality, and that absolute and immutable being belongs only to the rational and spiritual.

The ideal or rational can only be conceived as a function of the living and spiritual. When, therefore, Realism affirmed the distinct, substantial reality of genera and species, it gave currency to a false conception, in so far as it tended to suggest that these were so many numerically different rational "substances," possessing the same unintelligible brute particularity of existence which the stone possesses, and therefore needing the same explanation which it needs. But, on the other hand, inasmuch or in as far as the assertion of Realism was tantamount to a declaration that ultimate reality is attained *not* through the perceptions of sense, but through the conceptions of mind, it was the voice of true philosophy. It was only necessary that these conceptions should not be regarded as corresponding to so many distinct entities (a pseudo-idea in which the universal and rational is reduced under forms of particularity furnished by the sensuous imagination), but rather as pointing to ideal types, laws, purposes, creative acts of real, *i.e.* rational, will-endowed power, and this the power of absolute, divine spirit. Such " realism " were what we now and properly understand by positive, not negative or " subjective," philosophical idealism.

The opposite of all this was affirmed by Nominalism, and William of Occam was its influential spokesman. On the plea—quite justifiable from the point of view of that side or tendency of mediæval Realism, which I have just been criticising—that "entities must not be multiplied without necessity" (*entia non sunt multiplicanda praeter necessitatem*), he denied the substantive existence of universals (genera and species) as an hypothesis wholly impertinent to the explanation of individual existence. So far this was but a repetition, in substance, of one of Aristotle's criticisms of the Platonic theory of ideas (a criticism perfectly just, if in Aristotle's account of it that theory had been correctly represented). But William of Occam went further than this, and denied that in forming general conceptions the reason of man was actually and successfully stretching out toward the knowledge and comprehension of something more real than and explanatory of individual, sensibly-perceived phenomena. Properly speaking, the mind had, in William's view, no power of " stretching out," or of actively performing any other function. In all its cognitive operations it is strictly passive; it is led, not leads. It does not penetrate through the phenomenal to the real. It simply receives, through the senses, impressions; or it observes, not its own *actions* or nature, but simply the states which are superinduced upon it. In clear and definite impressions, he held, is given our best and most adequate knowledge of particular objects. Yet this knowledge is relative and uncertain. We cannot know that our impressions, or sensible ideas, are correct transcripts of real things. More likely they are not. At most we are only justified in believing our ideas to be *signs* of things, which for the rest are unknowable. Of these signs, spoken words are still other signs, just as, still further, written words are signs of spoken words. Our general conceptions are simply indefinite, but particular ideas, containing that which several particular objects (or sign-ideas) have in common, but lacking the definite lineaments or representative value of any of them. Thus all our ideas, particular and general, distinct and confused, being essentially nothing but (presumed) signs of objects which produce them, and words (*nomina*) being signs of these signs, the former are (as signs) of the same nature as the latter, and may hence be called by the same name as the latter (*nomina*, whence the term Nominalism, or *termini*, owing to which the name "*Terminists*" was also given to Occam and his followers).

It will be seen that this doctrine is purely critical and negative. It denies the possibility of knowledge of real existence, and restricts it to the realm of phenomena passively experienced and observed. The mind of man is no longer allowed to contain an element of active, and, in its sphere, authoritative reason. For the rest, it can know no more its own essence than that of the world or (except as matter of some probability) the existence of the absolute mind, or God. That, in maintaining these positions, William of Occam stands in the same rank with the most celebrated names in the later history of English speculation, is obvious, or will certainly become so before our studies are finished. Prof. Ludwig Noack, in his recently published Lexicon of the History of Philosophy, very accurately terms William of Occam "the most influential forerunner of his countrymen, Francis Bacon, Hobbes, John Locke, and John Stuart Mill."

Along with this philosophical negativism, William professed to keep his faith, and that, too, with more absolute, unquestioning credulity (for that it was, and this it is that generally and necessarily takes the place of philosophical convictions vainly sought or lost) than his partial master, Duns Scotus. In William's view the love of God is a duty flowing only from the sovereign will of God, whom no necessity of things compelled to require this love of us. Indeed, so absolute is God's power and freedom, that no truth of philosophy holds concerning him, and William simply revels in paradox while enumerating some of the physical impossibilities which are possible for God. Theological and "philosophical" truth are thus made utterly disparate and apparently contradictory. But there is no evidence that William, like so many a century or two later, while professing to accept both, was a dissembler with respect to his professed acceptance of the former. In this respect he only carried to the wildest extreme the tendency already commented on in Duns Scotus.

Literature, art, religion, a vigorous, moral, social and political life, are preëminently the works to which philosophy furnishes the corresponding theory. This correspondence was more perfect in earlier times, when the life of man was less complex and variously specialized, than to-day. The most flourishing period of the scholastic philosophy was coeval with the best, most confident, vigorous life of the Middle Ages in most of the directions just enumerated. Its self-extinction was contemporaneous with the beginning of a period of barbarity, into whose darkness the light of the Renaissance was destined finally to shine, with truly regenerating effect. The revival of learning and the reformation of religion were at once cause and sign of a new youth of the Occidental mind. Some of its grandest products we shall contemplate in our next chapter.

CHAPTER III.

ENGLISHMEN OF THE RENAISSANCE—SPENSER, DAVIES, HOOKER.

The revival of learning and the religious reformation reached their fulfillment in England in the sixteenth century. The tree of human life blossomed anew, and what magnificent and abundant fruit it bore in England is known to every student of the Elizabethan period of English literature. It is a matter of the deepest significance to note the precise nature of the nourishment, which quickened and supported this new and masterly life, and of the ways in which it actively, spontaneously, powerfully, successfully manifested itself.

The revival of learning meant, so far as it concerns the history of philosophy, the revival, and restoration to honor, of Platonism. And what was that, in distinction from Aristotelianism, which had been so completely absorbed, in form and substance, into the Scholastic philosophy? I admit — every careful student admits — no absolute contrast between Platonism and Aristotelianism. Aristotle was the true disciple, though a critical one, of Plato. Aristotle was the real continuator of Plato, more than the members of the Academic school, in which the tradition of his teaching was guarded. Both Plato and Aristotle held to the same fundamental truth of Idealism. For both, essential reality was not material, but spiritual; the material, as such, or absolutely considered, was nonessential, non-real. For both, life (*i.e.* being) was, in Aristotle's phrase, "energy of mind." Nor were it true to say that the way in which Aristotle conceived the same ultimate philosophical truth to be reached and apprehended, was inherently different from Plato's way. If for Plato this result was only reached through a dialectic of definition, and division, and hypothesis, by which the clouds of mere sensuous opinion were scattered, and the soul permitted either directly or through vivid reminiscence to behold the absolute reality, it is a similar work which, in Aristotle's view, is accomplished through analysis and reasoning; these simply clear the mental vision so that it may perceive, and directly know, what cannot be demonstrated. The difference between Plato and Aristotle is the difference between poetry and unimpassioned prose. Plato, in spite of his attribution of unintelligence (or rather of an "unconscious intelligence") to poets, is himself nevertheless the most remarkable specimen of an *intelligent* poet. He is the intelligent poet of philosophy, rapt with the moral power and fascination of philosophic truth, and in his wonderful dialogues bringing its resistless spell nearer home to the mind and heart of humanity than any other one whom this earth has been privileged to see. Accordingly, Plato's writings are real poems, exhibiting the highest power of unreflecting art, as well as the subtlest force of conscious reason. Note the point well. In the case of Plato reason is all aflame with feeling, but not mastered by it. He has not simply the acute perception, but the warm impression of eternal and essential being — of truth, beauty, goodness — as existing absolutely in a purely intelligible world (*i.e.* in a real world, for no "world," but such an one as adapts itself to *rational* intelligence, can for a moment substantiate its claim to be called absolutely real), and as the only sources of reality in the sensible world, and he is consequently enabled with the electrical effectiveness of a poetic touch to deliver this impression to mankind. With Aristotle, on the contrary, it is less the intoxicating sense of the transcendent glory of the absolute which lends him power, although even he exhibits a pathos of simplicity in his account of the blessedness of the divine life of pure thought. But he is no poet. The rather, he altogether clips off the wings of Pegasus. Plato's imagery is to him as nought, or else is so misunderstood by him that he mistakes it for strict, sober doctrine, and, in attacking it, attacks, accordingly, a man of straw. Aristotle is systematic, expository, following up in analytical detail the application of theory to concrete cases. In Plato we have philosophy and literature combined. In Aristotle it is philosophy in abstract, minutely reasoned, and thoroughly didactic form, that is presented to us. Broadly considered, the two philosophers supplement and complete each other. But in universal, intensive power, the power to address and to uplift men, Plato is as far superior to Aristotle as the whole, undivided, winged spirit is superior to exclusive, plodding, analyzing intellect. In as far, then, as the revival of ancient learning meant the restoration of the knowledge of Platonism and a renewed interest in it, it is obvious that it could not but be accompanied by a thoroughly renovating and regenerating influence upon every faculty of man. And this, particularly, when it fell upon soil previously prepared by the infiltration of the purest conceptions of christian faith. Once before, too, there had been a new, or revived, Platonism. It was in the last, dying centuries of Greek and Roman paganism, in the so-called Neo-Platonic school. But then it was pitted against Christianity, and although in its first developments, in men like Plotinus and Porphyry, it bore occasional fruits of burning, mystic ecstasy, yet its pure light was speedily quenched by a flood of foreign, earthy accretions, doctrinal and practical. But when, at the epoch of the Renaissance, it was taken up anew into the elements of our christian civilization, regarded no longer as *the sole* light of the world, but nevertheless at once and gratefully recognized as *a* light, and that a pure and grand, and, in its measure, vivifying one, then it not simply kindled a new flame, it also quickened a flame already existing — the flame of christian knowledge, faith, and aspiration, planted in the very nerve and sinew of the modern mind.

If Socrates, Plato's revered master, had made the maxim "Know thyself" the corner-stone of his teaching, the sum and substance of Platonism was that deeper and more accurate self-knowledge, which is the direct *way* to the recognition of the divine. True self-knowledge was the priestess of divinity. In like manner the purer christian doctrine made man at once the rightful son, and heir, and image of God. Obviously the renewed knowledge and love of Platonism could not but work to intensify and deepen the sense of the reality of the christian idea, held always, in the majority of cases, more or less as an arbitrary and peremptory, but not clearly intelligible, truth of revelation. An inward light would come to meet the light supposed to be purely external and simply authoritative.

I need not refer in detail to the incidents in the story of the revival of Platonism — to its first enraptured cultivation in Italy, when art was preparing for its loftiest, lustiest flights, to the schools founded for its study, and to the movement whereby it, as a part of "the Italian influence," was conveyed to English soil. It is enough that I recall here the "christianized Platonism" of that "poet's poet," Edmund Spenser, the first great thoughtful singer of the Elizabethan age. No soul more gentle than his, none more delicately alive to the impressions of horror or distress caused by the existence of abundant sin and sorrow, hypocrisy and all vice, in view of which his "Muses" cry out, in their "Teares,"

"So wander we all carefull, comfortlesse."

Yet not altogether "comfortlesse" was he. And you have but to turn to the "Hymnes" "in Honour of Love," and "in Honour of Beautie," and the hymns "of Heavenly Love" and "of Heavenly Beautie," to learn what the nature of this comfort was and whence derived. Everything about Spenser and his productions is "gentle" (in the poet's well-chosen phrase), and these "Hymnes" are a "gentle" quintessence of Platonic, poetic, christian faith (or rational *sight*). It matters not that the Platonism may have come to him through the Italian Petrarca, or that here and there a specifically Aristotelian definition creeps into his chaste lines; as, for example, in the second of the Hymnes above mentioned:

"For of the soule the body forme doth take;
For soule is *forme* and doth the bodie make."

The argument and the point of view are generally Platonic and christian. Here we find the same sense of contrast, as in Plato, between the imperfection and relative unreality of the earth and all which sense alone, or principally, perceives, and the perfection, the absolute worth and reality, of the intelligible, supernal, divine, between the spirit struggling to be free and spirit free indeed; between the semblance and the reality of "beautie."

> "By view whereof it plainly may appeare,
> That still as everything doth upward tend,
> And further is from earth, so still more cleare
> And faire it growes, till to its perfect end
> Of purest Beautie it may at last ascend;
> Ayre more than water, fire much more than ayre,
> And heaven than fire, appeares more pure and fayre."

Above the visible heavens are other heavens and heavens of heavens, of "fairness" ever increasing as we ascend.

> "Faire is the heaven where happy soules have place,
> In full enjoyment of felicitie.
> Whence they doe still behold the glorious face
> Of the Divine Eternall Maiestie;
> More faire is that where those Idees on hie
> Enraunged be, which Plato so admyred."
> And pure Intelligences from God inspyred."

Fairer still is the heaven of

> "Sovereigne Powres and mightie Potentates,"

and "heavenly Dominations." And yet still more fair, again, are the heavens of Cherubim and Seraphim, and of Angels and Archangels. But ineffably fair is that highest object of the mind's faith, the spirit's dim but still enraptured vision, God, the absolute beauty, the transcendent perfection.

> "Cease then, my tongue! and lend unto my mynd
>   Leave to bethinke how great that Beautie is
> Whose utmost [out-most] parts so beautifull I fynd;
>   How much more those essentiall parts of His,
>   His truth, his love, his wisdome, and his blis,
>   His grace, his doome, his mercy, and his might,
>   By which he lends us of himself a sight!"

> "These unto all he daily doth display
>   And shew himselfe in th' image of his grace.
> As in a looking-glasse through which he may
>   Be seene of all his creatures vile and base,
>   That are unable else to see his face," etc.

> "The meanes, therefore, which unto us is lent
>   Him to behold, is on his workes to looke,
> Which he hath made in beautie excellent.
>   And in the same, as in a brasen booke,
>   To read enregistred in every nooke,
>   His goodnesse, which his beautie doth declare;
>   For all that's good is beautifull and faire."

Yet here, as in the Platonic Symposium, the view of present beauty is but a stepping-stone to a higher point of vision, where sense is "robbed," reason "blinded," and the privileged gazer transported

> "from flesh into the spright."

For those who gain this point — and the "humanism" of the Renaissance would not deny this "sweete contentment" to any one —

> "Their joy, their comfort, their desire, their gaine,
>   Is fixed all on that which now they see;
>   All other sights but fayned shadowes bee."

Evidently, that explanation of beauty, which reappears in our day under the "advanced scientific" name of "physiological æsthetics," could not satisfy Spenser (however fully, under due restrictions, he might have recognized its scientific interest), who accordingly sings:

> "How vainely then doe ydle wits invent
>   That Beautie is nought else but mixture made
> Of colours faire, and goodly temp'rament
>   Of pure complexions, that shall quickly fade
> And passe away, like to a sommer's shade;
>   Or that it is but comely composition
> Of parts well measur'd, with meet disposition!
>
> "Hath white and red in it such wondrous powre,
>   That it can pierce through th' eyes unto the hart,
> And therein stirre such rage and restless stowre,
>   As nought but death can stint his dolour's smart?
> Or can proportion of the outward part
>   Move such affection in the inward mynd,
> That it can rob both sense and reason blynd.
>
> "Why doe not then the blossomes of the field,
>   Which are arrayed with much more orient hew,
> And to the sense most daintie odours yield,
>   Worke like impression in the looker's vew?
> Or why doe not faire pictures like powre shew
>   In which oft-times we see Nature of Art
> Exceld in perfect limning of each part?
>
> "But ah! beleeve me there is more then so,
>   That workes such wonders in the minds of men;
> I, that have often prov'd, too well it know,
>   And who so list the like assayes to ken,
> Shall find by trial, and confesse it then,
>   That Beautie is not, as fond men misdeeme,
> An outward shew of things that only seeme."

Thus the last lines intimate that this theory of beauty was for Spenser not mere theory. It was capable of being experimentally tested, and had been, in his own case, experimentally verified; not, however (and naturally), by sensible tests and with physical instruments and measurements, but in the living experience of the human spirit.

Such, then, was the "comfort" of Edmund Spenser. Nor was it exclusively prospective or individual. The insight which inspired it enabled him to see in the very, apparent, mutability of present natural objects the means by which they (in his language)

> "their being doe dilate;
> And, turning to themselves at length againe,
>   Doe worke their owne perfection so by fate:
> Then over them Change doth not rule and raigne:
> But they raigne over Change, and doe their states maintaine."

Thus, universally, the changing and phenomenal had the seat and type of its present, immediate life in the changeless efficacy of imperial mind.

The like inspiration nerved him to do hopeful and courageous battle in his poetry against all impurity and insincerity in the life of man in Church and State. The power of Spenser is that resistless power of gentleness which made the Hebrew psalmist "great"; it is the power of a new, fresh life, with that grasp of synthetic insight which, in its highest, most real and characteristic phases, necessarily accompanies and constitutes it; it is, finally, the power of that noblest "common sense," which seeks "reform" not simply through protest and the demand for "change of some sort," but by fitly feeding the fountains of intelligence, through which alone a true and authentic reform can be maintained.

An interesting and instructive illustration of the hold

which poetry and philosophy had upon cultivated men of affairs in this masculine epoch is furnished in a poem written by Sir John Davies, entitled "*Nosce Teipsum:* This oracle expounded in two Elegies. 1st, Of Human Knowledge; 2d, Of the Soul of Man, and the Immortality thereof." Born in 1569, educated at Oxford, early becoming an orphan, the author in his early manhood plunged into boisterous dissipation and was concerned with Christopher Marlowe in the publication of a book of scandalous verse, which "was condemned by the archbishop to be burned." Before he was twenty-five years old he had written a poem (which, whether it was ever completed or not, now exists only as a fragment) called "Orchestra; or, a Poem on Dancing." The conception of the poem should perhaps rather be called a *conceit,* charmingly imagined and gracefully executed, and at the same time characteristic of that joyous idealism which rides upon the crest of every high, massive, powerful wave in the progress of human culture. The argument requires us to admit that all the movements of the universe, *in magno* and *in parvo,* of worlds and of elements, of plants and animals, of men and angels, are but the movements, now grave, now gay and joyous, of one all-comprising dance.

> Dancing (bright lady) then began to be,
> When the first seeds whereof the world did spring,
> The fire, air, earth, and water did agree,
> By Love's persuasion, Nature's mighty king,
> To leave their first disordered combating;
> And in a dance such measure to observe,
> As all the world their motion should preserve."

Exquisitely and daintily, and with many a quaint fancy, Sir John describes what his poetic eye perceives of dancing motion in the zephyr-touched flowers, in the "turnings, windings, and embracements" of "the vine about the elm," in the water-nymph, which

> "arising from the land,
> Leadeth a dance with her long watery train,
> Down to the sea,"

in the "round dance" of

> "the two Bears, whom the first mover flings
> With a short turn about heaven's axle-tree,"

as also in all the other movements, "solemn, grave and slow," of stars and heavenly spheres. We easily follow our author as his imagination descries the semblance of a dance also in the physical movements of men, in

> "All pomps, and triumphs, and solemnities,"

and in the play of the poetic fancy. But when grammar and rhetoric, as instruments of poetry and eloquence, are found to illustrate the same theme, in

> "the parts
> Of congruent and well according speech,"

and in "tropes" and "figures," and "turnings every way," the smile, in which we find ourselves involuntarily indulging, springs, perhaps, from motives tinged quite as much by a perception of the ludicrousness as of the poetic truth of the conceit. But enough of this poem, which I mention thus particularly only as an illustration of the thoughtful and graceful buoyancy, which is among the more striking characteristics of the intellectual life of the Elizabethan era.

The philosophical poem of Sir John Davies, to which I began by referring, was first published in the year 1599, and a second edition appeared in 1602. Doubtless any one, who should now take up and read the poem, would demur to the judgment of the anonymous author of an edition of it published nearly a century later (in 1697), who, after mentioning that in it "are represented the various movements of the mind," adds: "at which we are as much transported as with the most excellent scenes of passion in Shakespeare or Fletcher." Sir John Davies was no Shakespeare! And yet, no thoughtful reader will wonder that, in the words of a writer in the last edition of the *Encyclopædia Britannica*, "its force, eloquence and ingenuity, no less than the modern and polished tone of its periods, made it at once extremely popular. It was to its own age all that Pope's *Essay on Man* was to the Georgian period."

After an exquisitely graceful Dedication to Queen Elizabeth, the author descants on the natural intellectual blindness of man as now constituted, in contrast with his first estate. Our first parents, with intellectual eagle's eyes could look on the eternal; but, through their "desire to learn" the knowledge of evil,

"Bats they became, that eagles were before."

Now the soul shrinks from contemplating and knowing herself, on account of her present deformity. Still, affliction can make her withdraw in upon herself, and, adds Sir John, quaintly,

"This mistress lately plucked me by the ear,"

leading him to reflection and to intellectual discernment.

A full account of the psychology expounded in this poem and of the arguments advanced for the immortality of the soul, would be wearisome and beside my present purpose. I mention only a few points, either important for our argument, or curious.

First, then, genuine self-knowledge, the knowledge of the reality and nature of the soul, by itself, is a thing concerning the possibility of which the poet has no question. True, this is not possible without some infusion of a light divine, which is to the mental eye what the sun-beams are to the physical one. But guard against supposing that Sir John Davies could be led to assert the indispensableness of this light only out of deference, or from blind subjection, to the dictum of a revealed or currently established theology. Christian philosophy does indeed assert this, but, not only christian philosophy, all systems of affirmative (not negative, empirical, "subjective") Idealism, be they called after the names of Plato or Aristotle, of Descartes, Spinoza or Leibnitz, of Berkeley, Kant or Hegel, also assert, in some form, and of necessity, the same thing. The very sense of philosophical Idealism is to put and represent man in direct relation with the Absolute Mind, so that his light is its light, and its strength is made his. On the other hand, the unhesitating conviction of the reality of self-knowledge must at once be recognized as one of the most obvious elements of intellectual and moral strength. It is contained, however unconsciously — and it would indicate a morbid condition to be too conscious of it — in every vigorous manifestation of the life of men, and most in those oases in the history of civilization, when hope, and confident courage and resolve, in all the characteristic directions of man's best life, run high and execution follows close after — or, in other words, in what may be termed the blossoming-times of human culture. In this respect it is in marked contrast with that impotence of uncertainty, or of agnosticism, which, in the long winters that have generally followed these times, has sprung up on the soil of a sensualistic psychology, proclaiming that the soul can only know itself as a series of states or as a " bundle of perceptions."

"The soul a substance and a spirit is," says Sir John Davies. The senses are its servants, not separate from it, but a power "within a greater power." They furnish materials which the soul elaborates, controls, and, if need be, corrects. Happily writes our author:

> "Sense outside knows, the soul through all things sees:
> Sense, circumstance; she doth the substance view;
> Sense sees the bark, but she the life of trees;
> Sense hears the sounds, but she the concords true."

The soul is then defined in its distinction from the body, and, after Aristotelian and scholastic precedent, vegetative, sensitive and intellectual powers are attributed to it, of the first of which it is said,

> "This pow'r to Martha may compar'd be,
> Who busy was, the household things to do."

Poor "careful and troubled" Martha! What would she have said if, in addition to the other ignominious purposes of comparison for which she has been obliged these long centuries to serve, she had known that the flagging fancy of an English poet-philosopher would one day alight upon her name to illustrate the vegetative function of the soul? In wrestling with the subject of the five senses, in their order, the muse is fairly worsted. At least she pants and limps in a manner painful to observe. Still, while on the subject of the sense of taste, our author manages to attract our attention, by observing that it, since the invention of the art of cookery, has proved more murderous than "sword, famine or pestilence." And as regards the sense of smell, his conclusion is comparatively derisive, one would say, for he declares that—

> "They smell best that do of nothing smell."

There follow excellent stanzas relative to "Wit" (or Intellect) and "Will," the former "the pupil of the soul's clear eye," and the latter the "emperor" among the soul's faculties; to truth and goodness, as the object of wit's discriminating search and of the will's choice, in which connection we read,

> "Will is the prince, and Wit the counsellor";

and finally to God, who is

> "Alpha to Wit, Omega to the Will."

In an extremely beautiful comparison, extending through several stanzas, Sir John Davies likens the soul to a princess who accepts the attentions of many, but gives herself finally to a foreign prince whom she has not seen, and of whom she knows through his ambassadors. This foreign prince is God. His ambassadors are all objects of knowledge.

With considerable appositeness of argument, and clearness of exposition, Sir John Davies sets forth his thoroughly spiritualistic psychology, and develops numerous considerations tending to establish the doctrine of the soul's immortality, all founded on the best philosophy the world had produced, and pervaded by an obvious breath of sincere and independent conviction; this, too, in spite of the apparent over-confidence (and very mediocre poetry) of the concluding stanza:

> "And if thou, like a child, didst fear before,
> Being in the dark, where thou didst nothing see;
> Now I have brought thee torchlight, fear no more;
> Now when thou dys't, thou canst not hood-winked be."

The poem may stand as a document to prove what was the thoughtful faith of the best type of English gentlemen in his day. Such faith, or the like of it, made the Spensers, the Sidneys—I will even add in the same breath with these choice names, the Davieses of the Elizabethan era, England's golden age. Of it, and of the whole grander and more comprehensive philosophy of existence which it implies, considered as verifying itself in the lives and actions of those who live in practical conformity with it, and so live successfully, or else, denying and sinning against it, live in vain, William Shakespeare is the historian and mouthpiece. It was the true gold of England's "golden age," as it is also the principle of all that is truly golden in the life and history of mankind.

I may mention as of interest, before leaving Sir John Davies and his poem, that the author subsequently devoted himself with active zeal to political affairs, holding distinguished positions of trust in the gift of the crown, serving the nation in parliament, dying in 1626, shortly after his appointment as Lord Chief Justice of England, and leaving behind him an enviable reputation for trustworthiness and uprightness.

Along with the revival of learning I mentioned, at the beginning of this chapter, the religious reformation of the sixteenth century as one of the most noteworthy factors in the movement by which the Occidental mind was regenerated. The two factors wrought indeed together and aided each other. No genuine *Renaissance* through the restoration of letters and learning, and no genuine renovation in religion was possible, which should have reference to, or affect, externals alone. An ostensible *Renaissance* of this kind could, in the realms of letters and philosophy, at best, eventuate in nothing more than mere, unenlivened erudition, in that dry-as-dust formalism of scholarship, which

> * * * " evermore to empty rubbish clings,
> With greedy hand grabs after precious things,
> And leaps for joy when some poor worm it fingers."

A real revival of learning and of letters could be deemed to take place, not simply when new materials (or old materials restored) were placed in scholars' hands, but only when in the minds of scholars themselves there was a revived sense of spiritual dignity and creative power, sufficient to use these materials as means and occasions for new exhibitions of that inexhaustible genius which is in man, and which, in the highest sense, constitutes him. And this is precisely what happened in the time termed " of the Renaissance," and it is also precisely in this self-regenerating movement of the human mind that the significance of the Renaissance consists, and not in any accidentally-occasioned emigration of Greek scholars and importation of ancient manuscripts from Constantinople: the demand for these scholars and manuscripts preceded the supply, and it has been well remarked that, had not the taking of the capital of the Eastern empire by the Turks driven the scholars westward, they would have been induced to go in that direction with their treasures by the growing demand for them.

In like manner the religious reformation, if it had any significance, did not derive this from changes effected in the forms of worship or the wording of dogmas alone. Its iconoclasm is only its negative and accidental side. Its positive side, its strength and life, lay in the new and better life in morality and religion, of which living man felt the possibility, for which his deepest aspirations were stirred, and of which, with something of a sense of creative power to will and to do (while God wrought in him), he was resolved to secure the realization.

In England the Reformation fell upon a soil of national disposition and political circumstance well fitted to receive it. Both in poetry and in theology it had more than one forerunner among the English. It is enough if I mention the poet Langland, whose "Vision of Piers the Ploughman" spoke the language and the mind of the English common people, and became, says Stopford Brooke, "the book of those who desired social and church reform," and John Wyclif. On the other hand, against the danger which every reformation runs, of evaporating in mere words of noisy protest, or degenerating into simple iconoclasm or pure antinomianism, no safer barrier could anywhere be found than in the minds and hearts and habits of a people who, on the one hand, were deeply in earnest and sincere, and, on the other, pointed, as to one of their greatest glories, to a *Magna Charta*, a Great Charter, or lesson, at once of rights and of duties, or, in other words, of *law*. The nation whose public, political life had imbedded itself in an entity like the British Constitution, not one written instrument, but an organic growth of multitudinous roots and branches, and still unfinished, a body of precedent, and definition, and prescription, at once the outcome and the support of the spirit of *order*,—that nation had peculiar qualifications for taking up the work of the Reformation, and, by fixing it in forms of positive faith and institution, protecting its light and life from the destructive excesses, the chaos and darkness, of pure lawlessness.

And, indeed, in the epoch which we are considering, *i.e.* during the reign of Queen Elizabeth, one of the best representatives of what may be termed *the spirit of order in Protestantism*, Richard Hooker, stood forth, equally conspicuous for his learning and his eloquence, at once to explain and defend the authority of *law* and to illustrate the power and riches of the English tongue.

Born in the year 1554, Richard Hooker, still in the prime of life, died in the first year of the following century. He was favored after his death with having for his biographer a person of no less celebrity than quaint Izaak Walton, whose pictures of Hooker's alleged bashful humility and meekness are deemed to bear the impress more of the writer's peculiar imagination than of reality. These qualities, indeed, if we may trust Walton, must have had something to do with the unfortunateness of Hooker's married life; for, says his biographer, "the reader has liberty to believe that his modesty and dim sight were some of the reasons why *he trusted Mrs. Churchman to choose his wife.*" If Hooker's sight was "dim," it was not dimmer than the sight of Love, who notoriously is blind and yet never blunders. Hooker evidently erred in not choosing his own wife himself. Placed, as a minister of the Established Church, in a position which made it necessary for him to enter the lists of controversy against Puritanism, he did this, in Hallam's phrase, "like a knight of romance with arms of nobler temper." But mere controversy, and especially of a personal kind, could not but be flatly odious to him. Accordingly, at his own request, he was removed to a living in the country, where, in his own words, he could behold God's blessing spring out of his mother earth and eat his own bread without oppositions. His mind meanwhile was teeming with the conception of a vast work which should remove grounds of controversy by setting forth truth in her larger, grander, catholic lineaments. The work was to be entitled "Eight Books of the Laws of Ecclesiastical Polity," and of the eight five were completed and published in the author's lifetime. Of these, again, it is the first one, "Concerning Laws and their several Kinds in General," that chiefly interests us here.

On the nature of Hooker's greatness I quote here a page from the Introduction prefixed by Mr. R. W. Church to his recent edition of Book I of Hooker's work.

"No one [before Hooker] had thought of more than attack or defense, on the well-known ground and with the customary well-known arguments, turned to such account as each writer's skill and resources allowed. The grasp and largeness, the peculiar power which was attracted by great ideas, and also at home among the minute intricacies of scholastic argument, above all, the poetical fire, the self-devotion and enthusiasm of literary creation, the romantic belief in the deep and universal interest which was masked under what seemed dry and subtle questions, and the romantic passion to accomplish a work which should bring out their significance in regard to what all men understand and wish for,—this had been wanting; for all this means really genius; and the marked ability which is to be seen in the controversialists on both sides was something much short of genius. . . . The story told by Walton of the learned English Romanist, Cardinal Allen or Dr. Stapleton, who said to Pope Clement VIII that he had never met with an English book whose writer deserved the name of an author till he read the first four books of a 'poor obscure English priest, on Laws and Church Polity,' at least expresses the fact that Hooker is really the beginner of what deserves to be called English literature, in its theological and philosophical province."

In carrying out his work Hooker displays a profound knowledge of philosophy in its best historic forms, but his power and originality lie especially in his own quickened and quickening sense and comprehension of the notion of law and all that it implies. Well may Mr. Church say:

"The fundamental idea of law, with its consequences and applications, . . . appears to have absorbed and possessed him,"

adding that

"it shines through all his writings: what we have of his may be described as one great work on this theme, beginning with fragments, such as the Sermons; then, with one completed portion intervening in the middle, the first five Books on the Laws of Ecclesiastical Polity; and ending with fragments, the uncertain or unfinished Books VI to VIII."

That the realm of law is coextensive with the realm of existence, so far as this is open to rational comprehension, is it at once obvious. For existence is activity, and only that activity which is agreeable to law is orderly, and only that which is orderly is intelligible; chaos is to human, or any other, reason identical with darkness or nought. Law, then, is an expression, a requirement, and a fulfillment of order, and so of reason, and so of life or being. But how is law established? By chance, by an inherent fatal necessity of things, by an arbitrary, unreasoning fiat of absolutely sovereign divinity? None of these hypotheses, popular as one or all of them may at times have been or still be, will satisfy for a moment the requirements of healthy reason. Healthy reason is vitalized reason, and vitalized reason is self-conscious spirit, the characteristic essence of man, and the true and only agent of specifically philosophic cognition. I may call it, therefore, preëminently philosophic reason, in distinction from purely discursive ratiocination. If the latter moves in logical distinctions, pulling ideas or groups of ideas apart, isolating, discriminating, and then comparing and arguing from single relations apparent among the ideas, or parts of ideas, dissected, it is the function of the former to *grasp*, and to grasp *wholes*, of which the ideas in question are but the partial framework, to seize the richly colored *life*, of which they are, taken separately, the achromatic and oft misleading symbols, *the simplicity of truth*, in the light of which their complexity is resolved into a ministrant harmony. And my declaration is, that reason, so considered, finds and can find in all the objects of its contemplation only itself, or that which is cognate to itself. It knows no *existence* of which spirit is not the power and the life. It knows no activity of which reason, the light of spirit, does not prescribe the law. It knows no law, the operation or observance of which does not tend to good, to harmony, to beauty, and which has not, therefore, literally or virtually, the sense of a requirement. For it, accordingly, accident, or fate, or the brute might of unrestrained, unenlightened will can be no source of law, and it can only regard those who, in any attempted explanation of law, have recourse to them, as taking refuge in an *asylum ignorantiae, i.e.* as explaining nothing. Nor is this view peculiar to philosophic speculation merely; it is (at least implicitly) that of the mind of man when it asserts itself in its healthiest, most unrestrained, and hence most natural, rational and necessary acts of knowledge, and we need not, therefore, be surprised to find it asserted anew in that period of the modern mind's new life, self-knowledge and intellectual mastership, a section of which we are now contemplating.

It is this view which Hooker, with rare eloquence and unusual learning and penetration, sets forth. On the one hand, the empire of law is universal. On the other, its source is to be found in reason divine. The laws which God, the possessor and impersonation of this reason, has established, are not ordinances proceeding from a sovereign will, wrested from the control of perfect reason (as William of Occam, for example, had taught). "They err," declares Hooker, "who think that of the will of God to do this or that there is no reason besides his will. Many times no reason is known to us; but that there is no reason thereof I judge it most unreasonable to imagine, inasmuch as he worketh all things κατὰ τὴν βουλὴν τοῦ θελήματος αὐτοῦ, not only according to his own will, but *the counsel of his own will.*" But the ends which perfect reason can propose to itself, can only be ends of beauty and goodness, and a law necessarily relating, not to things at rest, but to movement, change, "operation," we have the elements of the following definition: "A law, therefore, generally taken, is a directive rule unto goodness of operation." There is here, it will be noticed, a conspicuous absence of that secondary notion of law which is given in the perfected results of the experimental and observational sciences of *phenomena*, namely, the notion merely of a rule or order which is discovered to hold good, as far as observation has extended, concerning the visible succession or combination of phenomena; which rule, order or so-called law is then often by unscientific interpreters termed at once, without further discussion, an "ultimate fact," and is hypostatized and treated in discussion as if it were a sort of independent entity, a little God, as arbitrary and stubborn as fate, and forcing the "events" (still other hypostatized abstractions), which occur in accordance with it, to be what they are and to occur as and when they do with inexorable, but otherwise absolutely inexplicable, unintelligible necessity. Neither laws of nature, nor any other laws, are, rightly regarded, laws of *happening;* but of doing, of operation, of action for which there is a reason. Whatever is done in accordance with and in consequence of them is done because reason directs it, and reason directs it because it is good. "A law is a directive rule to goodness of operation." Is, then, nature a reasonable being to whom laws, "rules of operation," considered as prescriptions of reason, can be addressed, and that with the expectation that she will fulfill the moral obligation which they imply to act according to them? No, the laws which we may figuratively conceive and describe as addressed to nature, are the laws which divine reason prescribes to the operation of divine power.

Nature is no entity with power to understand or to do. The works of nature are God's works. "Those things," declares Hooker, "which nature is said to do, are by divine art performed, using nature as an instrument." Nature the "instrument" of divine reason: this is the language of philosophic Idealism in all ages, and of the religious Idealism which flows from the very nature of man the world over, with, at most, only a difference in what may be termed the intellectual scenery of the conception. (Compare, for example, Plato and Hooker together on this point.) The invariability of natural law (it were better to say, of nature's visible or apparent obedience to law) follows, with Hooker, from the immutability of the perfect reason of divinity; but has also its particular, intrinsic reason in the necessity of such invariability (of "law," or rather of *obedience*) for the subsistence of the universe. "The obedience of creatures unto the law of nature is the stay of the whole world." Finally, the "goodness of operation" of nature's laws is attested by the fact which Hooker proclaims, that the works of nature "are all behoveful, beautiful, without superfluity or defect."

It is not necessary, however interesting and inspiring it might be, to follow Hooker through the whole course of his development of this grand, because genuine and reasonable, conception of law, in its application to the inner workings and relations of the divine nature, the superior knowledge and willing obedience of angels and archangels and of saints in glory, and to the case of men on earth, for whom knowledge is attainable only through a mental travail, which is painful, and hence repulsive, to the natural man, and whose obedience, even when knowledge is not wanting, is rarely without let or hindrance. Only, as regards those mysteries of the divine nature concerning which our silence is our best eloquence, Hooker is convinced that they are mysteries only for man's limited reason, but not for absolute or perfect reason. And as regards the laws which are to govern man, laws of nature and morality, of religion and (when conformed to its true intention) the state, none of them, either, are arbitrary. They are an expression of reason, and are to be rationally apprehended and justified. The general law of man's being is determined by that which is for man his peculiar good or perfection. And this consists in nothing less than a certain present realization of the divine within the limits of the human. It is perfect union with God and enjoyment of him, so that "by being unto God united, we live, as it were, the life of God." This is our "felicity and bliss," but is not absolutely attainable in this life. "Under man," says Hooker, "no creature in the world is capable of felicity and bliss. First, because their chiefest perfection consisteth in that which is best for them, but not in that which is simply best, as ours doth. Secondly, because whatsoever external perfection they tend unto, it is not better than themselves [namely, divine], as ours is."

In conclusion, I cannot refrain from rehearsing the paragraph, oft-cited, but never sufficiently to be admired, with which Hooker splendidly sums up and concludes the argument of his first book:

"Wherefore, that here we may briefly end: of Law there can be no less acknowledged, than that her seat is the bosom of God, her voice the harmony of the world; all things in heaven and earth do her homage, the very least as feeling her care, and the greatest as not exempted from her power; both angels and men, and creatures of what condition soever, though each in different sort and manner, yet all with uniform consent, admiring her as the mother of their peace and joy."

This is a specimen of the best idealism, not only of the English, but of the universal human mind; and the First Part of Hooker's work is enough of itself to disprove any pretense that in the English mind there is no capacity for true philosophical *speculation* ($=vision$).

CHAPTER IV.

WILLIAM SHAKESPEARE.

Shakespeare, of name undying!
Thy fleshly heart, low lying,
Responsive beats no more,
As in the days of yore,
To vexed humanity's deep sighing.

But, in thy living pages,
'Twill need no keen-eyed sages
Forever to descry
Such life-blood coursing high,
As feeds the strength of all the ages.

ONCE, when I was instructing, with a German text-book as guide, a class in the history of German literature, we came across the statement that a certain man, of great note in his time, held at one of the German Universities a professorship of "philosophy and poetry." The combination of subjects was sufficiently uncommon to be striking, and I asked one of my most thoughtful pupils the question, whether in his view such a combination was not incongruous; is there anything in common between philosophy and poetry, so that these two may legitimately be brought together as constituting one homogeneous topic of study and contemplation? The answer which I received was the same which, I doubt not, would be given, at first thought, and without deeper reflection, by ninety-nine out of any hundred persons, who have no ideas concerning philosophy and poetry, except such as are unconsciously imbibed from the common atmosphere of opinion which surrounds us all. To mention philosophy and poetry in the same breath was regarded as a ludicrous anomaly.

And indeed it is difficult to conceive of a contrast more absolute than that which exists between the too prevalent manner of what is termed philosophy and the characteristic manner and spirit of poetry. The one dryly argumentative and expository, often appalling by its technicalities of terminology, and too often, though illegitimately, confined to the analysis and labored digestion of dry bones or husks, from which life has long since fled; the other, instinct with the warmest human vitality, the passion, the hope, the despair, the love, the hate, the aspiration, the vision of the human heart. But what if the subject, the method, the end of philosophy were too generally misconceived, not only by laymen in learning, but also by a large number of those whom we are accustomed to honor with the name of philosophers?

Need I remind the reader that there are two things which, although absolutely distinct, and even contrasted, in their immediate aim, subject-matter, point of view, and method, are yet so closely related (being indeed correlates, complementary subdivisions of the whole of human knowledge) that they have, to the greatest extent, in the history of human thought, been confounded with each other? I refer to physics and metaphysics, or to physical science (with all its subdivisions, exact and descriptive, or both combined) and philosophy — the former having to do with sensibly verifiable *phenomena*, their classification, their mechanical explanation, and their perfect expression in mathematical formulæ, and the latter with rationally apprehensible *realities*, with the living causes of phenomena and their rational explanation; the one dealing with apparent form, the other with vital substance, the one with sensible fact, the other with rational, ideal, spiritual truth, the one content simply to take the measure of the sensibly actual, however imperfect, the other testing all by the standard of the ideally perfect and so prescribing to the imperfect the law of its progress to perfection; and, finally, the one — Science — tending to the present material utilities and, in certain branches, humanities of life, the other to that still higher, sacred utility, the present and eternal development and conservation of humanity itself — the actual realization of the ideal Man, in feeling and in reason. These two, I say, philosophy and physical science (in which I include constantly mathematics, the special organon and methodological ideal of physical science), are complementary to each other, having each its peculiar province and inner justification, and yet so organically related that each leads to, implies, demands the other. But the time has never yet been when the distinction, or at least the true relation, between the two was clearly and universally perceived and respected. In ancient times the philosophical problem was first approached, and rightly, for reasons involved in the nature of the case, and especially of man, who, considered in his vital relations, constitutes the first and most absorbing and indeed (if you consider all that is involved in the true knowledge of man) the whole theme of philosophy. And, by the way, the utter short-sightedness of the Baconian complaint concerning the alleged barrenness of ancient philosophy — its failure to bring forth "fruits"

—is at once apparent when one considers its inestimable influence in giving to life and civilization—either directly or indirectly (in the latter case as the hand-maid of religion)—whatever of ideal perfection these have possessed down to the present day. Is a noble life, the inspiration of ideal insight, the moulding of the world's moral and artistic life (*i.e.* its greatest values) no fruit? Bacon needed but to reflect upon the moral sources of the literary power of the Elizabethan era, of which he was an ornament, to perceive that that wonderful epoch in the higher life of England was but part and parcel of a *Renaissance* and new life of the best spirit of ancient speculative thought.

However, not to insist now at greater length on this point, it is unquestionable that while concrete physical science was by no means unknown, in substance and in the elements of its method, to the ancients, yet its cultivation remained far behind that of philosophy proper, and it was, and continued for centuries to be, regarded (what there was of it) as an integral portion or a loose adjunct of philosophy and designated by the same name. The history of modern thought has exhibited precisely the contrary state of things, notably in England. The very conception and method of philosophy have been borrowed from physical science (termed natural philosophy;—we shall see this in detail in the following chapters). In other words, instead of science being swallowed up by philosophy or, to use the hateful cant expression, "in bondage to philosophy," philosophy has been held mostly fast in the fetters of the presuppositions and methods of physical science, from which she has not yet succeeded in completely rescuing herself.

My present point is this: Philosophy is a positive thing, as positive as existence itself. But it is not a mere knowledge of details and minute relations. Its characteristic function is not numbering or measuring. It is not anatomy. It does not, if true to itself and its aim, place the objects of its investigation in a vacuum of abstraction fatal to life (which physical science really does). Its problems are problems of life, because they are problems of essential being and of active power. Its problems are synthetic and organic, because life is synthesis and organism. They are ideal and rational, because, first, the knowing mind, the living reason, of man, which is the organ of philosophy, can grasp only that which bears the marks of reason (everything else being incommensurate with it and absurd), and, secondly, because all life turns out for philosophy to be what it was anciently defined, namely, "energy of intelligence," or, in the language of religion and poetry, "energy of love."

Now, philosophy proper being *theory of life*, in the broadest and highest sense of this term, I affirm that poetry is the *exposition of life*, whether life of man or of nature. On the side of their insight the philosopher and the poet are brothers, with somewhat of the difference which Plato puts between them, namely, that the former is explicitly conscious of the theoretic sense and import of the vision, and the latter not, though this difference is only relative. Both bring the same message, for both report the same simplicities of being, the same eternities of truth — only, the one in forms of demonstration, calculated to produce a reasoned conviction; the other in forms of living fancy, adapted to enhance the fascination of the message. Let no one, however, suppose that the creative power of the poet extends over the philosophic truth, the real and essential substance, of what he sings. Over this he has no control. As to this, he is inspired by the truth, the substance, itself, which is uncreated and unchangeable; he is simply its organ, or instrument (as Pope so finely said of Shakespeare, that he was nature's instrument; and as Schiller says of all real poets: " Die Dichter sind überall, schon ihrem Begriffe nach, die *Bewahrer* der Natur"); he is a seer and can only tell what he sees. Of what use were it if (to suppose the absurd) he could create new truth, new essential reality, new ideal substance? His creation would be unintelligible to any but himself; nay, he himself could not understand it, nor could any god.

The rather, the very reason why the poet speaks a universal language, intelligible to the universal heart and mind of man, is that he reports concerning things which are genuine, abiding, eternal, intrinsically real, and which, therefore, on the one hand, he cannot change, and on the other are the soil in which human nature and the nature of things are so deeply, however unconsciously, imbedded, that once mentioned they seem to us as though we ought always to have known them — supremely "natural," as we say, a kind of revelation of grand simplicities which virtually we had always known. This work of the poet is that "one touch of nature," of reality, of being, which "makes the whole world kin."

Creative the poet is at most only in regard to the form in which his story is told. I conclude, then, that the true poet is the agent and messenger of immortal truth, of eternal reality, of God, and that the real sense of his song consists precisely in this, that it is a communication of fascinating glimpses of the source whence inspiration is derived; it is in its measure, as I began by saying, an exposition of living truth, or of truth of life.

The true, grand poet has in him then the substance of the true philosopher, only that he sings, freely, uplifted and borne by his message, not held down by it as by a weight, with an appearance of unconsciousness or irreflection; in short, as Goethe puts it, "as the bird sings," while the philosopher aims at systematic, discursive exposition, and employs, more especially (though not necessarily, as witness, above all, Plato), the dialect of unadorned, reflective prose. The philosopher observes and thinks, and makes exhibition of his thought as such, in such reasoned form as is judged best adapted to force assent to its theoretical correctness. The real poet is careless of assent, and yet sure of it, for his words are but as the vibration of the universal nature of man and of things, and cannot but awaken responsive and consentaneous vibrations in the soul of every hearer. Of such an one we may well say that, knowing and portraying the secrets of *Life*, he has furnished the data and tests of philosophy, even though he were no theoretical philosopher.

I would fain exhibit now, though briefly, William Shakespeare as a poet in the sense just explained. For, within the limitations fixed by the definition given of the poet's nature and function, I see in him the supreme exponent of the philosophic thought of his age and nation; indeed, a true prophet of mankind in all ages and all nations. (Coleridge: "Shakespeare is of no age.") His work is a vindication of the possession by the English mind of the faculty of truest philosophical insight, and at the same time swells with

Such life-blood coursing high,
As feeds the strength of all the ages.

With this end in view, and bearing in mind that what we are searching for we must, from the nature of the case, expect often to find, less in the form of explicit statement than of obvious and necessary implication, we may naturally and properly ask, first, whether in the world of Shakespeare's thought supreme reality is ascribed to that which the senses are supposed to perceive, or to that which the rational spirit alone apprehends, and whether the power which gives laws to events and shapes their issue is confusedly conceived as blind and irrational, and incapable of love or mercy (a "persistent," mechanical "force"), or clearly apprehended as spiritual and holy; and secondly, and particularly — for Shakespeare is still more directly the poet and historian of man than of the nature of things — in what he finds the specific nature of man — of perfect manhood — to consist, whether in flesh and blood, in sense and mechanically acting, and hence uncontrollable passion, or in the living, spiritual realization, through the free activity of a reasonable will, of an ideal purpose. And let me beg the reader to consider, in passing, with reference to this latter point, that if Shakespeare is what the whole civilized world admits, and his unquestioned power over the heart and mind of man proves him to be, he, if any mortal, must have known what man is, not simply in his imperfect actuality, but also — and this is the essential thing — in his proper reality, his true intent, his ideal perfection. For what has Shakespeare written? He has written Histories, Comedies, Tragedies; he is a dramatic historian, comedian, tragedian, and this supereminently, without a rival, as "nature's instrument," or better, like all true genius, as the instrument of divinity. But of what is he the historian? Not, surely, of the kings and wars and of the life, high and low, of the English people, and of these alone. The statistical element, the element of special historic actuality, is certainly not wanting. But this is the least important part in Shakespeare's historical dramas. Shakespeare is more than an English historian; he is the historian of the modern mind, he is the historian of man. More strikingly does this appear true when we include in the account the comedies and tragedies of Shakespeare. In order that one may be, as nearly as possible, the ideal comedian, the tragedian *par excellence*, what must one know, if not man? What are comedy and tragedy, if not the representation of that which is characteristically affecting for man? To what may they be better likened than to chemical tests, skillfully and intelligently chosen, which excite in man certain reactions that exhibit, in their measure, accurately the nature of man? The perfect comic and tragic author must therefore know what is comical and tragical *for man*. For this purpose he must know man's true nature, and his work will be in the broadest and best sense the history, or exhibition, of man. Such knowledge Shakespeare certainly possessed, and accordingly one source, and indeed the great and commanding source, of the power and fascination of Shakespeare's dramas lies in the fact that *man* finds himself in them. Shakespeare "holds the mirror up" especially to man's "nature," revealing man to himself, not merely in his coarse, unpleasing, semi-irrational actuality,—for this neither poet nor philosopher is needed; any observant scribbler can do this,—but in his ideal reality, his possibility, his required nature, in that divine purpose, in proportion only as he realizes which, man is himself, or possesses character, *i.e.* true human substance. It is only in the light, or by comparison with the standard, of this perfect image that man measures his actual perfection, or recognizes his imperfection or distortion. It is by this standard that in Shakespeare's plays his own characters are obviously—however unconsciously, in many cases—judged.

I return now to the queries above raised concerning Shakespeare's thought, and consider, first, his conception of nature.

The sum of concrete existence we term nature. Analytic, studious, investigating man, theorizing concerning it, arrives, according to his moral and intellectual point of view, at various conclusions respecting its real substance and the order of its functions. The one, following the suggestions of sense and reasoning from a few incomplete analogies, sees in nature only a machine stored with unintelligent force, which, working day and night, brings forth in restless activity successive forms and specimens of living creatures, which come into existence only to be directly swallowed up again in the mills of this blind god. Thought and feeling, fancy, faith, prayer, hope, love, are only delusive, accidental products of its mechanical energy,—glittering bubbles, destined to prove their impotent insubstantiality by bursting! Another, strong in the self-conscious assurance of the reality of mind (*i.e.* individual consciousness), and aware of the mutability and relativity of sensible perception, leaps (we will suppose) to the conclusion that the latter is absolutely deceptive, that the belief in externality, a world of real space in three dimensions, is an illusion, and that time is nothing but a subjective phenomenon. Instead of treating time and space as dependent functions of real, universal mind, and thus possessing derivative reality, he makes them purely illusory "ideas" of individual, phenomenal mind, and ascribes reality only to a ghostly abstraction. Shakespeare's vision is more comprehensive than either of these. On the one hand, he is not like the German poet upon whom Schiller passed the criticism, that whatever he treated he stripped it of its body, leaving it pure spirit. This is not Shakespeare's art. The world of his dramas is the present world of embodied life and action, in space and time, and not a timeless and spaceless world of — from man's present point of view — abstraction. Nay, the very substance of his art consists in this, that to the "forms of things [sensibly] unknown" — ideal values, truths of character, spiritual realities — he gives present intelligibility for men still held in physical nature's arms, by assigning to them a "local habitation and a name." Such localization in space, and such naming, are the language in which he enables us to read — more than "a little" — in the "infinite book of secrecy" of the nature of final and commanding realities. On the other hand, Shakespeare is just as far removed from supposing that the mere sensible identification of phenomena, and of their order, in time and space, and the naming of them, contains the whole sum of interesting and useful, or marks the outermost limit of possible, knowledge.

"These earthly godfathers of heaven's lights [the astronomers]
That give *a name* to every fixed star,

> Have no more profit of their shining nights
>   Than those that walk, and wot not what they are;
> Too much to know is to know naught but fame:
>   And every godfather can give a name."
> *L. L. Lost*, I, 1.

Shakespeare here satirizes, in effect, as a narrow perversion of the real nature of knowledge, those same methods and practical assumptions which Goethe, through the mouth of Mephistopheles, covers with irony in his Faust tragedy: the *method*, which is content to enumerate, to determine analytically the order in time of the successive states of action which, in life or nature, are bound up in one organic, synthetic act, and the form and mechanical function of each of the parts of a dissected organism, and the *assumption* that this is complete and final knowledge of ultimate reality. Nay — Bacon, Shakespeare's renowned contemporary, to the contrary notwithstanding — there are more things in heaven and earth themselves than are dreamt of in such physical "philosophy." Space and time, figure, motion, the sensibly known, although the form in which nature presents objects to us, are but the form, and not the life, not the substance. Easily may they deceive us. "O place, O form!" cries out Angelo, in *Measure for Measure:*

> " How often dost thou with thy case, thy habit,
>   Wrench awe from fools and tie the wiser souls
>   To thy false seeming!"

And so accurately, and in such manifold figures, has Shakespeare described the various "paces" of time ("Time travels in divers paces with divers persons"), and so, by implication, its relativity, that one of the latest interpreters of Shakespeare's thought claims him as a forerunner of Kant, in holding that time is *only* a subjective form of human sensibility.* Not this, I imagine, is Shakespeare's thought, but that time, as a form of physical existence, shares, except in as far as both are informed with the power of spirit, in the impermanency and insubstantiality of such existence. The fundamental reality of physical existence is not sensibly discerned — in this negative conviction Shakespeare's compatriots of to-day, the "experiential" and physical (or "scientific") philosophers of England, agree with him unanimously, but here, too, their agreement with him is prone to stop;— the material constitution of nature is but a matrix, a temporary instrument of generation, in the hands of an ideal life. For it the same thing holds true, which Shakespeare, in the lines I shall presently quote, plainly teaches concerning man. Its being is not in what it *has*, its material body, a mere instrument, or integument, but in what it *does* (according to the energetic axiom of Leibnitz, "*Substance is* ACTION"), or in the *life* which it lives. In Love's Labour's Lost, Biron, the merriest and most clear-seeing courtier of them all, declares:

> "So study evermore is overshot;
> While it doth study to *have* what it would,
> It doth forget to *do* the thing it should;
> And when it hath the thing it hunteth most,
> 'Tis won, as towns, with fire; so won, so lost."

This mistake, nature of her own accord never makes.

---

* Just as strong, but also, it must be said, just as unconvincing, an argument could be drawn from Shakespeare's imagery, to prove that he held space to be nothing but a subjective form of human sensibility. Compare the intensely forcible ejaculation of the enamored Antony, in Cleopatra's palace: "Here is my space!" and Hamlet's "O God! I could be bounded in a nutshell, and count myself a king of infinite space, were it not that I have bad dreams."

Were she for a moment to "forget to do," and only "study to have," her fate were sealed at once; and this, one day, will be her fate, when exhausted with doing, all her most brilliant and seemingly-solid having shall fade into nothingness. "All is mortal in nature." And Gloucester, soliloquizing over the wrecked mind of King Lear, bursts forth,

> O ruin'd piece of nature! This great world
> Shall so wear out to nought."

And Prospero, whose command of nature was most complete, in well-known lines:—

> "The cloud-capp'd towers, the gorgeous palaces,
> The solemn temples, the great globe itself,
> Yea, all which it inherit, shall dissolve
> And, like this insubstantial pageant faded,
> Leave not a rack behind."*

Plainly, that which to the eye of the greatest poet's discernment is from everlasting to everlasting is not matter, and, consequently, not blind force.

Of what character, now, is this life which nature leads? In what forms is it apprehended by us, and what is its source?

What is Life? Every age has its circle which it seeks to square, its problem, absurd in the terms in which it is stated, that it seeks to solve. Perhaps in our day no more striking illustration of this truth is furnished than in the attempts to comprehend the nature of life by

---

* Mr. Herbert Spencer (First Principles, p. 173) finds in this passage evidence, not of poetic nor of philosophic insight, but, rather, of an unfortunate ignorance, on the poet's part, of the scientific law of the indestructibility of matter! I know not whether Shakespeare's muse, if appealed to, would confess herself more grieved or amused at this criticism.

physical analysis or chemical composition. A Don Quixote of science, selecting inferior organisms, in which life is at its lowest ebb — slumbering, so to speak — and armed with microscope and retort, glass jars and balances, goes to work to pull apart the animate mechanism, to number and classify and name its molecules, to ascertain all the facts of organic structure, and all the visible conditions of life, with a view to creating, subsequently, by artificial means, a similar structure, supplying all these conditions, and seeing life appear. The experiment meets thus far with indifferent success, it is true, but the experimenters have an audacious faith in final victory. And indeed there is a sense — the only one to which genuine, intelligent science pays attention — in which this faith may, for aught I know, be well founded. It may indeed be that some day the ingenuity of man will succeed completely in bringing together all the conditions without which physical life does not exist, and that this success will be rewarded by the vision of physical and chemical motions apparently passing over into, or having added to them, vital motions. But this would prove nothing concerning the nature of the power by which that change was effectuated. And life is *power*, not merely vital *motion*. The latter, as being a phenomenon, physical science may and must observe and trace; the former, as being the cause of phenomena, is confessedly beyond the range of its vision. Further, physical life is conditioned power, or power exerting itself instrumentally. This is the utmost, speaking summarily, that the laboratory can teach us respecting the philosophy of the question, and this is virtually nothing; for who did not know it, who denied it, beforehand? Shakespeare knew it, and also that it was utterly irrelevant as an answer to the question as to—not *how* but *what* life is. "Thou art not thyself," says the Duke, disguised as Friar, who would prepare Claudio for death; *i.e.* Thou, as a being physically constituted of flesh and blood, a mass of visible protoplasm, art not thyself.

> " For thou exist'st in many a thousand grains
> That issue out of dust."
> Meas. for Meas., III, 1.

The enumeration of these grains is not the enumeration of the elements of thy life, nor is the whole sum of them the sum of thy life, and that because, among other things, life is not divisible into physical elements of any kind; it is not anatomically or atomically constituted; it is an indivisible and invisible power, incapable, as such, of mechanical destruction or construction.

After the worker in the laboratory comes the alleged philosopher of the laboratory, and after having warned us and demonstrated to us that neither he nor we can tell what anything really is, but only how and under what laws it appears, edifies us with the assurance that life (as a phenomenon) is "the definite combination of heterogeneous changes, both simultaneous and successive, in correspondence with external coexistences and sequences." We accept the statement in the spirit in which it is offered, as a description, more or less lucid, of what visibly goes on when life is present, and note the alleged "correspondence" or harmonious correlation of different factors, as indicating that life is a power behind and above them all, since it controls all. But the philosophical question is, not what is life as a phenomenon, but what is it as noumenon, a "thing-in-itself," what is it in its essential reality?

To this question no one but the genuine poet, or the real philosopher with true poetic insight, can give an answer. The former necessarily sees, and those who rightly hear him singing cannot but perceive that he sees, and how he sees, what and where life is; and this, even though he make no attempt expressly to tell it. The philosopher sees, and expressly labors to report and persuade of the truth and genuineness of his vision. And the answer which they both unite in giving concerning the nature of life contains the key to all philosophy of being. For *life is being*, which latter is not inert impenetrability (as of material atoms), but the activity of self-exerting, self-evidencing, self-directing power; or rather it is such power (a synonym for life) itself. But "self-directing power," what is it but another expression for spirit, of which reason (intellectual, moral, and æsthetic) is the guide, and will the motive force? This, then, is what the poet and philosopher agree in saying, namely, that as all activity betokens power, so all power betokens, and is (though, it is true, in different grades), the direct function of mind. And so, then, life, which is power, is *energy of mind*. Since now all power is referred to mind — and to what else should it be referred? — physical science confesses that it knows naught of power, or force, as such, but only of phenomena of motion, and the only rival theory to the one just announced is a theory which renounces the task of comprehending, and so explaining, power, and simply accepts it as a brute fact, endowed (as is supposed) with the attributes of fate and mechanical necessity — since, I say, all power is referred to mind, and since all energy of mind is life, it follows that all real power is living (real "*vis viva*"), and that the connotation of the term life must be extended so as to make it coextensive with the whole realm of existence; for the realm of existence extends not where there is no living power, where, to repeat our previous phraseology, there is no *doing*. Life, then, in view of all that has been said, appears as the omnipresent demonstration, in the midst of the phenomenally actual, of the commanding reality of the ideal — *i.e.* of rational, spontaneously active, ever directly or indirectly creative spirit, as that to which essential being alone belongs, and of which alone the "ideal" is the product and vital function.

Our concern here is immediately with the universal life of nature, and not with the conscious personal life of the human spirit, that form of finite existence in which life rises nearest in resemblance to God, its perfect exemplar and giver. We set out to inquire in what forms the life, which Shakespeare recognizes as the essential and constitutive thing in nature, manifests itself and is known to us. Shakespeare's answers are in accordance with the requirements of the foregoing analysis. If life is a function of rational spirit, it can appear and be known only in forms of intelligible order, and in services of goodness and beauty, such as reason can alone understand, propose, and delight in. And thus it is in Shakespeare's world. So completely is *order* the essence and mainstay of the universe that the enraged and desperate Northumberland (in K. II. IV, Pt. II) can pronounce no more frightful imprecation than "Let order die"; with order, reason's living work, all cognizable existence, dies, vanishes into the primæval "darkness," which accordingly the poet leaves to "be the burier of the dead." Living power is gone: created light gives place to undefinable darkness;

the created "something," the round world, shrinks into its original or (sensibly considered) its essential nothingness. Further the life of nature manifests itself in services of goodness and beauty. Take, in illustration of this statement, the 3d sc. in Act II of Romeo and Juliet. It is Friar Lawrence who speaks, and it is related that Shakespeare himself used to assume upon the stage this rôle, as one with which, presumably on account of the sentiments (concerning nature and human life) uttered in it by the keen-visioned and broad-visioned friar, he was in peculiar sympathy.

> "The grey-ey'd morn smiles on the frowning night,
> Check'ring the eastern clouds with streaks of light;
> And flecked darkness like a drunkard reels
> From forth day's path and Titan's fiery wheels.
> Now, ere the sun advance his burning eye
> The day to cheer, and night's dank dew to dry,
> I must up-fill this osier cage of ours
> With baleful weeds and precious-juiced flowers.
> The earth, that's nature's mother, is her tomb;
> What is her burying grave, that is her womb;
> And from her womb children of divers kind
> We sucking on her natural bosom find:
> Many for many virtues excellent,
> None but for some, and yet all different.
> O, mickle is the powerful grace that lies
> In herbs, plants, stones, and their true qualities:
> For nought so vile that on the Earth doth live
> But to the Earth some special good doth give;
> Nor aught so good, but, strain'd from that fair use,
> Revolts from true birth, stumbling on abuse:
> Virtue itself turns vice, being misapplied,
> And vice sometime's by action dignified.
> Within the infant rind of this weak flower
> Poison hath residence, and med'cine power:

> For this, being smelt, with that part cheers each part;
> Being tasted, slays all senses with the heart.
> Two such opposed kings encamp them still
> In man as well as herbs, grace and rude will;
> And where the worser is predominant,
> Full soon the canker death eats up that plant."

It is not without reason that I have twice employed, with reference to nature as it reappears in Shakespeare's thought, the expression, "*services* of goodness and beauty." For as the *virtues* of natural objects are active powers, directed to right uses, so natural beauty is the accompaniment of a service rendered to the universal order, or to man, the created earthly head of that order. The sun is "glorious," indeed, but only as it "completes" its "courses," only as it is a shining sun, a "blessed breeding sun," an "all-cheering sun." The "smallest orb that thou behold'st" sings "like an angel," yet not in idle rest, "but in his motion." This idea is strikingly developed in one of Shakespeare's sonnets (54):

> "O, how much more doth beauty beauteous seem,
>   By that sweet ornament which truth doth give!
> The rose looks fair, but fairer we it deem
> For that sweet odour which doth in it live.
> The canker-blooms have full as deep a dye
> As the perfumed tincture of the roses;
> Hang on such thorns, and play as wantonly
> When Summer's breath their masked buds discloses;
> But, for their virtue only is their shew,
> They live unwoo'd and unrespected fade;
> Die to themselves. Sweet roses do not so;
> Of their sweet deaths are sweetest odours made."

Natural beauty is the ministrant and fainter type of the beauty of moral beings—of men, more immediately

—which consists precisely in, or is the inseparable and indispensable garb of active moral perfection, and of which Shakespeare sings, "Virtue is beauty," "Beauty lives with kindness," and (of Portia) "She is fair [*i.e.* in the 'shew' mentioned above in the sonnet], and, fairer than that word, of wondrous virtues." It is *man* whom Shakespeare terms "the beauty of the *world!*"

Shakespeare is far enough removed from that sentimentalism, prevalent in later times, which is prone to revel in descriptive praises of "nature," as of an immense pictorial "shew," which spreads itself out periodically for the idle delectation of human beholders—a panorama whose whole significance is exhausted in the impression which it produces on the organs of human sensation—a sort of *article de luxe*, mysteriously, or, rather, to all intents and purposes, accidentally, just because incomprehensibly, provided for lazy, intellectual sybarites—an object to be "returned to," after a period of unnatural estrangement, with forced and hence sickly "love," or over which (to apply a phrase of Goethe's)

"Sich staunend zu ergötzen"

(translated freely: "to revel in the luxury of astonishment"). It is this mental—or sentimental—attitude with reference to nature, the prevalence of which in modern poetry Schiller, in a well-known essay, deplored and contrasted with the healthier simplicity of Homer and Shakespeare, whose power and real insight lay in the fact that *their feeling was natural*, while ours is an artificial plant, a hot-house growth of professed "love" and often all but deifying "admiration" *for nature*. ("*Sie empfanden natürlich; wir empfinden das Natürliche.*")

For Shakespeare, as for Homer, nature is not the object of supreme interest, whether morally or æsthetically. But whatever interest she does possess, arises from the circumstance that the uses and beauties of nature foreshadow and are auxiliary to the excellences and beauties of human character. And this, again, they do and are, because they are the manifestations of a life communicated in common to nature and to man, her crown,— though in lower potency to the former than to the latter. In short, they are, in accordance with our foregoing definition, revelations — direct works — of an "energy of mind." The life of nature is the power of God. And it is a wonderful touch of nature's art in Shakespeare, that, to the height of this grand, but simple, argument — (for, after all, it is only the argument of *living* sight) — he represents, in a passage redolent as with a fresh breeze of healthy, open-air delight, not man, but a being belonging peculiarly and alone to "nature," as rising :—

> "But what a point, my lord, your falcon made,
> And what a pitch she flew above the rest,
> *To see how God in all his creatures works!*
> Yea, man and birds are fain of climbing high."
>
> 2 *K. H. VI, II, 1.*

Nature lives, but not through herself. She lives in God, through the power of divine spirit. Her rational and fixed order, her virtues, her beauties, all bespeak the immediate energy of mind. Hence that which is "a fault to nature" is also "to reason [the function of mind] most absurd."

The remaining portion of our present theme — respecting Shakespeare's conception of essential or perfect manhood — is nearly as inexhaustible as his works themselves.

I can now only recall hastily some of the leading elements in that conception, and seek to emphasize a point or two of capital importance, to which Shakespeare himself, by the striking emphasis of his language, directs the attention even of the unwilling.

Note, then, that in the world of Shakespeare there is no question whether man is simply a physical phenomenon or a spiritual reality, whether his mind is originally a *tabula rasa*, and subsequently a mechanical growth, or a living power, possessing a nature and faculties of its own, nor, consequently, whether he is in his action automatic or free. By as much as man is man, Shakespeare perceives that the second, in each of these pairs of alternatives, is true of him. But Shakespeare also perceives that the actual man may only be half a man, and almost no man at all; and, in general, that manhood is a problem, which every one is called upon, on pain, if he neglect this, of being less than man, to solve; a work, in which all men, with more or less of intelligence and success, are engaged, or else are fatally neglecting; an ideal, the free and willing realization of which marks the true man. Nor is he, also, unmindful of the circumstance that although essential manhood is an ideal value, a spiritual life, yet the means of its present manifestation, nay, more, of its present *realization*, is the "natural man," as existing in and determined by flesh and blood, with his manifold peculiarities of temperament, and advantages or disadvantages of *milieu* or environment, the whole constituting a mechanism which at once serves as a check or foil, but also as an instrumental lever and fulcrum, to the spiritual man. And so accurate is Shakespeare's knowledge of the phenomenology of the natural or (in modern phrase) physiologico-psychological man, that in this respect, too, the full truth, as it regards Shakespeare, of Herder's belief is sustained, that "Homer and Sophocles, Dante and Shakespeare have furnished more material for psychology and the knowledge of man than even the Aristotles and Leibnitzes of all nations and times." No one is better acquainted than Shakespeare with the degree to which the heart—

"Corrupt, corrupt, and tainted in desire"—

and not only that, but the "pale cast of" intellectual "thought," blinds the eye to the true self, and sicklies o'er the native hue of the spirit's resolution. None know better than he to what degree "nature must obey necessity." Yet this knowledge does not mislead him for an instant, or by the distance of a hair's breadth, toward the identification of manhood with automatism. Imagine for an instant the impossible, and suppose the men and women of Shakespeare's dramas to be mere automata. Can a more profane travesty of the poet's noble, all-persuasive thought be conceived? Enter the portals of his splendid, truthful visions, and your brow is cooled, your spirit invigorated at once with the breath of a freedom, a responsibility, a glad and sacred possibility, which is neither the slave nor the enemy, but the facile and rightful mistress and user of the earthy. The "necessity" of bent, of passion, of external influence is only apparent. It is a sham. It is a lion in the way of the moral sluggard. To genuine manhood it offers, in its various forms, steps and stimuli, means and instruments.

"Our mere defects" may
"Prove our commodities."—*Lear*, IV, 1.

The only true necessity, as Shakespeare will illustrate for us, is that which a reasonable will, not submits to, but creates.

But it is time that Shakespeare himself be allowed to express himself on these various points. I am aware how delicate a matter it sometimes is to select from the works of a dramatic author, where the exigencies of the case require him to bring before his public persons actuated by and giving expression to all varieties of sentiment, passages in which the author is to be considered as expressing his own views. Of course I would venture upon nothing of the kind were I not convinced that the citations I make are fairly representative of the main direction of the poet's own thought — a conviction which must, naturally, depend quite as much, or more, on a certain comprehensive and sympathetic perception of the elements of the general moral atmosphere which pervades Shakespeare's dramatic world, as on the analysis of single texts. I willingly accept the responsibility for my own judgments in the present case, with no fear of their being contradicted either by the general consensus of Shakespearean criticism or by the common opinion of all intelligent lovers of Shakespeare.

First, then, we are not characteristically ourselves when, or so far as, our lives are absorbed in sensual functions: the self to which Shakespeare, through the mouth of Polonius, bids us be true ("to thine own *self* be true"), is an ideal possibility and requirement, a spiritual entity— for it is endowed with reason to perceive, and will to execute, and heart to love, the ideal truth, and goodness, and beauty.

> "What" [says Hamlet] "is man
> If his chief good and market of his time
> Be but to sleep and feed? a beast, no more.
> Sure, He that made us with such large discourse,
> Looking before and after, gave us not
> That capability and godlike reason,
> To fust in us unus'd."

The perfect (or, in Plato's language, which Shakespeare also imitates, *kingly*) state of man is when each "office" does

> "Distinctly his full function."

This were a harmony of sense and reason, which, however, in view of the unbridled lusts of the former, is not to be effectuated but by the use of reason to bridle and control sensuous passion. Hence, the excellent advice which Northumberland, in K. H. VIII, I, 1, gives to Buckingham, is an elementary principle of ethics, or of practical truth to self:

> "Ask God for temp'rance."

> "Let your reason with your choler question
> What 'tis you go about. To climb steep hills
> Requires slow pace at first: anger is like
> A full-hot horse, who being allow'd his way,
> Self-mettle tires him. Not a man in England
> Can advise me like you. Be to yourself
> As you would to your friend."

Buckingham has, namely, the knowledge and the faculty requisite to guide and control himself as his own manhood requires. Again:

> "Be advis'd:
> say again, there is no English soul
> More stronger to direct you than yourself,

> If with the sap of reason you would quench,
> Or but allay, the fire of passion."

The same lesson is familiarly known to, or practiced by, Prospero, the intellectual hero of that play which, in Prof. Dowden's language, "expresses Shakespeare's highest and serenest view of life." Says Prospero:

> "Though with their high wrongs I am struck to the quick,
> Yet with my nobler reason 'gainst my fury
> Do I take part: the rarer action is
> In virtue than in vengeance."

Even Iago, who is just as little a fool as he is a consummate villain, will tell us: "If the balance of our lives had not one scale of reason to poise another of sensuality, the blood and baseness of our natures would conduct us to most preposterous conclusions; but we have reason to cool our raging motions, our carnal stings, our unbitted lusts." Aye, "to most preposterous conclusions" are we in fact conducted when, not deprived of, but displacing, the "scale of reason," and neglecting that moral work by which character is formed, the natural man is allowed to have his own way (a too common error now-a-days, not only in self-discipline — by reason of the common absorption in the chase for secondary goods, as place and wealth, and physical comfort — but also in the discipline of children, who, dear creatures, must not have their wills, *i.e.* their unreasoning passions, crossed, lest they lack "spirit"; as though "spirit" were not a deadly thing, without the kingly power to rule it!). For then are we not simply "not ourselves" — as is the case

> "When nature, being oppressed, commands the mind
> To suffer with the body"

(*i.e.* when, through natural causes, complete functional derangement supervenes) — but worse. For

> "Sometimes we are devils to ourselves,
> When we will tempt the frailty of our powers,"

i.e. of our lower powers, and that by relaxing our hold upon them. Nay, then we are "merely our own traitors. And as in the common course of all treasons, we still see them reveal themselves, till they attain to their abhorred ends; so he that in this action *contrives against his own nobility, in his proper stream o'erflows himself*" (All's Well That Ends Well, IV, 3.) We "pursue

> (Like rats that ravin down their proper bane)
> A thirsty evil, and when we drink we die."
> *Meas. for Meas.*, I, 3.

Now that in such a course of active personal degradation, when we

> "In our own filth drop our clear judgments," and "strut
> To our confusion,"

there is much that is automatic, is perfectly known to Shakespeare, as to every thoughtful man. But precisely therein lies, not the excuse, but the disgrace and the condemnation of him who thus errs. The lower nature of man is precisely an automatic mechanism, and uncontrolled it moves at last with a power practically irresistible.

> "What rein can hold licentious wickedness,
> When down the hill he holds his fierce career?"

cries out Shakespeare's favorite hero, King Henry V. But also, precisely in the circumstance of our allowing the automatic mechanism to run without restraint consists the very treason to ourselves above noted. We abdicate our own manhood by submitting to be controlled by, and practically absorbed in, a mechanism which (unhappily) will move on, with ever-increasing and dangerous speed, without waiting for any direct impulses on our part. We are not true to our real selves; we consent, as much as in us lies, not to be ourselves. It is then that life appears — and rightly — as it did to Macbeth, when by crime he had divested himself of his proper humanity, as

>"A walking shadow
>. . . a tale
>Told by an idiot, full [indeed] of sound and fury,
>[But] signifying nothing."

But our condemnation remains, for the automatic part is originally not put in possession of us, but we are placed in possession of it, and it is ours to maintain and confirm our control of it. It is of no avail for us to declare, with reference to its power over us (with Roderigo), "it is not in my virtue [power] to amend it." The answer is: "Virtue? a fig! 'tis in ourselves that we are thus or thus. Our bodies are gardens, to the which our wills are gardeners; so that if we will plant nettles, or sow lettuce; set hyssop, and weed up thyme; supply it with one gender of herbs, or distract it with many; either to have it steril with idleness, or manur'd with industry; why, the power and corrigible authority of this lies in our wills" (Othello, I, 3.) If we sow we shall reap, and the crop will grow automatically; but it is for us to determine how and what we will sow. This is our responsibility, but also our privilege. (A like subterfuge of human frailty is powerfully castigated by Edmund, in King Lear, I, 2: "This is the excellent foppery of the world, that when we are sick in fortune (often the surfeit of our own behavior), we make guilty of our disasters the sun, the moon and the stars, as if we were villains by necessity, . . . and all that we are evil in by a divine thrusting on.") In short, Shakespeare's characters are endowed with free will, and it is preëminently because they are thus endowed that all men everywhere recognize themselves in them. The poet, reading human nature with his divinely given insight, finds there what philosophy and the common sense of mankind agree in finding, freedom, spontaneity, and true, and in its measure independent, life, undisturbed by the utterly irrelevant circumstance (which yet seems to disturb so many excellent people now-a-days) that the analytic science of mental *phenomena* (not of mental *life*) discovers nothing of the sort. And further, and more particularly, notice that Shakespeare — the all-seeing, we are tempted to say — has expressed, with wonderful effect, in one line, a truth which is a commonplace for all profound and consistent philosophic thought, namely, that for will — which, in the last resort, is the only and sufficient explanation of all real power or "force," and hence, in conjunction with reason, its inseparable companion, of all things — there is no necessity whatever but such as itself creates; true necessity is not imposed, it is *made*. This, in its relation to man, is expressed by one of Shakespeare's characters in these words:

"Look, what I will not, that I cannot do!"
Meas. for Meas., II, 2.

Plainly enough, for Shakespeare, the specific nature of man consists (in the phraseology which I used hypothetically near the beginning of this chapter) in the living, spiritual realization, through the free activity of a reasonable will, of an ideal purpose. At the same time Shakespeare forgets none of the conditions on which the best activity of reason and will depend, or means by which they are disciplined and made effective. Reason must be enlightened, else were it not reason, and would not accomplish its due function.

> " Ignorance is the curse of God,
> Knowledge the wing wherewith we fly to heaven."
> 2 K. H. VI, IV, 7.

Such knowledge, not a merely passive acquisition of the intellect (not mere information), but a main-spring of action to the will which it illuminates, is, partly, it is true, a virtual endowment, but partly, also, and no less essentially, a cultivable growth.

> "Nature, crescent, does not grow alone,
> In thews and bulk, but, as *this temple* waxes
> *The inward service of the mind and soul*
> Grows wide withal." *Hamlet*, I, 3.

It does not all accrue from sense-impressions. It involves self-knowledge, through solitary communion of the soul with itself — whence its language is (K. Henry V is the speaker):

> "I and my bosom must debate awhile,
> And then I would no other company."

The will of man itself is not a faculty of wonder-working omnipotence, but works through means which, on the one hand, limit and define its scope, and, on the other, are its own creation. The enlightened will *makes* habit and uses it as its instrument.

> "Refrain to-night,
> And that shall lend a kind of easiness
> To the next abstinence: the next more easy;
> For use almost can change the stamp of nature,
> And either curb the devil, or throw him out
> With wondrous potency."   *Hamlet, III, 4.*

But will, enlightened, must act promptly, otherwise it wastes its own energy.

> "That we would do,
> We should do when we would; for this *would* changes,
> And hath abatements, and delays as many,
> As there are tongues, are hands, are instruments."

Nor, finally, does Shakespeare forget that the divine in man is organically related to the supreme divine. The divine purpose in man is indeed self-realizing, but only through the ever-ready help of God.

> "Every man with his affects is born,
> Not by might master'd but by special grace."
>   *L. L. Lost, I, 1.*

Over the righteous cause of the individual or the nation the ægis of divine protection is represented as constantly hovering. The faintest endeavor, if sincere, to work righteousness, God not simply approves, but aids. This sentiment (in general terms) shines throughout Shakespeare's histories: "Heaven is above all yet" (K. H. VIII, III, 1); "Heaven still guards the right" (K. R. II, III, 2); and no less in his tragedies; to cite further illustrations were to draw from a well-nigh inexhaustible mine.

So, then, the end of all human perfection is — not "vanity" — but the undemonstrative majesty of ideal character, whose "greatest help" — and strength — "is quiet" (2 K. H. VI, II, 4); whose "crown is called content" (3 K. H. VI, III, 1), to which not seldom "nothing" brings "all things" (Timon of Ath., V, 2), which knows at the right time "the blessedness of being little" (K. H. VIII, IV, 2); and yet, made "bold and resolute" through the consciousness of its own "innocence," can, in the defense of a right cause, demonstrate greatly its own imperial power. Concerning which let us conclude by hearing two characters whom we may rightly judge to be among the most *Shakespearean* of all those who people Shakespeare's wonderful transcript of the moral world. And first, Hamlet:

> "Rightly to be great,
> Is *not to stir* without great argument,
> But *greatly* to find quarrel in a straw,
> When honour's at the stake."   IV, 4.

And K. Henry V, of whom Shakespeare, in the chorus-prologue to Act IV, cries, "Praise and glory on his head":

> "In peace there's nothing so becomes a man
> As modest stillness and humility;
> But when the blast of war blows in our ears,
> *   *   *   *   *   *   *
> Stiffen the sinews, summon up the blood,
> *   *   *   *   *   *   *
> Then lend the eye a terrible aspect;
> Let it pry through the portage of the head,
> Like the brass cannon; let the brow o'erwhelm it
> As fearfully as does a galled rock
> O'erhang and jutty his confounded base,
> Swill'd with the wide and wasteful ocean.
> *   *   *   *   *   *   *
> *   *   *   bend up every spirit
> To his full height. On, on, you noblest English.
> *   *   *   *   *   *   *

* * *   The game's afoot:
Follow your spirit [not, yield to an automatic impulse],
   and upon this charge
Cry, 'God for Harry, England, and St. George!'"
                                                    III, 1.

But this discussion must end here, even though abruptly. I trust I have done something to show that Shakespeare the poet reads life — in the broadest acceptation of the term — as the universal mind of man reads it, as the heart feels it, as philosophy interprets it. Shakespeare, as a true poet, supplies philosophy with its peculiar data and tests. He supplies one of the first and grandest proofs of the native endowment of the English mind with the first and grandest prerequisite of genuine philosophy; I mean with the power of *living* — which is spiritual — insight.

CHAPTER V.

FRANCIS BACON.

WE come now to the consideration of a name which Englishmen at large have been wont to honor as one of the proudest in their annals; to one whom they are proud to regard as typical of all that most entitles their nation to the intellectual respect and substantial gratitude of mankind. Not, however, as we shall see, without variation and marked exception; and it will be our endeavor to seek to indicate in general what estimate is really to be placed upon his spirit and his work.

William Rawley, D.D., "His Lordship's first and last Chaplain," begins his brief "Life of the Honourable Author" as follows:

"Francis Bacon, the glory of his age and nation, the adorner and ornament of learning, was born in York House, or York Place, in the Strand, on the two and twentieth day of January, in the year of our Lord 1560 [old style; new style, 1561]. His father was that famous counsellor to Queen Elizabeth, the second prop of the kingdom in his time, Sir Nicholas Bacon, knight, lord-keeper of the great seal of England; a lord of known prudence, sufficiency, moderation, and integrity. His mother was Anne, one of the daughters of Sir Anthony Cook, unto whom the erudition of King Edward the Sixth had been committed; a choice lady, and eminent for piety, virtue, and learning; being exquisitely skilled, for a woman, in the Greek and Latin tongues. These being the parents, you may easily imagine what the issue was like to be; having had whatsoever nature or breeding could put into him."

He, into whom nature and breeding had really put

their best work, might well consider himself made for the greatest things: a view, which, as we shall see, Bacon indeed took of himself. Note, further, particularly that Bacon was born into the atmosphere of courtly station, and that, too, when life in such station must rest upon a strong and solid sense of generous and just power. For it was in the "golden days of good queen Bess," from which, in the words of Mr. E. A. Freeman, the "completed national character of England mainly dates;" a very and noble "*partus temporis*" (to apply a phrase of Bacon's), or "*birth of time*," when convergent lines of political and religious life met, crystallized, and manifested themselves in demonstrations of conscious political and moral energy and wholeness, unparalleled in the history of England, and in which sovereign and nobility participated, not as idle or indifferent spectators, but, very essentially, as true leaders of the people. His mother, too, like Spenser's "Gloriana," Queen Bess, was "exquisitely skilled in the Greek and Latin tongues." That Renaissance love of letters which helped to kindle that other larger, freer, more spontaneous and more energetic "love of the soul," the fire of genius, whose light in English literature was then beginning to burn more intensely than ever before or since, was, then, among the fires which burned on Bacon's domestic hearth. A happy augury, one would say, indeed!

However, we find Bacon — with whom as a boy Queen Elizabeth is said to have "delighted much to confer . . . and to prove him with questions"; who, then, "delivered himself with that gravity and maturity above his years that her majesty would often term him, *The young lord-keeper*" — we find him, I say, just past the age of twelve years, in the spring of 1573, entering Trinity College, Cambridge, where he remained as a diligent student for three years. Just what the nature of the instruction was, which he received in philosophy — from which in those days natural science was not sharply separated as now — we do not know. The doctrine taught was, however, termed Aristotelian, doubtless with a large admixture of scholastic form and interpretation. It failed to satisfy the youthful mind, and, doubtless, rather immature judgment, of Bacon, but not, certainly, for the same reason for which, a little later, the Frenchman Descartes turned away from the like instruction unsatisfied. What Descartes missed was a basis of absolute certainty for philosophical knowledge — the knowledge of *being* — of God, of spirit and matter, of soul and body, and, by implication, of those moral and æsthetic sciences which depend on such knowledge. Bacon, on the other hand, was discontented at the material fruitlessness of the doctrine taught him, at the absence (to employ an expression subsequently used by himself) of "industrious observations, grounded conclusions, and profitable inventions and discoveries." Not the ontological question as to the absolute nature of reality, no unsolved, or apparently unsolved, riddle of "fate, free-will, and providence" troubled him or occupied primarily his attention. His thoughts were concentrated, or beginning to be concentrated, on the knowledge of physical phenomena and the uses to be derived from such knowledge.

Shortly after leaving the University we find Bacon accompanying Sir Amyas Paulet, the English ambassador, to Paris, and, during the two years and more of his residence in France, travelling extensively in the provinces of that country. Returning in 1579, upon the death of his father, and being obliged, owing to the slightness of the fortune left him, to choose some profession by which to earn his living, he adopted the law. His devotion to the study of the law did not keep him from having a prudent eye to the chances for political advancement and preferment at the court. Indeed, Dr. Rawley, his friend and biographer, very naïvely, and with a quaint air of truth, remarks, "Notwithstanding that he professed the law for his livelihood and subsistence, yet his heart and affection were more carried after the affairs and places of estate"; he made the law "(as himself said) but as an accessory, and not his principal study."

In 1580 began the correspondence with his uncle, Lord Burghley, the queen's lord-treasurer, asking that his influence might be exerted in the writer's behalf. In 1584 he entered parliament as member for Melcombe, in Dorsetshire. His advancement at the bar was rapid. "His birth and other capacities" brought him frequently to court and to "the queen's eye, who would often grace him with private and free communication, not only about matters of his profession or business in law, but also about the arduous affairs of state; from whom she received from time to time great satisfaction. Nevertheless, though she cheered him much with the bounty of her countenance, yet she never cheered him with the bounty of her hand." In other words, the queen honored but did not enrich him, save only (through Lord Burghley's influence in 1589) with "one dry reversion of the register's office in the Star Chamber, worth about £1,600 *per annum*, for which he waited in expectation fully, or near, twenty years [till 1608; he then administered it by deputy]; of which his lordship would say in Queen Elizabeth's time, *that it was like another man's ground buttaling on his house,* which might mend his prospect, but it did not fill his barn." And it was or seemed of special consequence to Bacon that *his* barn should be filled, partly because he was and ever remained in the uncomfortable position of a man in debt, and partly because he had undertaken what was, in his view, to be the most vast of conquests, the plan for which he had roughly announced in a tractate (now lost) somewhat ambitiously entitled "The Greatest Birth of Time" (*Temporis Partus Maximus*). Bacon, namely, carrying over into the domain of mind a certain lordly instinct of domination and world-conquest, which it is instructive to note, had, in a letter to the lord-treasurer, his uncle, written at the age of one-and-thirty, made use of these words: "I have taken all knowledge to be my province." It was his purpose to clear this province of roving invaders, and, taking possession of it, to put it under such an excellent system of administration that its peace and prosperity should be henceforth assured. "This," he continued, "whether it be curiosity or vainglory, or nature, or (if one take it favorably) *philanthropia*, is so fixed in my mind as it cannot be removed." Evidently the fixed idea of the reformer possessed Francis Bacon. But in order to execute the proposed plan of subjugation and reform, leisure and freedom from distracting material anxieties seemed indispensable, and to secure such leisure and freedom, no way appeared likely to be shorter and quicker, and none more consonant with the aspirations and conscious desert of one born in Bacon's circumstances and with his peculiar nature, than to seek for some position in the gift of the crown, upon the emoluments of which he could support himself with dignity, while time should be left him for the peculiar work he had undertaken. Hence we can understand that the failure, from whatever cause (the secret opposition of his cousin, Robert Cecil, is alleged), to obtain advancement in the service of the crown, could not but be doubly disappointing.

However, as years pass on we find Bacon still in public life. In the parliament summoned in 1593 he sat as member for Middlesex. Grave questions of constitutional privilege and precedent were brought before that body, and in the discussion of them Bacon took an important and influential part, guided, apparently, by a regard for the true interests of the country and its liberties, and to the detriment of his own immediate fortunes. We can easily imagine what must have been the style of argument of the man who, in addition to his well-attested legal acumen, possessed that knowledge of history and that practical insight, of which, in his Essays (first published four years later, 1597), he was destined to give the world such illustrious evidence. "Rare Ben Jonson" has described his eloquence, saying:

"No man ever spoke more neatly, more pressly, more weightily, or ever suffered less emptiness, less idleness, in what he uttered."

Some time before this had begun the famous friendship with the Earl of Essex, the issue of which was destined to do so much to justify, in popular estimation, the last of the epithets applied to Bacon in Pope's famous line:

"The wisest, brightest, *meanest* of mankind."

Those who, delighting in malice, and determined to thwart Bacon's bequest of his name and memory to "men's charitable speeches," are resolved that this and other passages in Bacon's life shall read as a story of unmitigated shame, will read and accept the accounts given, for example, by Macaulay in his essay on Bacon, or Campbell in his Lives of the Lord Chancellors. Less passionate, and more just and favorable to Bacon, are the maturer judgments of such men as Mr. Spedding (*Letters and Life of Francis Bacon*) and Prof. Adamson (Article *Bacon*, Encycl. Brit., 9th ed., Vol. III). At best, the story of Bacon's relations with Essex is melancholy enough. For it represents him as receiving for years the affection and substantial favor of the Earl, advising and at times warning him faithfully, and finally, when the latter had made himself manifestly, and by his own final confession, guilty of inexcusable treason, compelled as a servant of the crown and of truth to take part against his former friend in the proceedings which resulted in his conviction and capital punishment. The most, as it appears to me, that can be said against Bacon, in connection with this affair, is that the conflict of old affection, and the coincidence of immediate personal interest, with the final obligation to proceed actively against Essex, did not, as far as I have learned, produce, on the one hand, any violent laceration of feeling or, on the other, any signs of morbidly conscientious self-questionings in Bacon's breast.

Though under Elizabeth Bacon's standing was that of one of the learned counsel, yet he was not a salaried officer, and his pecuniary fortunes languished. At one time he contemplated mending his condition by marriage with a wealthy, but in other respects undesirable, widow. This, however, did not succeed, and in the year 1598 he was once arrested for debt and taken to a sponging-house. "But," as Rawley, his chaplain-biographer, curiously puts it, "though he stood long at a stay in the days of his mistress Queen Elizabeth, yet after the change, and coming in of his new master King James, he made a great progress; by whom he was much comforted in places of trust, honour, and revenue." "Nine times," indeed, according to Bacon's own enumeration, did his royal master raise and advance him; "thrice in dignity and six times in office." Soon after the accession of King James, Bacon was knighted. He was also continued in the same standing which he had held under Queen Elizabeth, as Counsel Learned Extraordinary. His subsequent appointments were as follows: in 1607, to be Solicitor General; in 1613, Attorney General; 1616, Privy-Councillor; 1617, Lord Keeper of the Great Seal; 1618, Lord Chancellor. In 1618 he was created Baron Verulam, and in 1621 Viscount St. Alban's.

Bacon was not merely a student and a man of reflection; he was also a politician and knew and used the arts of the politician. He was throughout his whole career a pertinacious wire-puller. He prudently and energetically kept all his irons constantly in the fire. He flooded the king and all his influential friends with letters urging his own fitness for important offices. (And in urging his claims Bacon always knew how to quote not only the ancients in general but also, in particular, "Scripture to his purpose"; as, for example, when, in a letter to King James, he says that "Perceiving how, at this time, preferments of law fly about mine ears, to some above me, and to some below me, I did conceive your majesty may think it rather a kind of dullness, or want of faith, than modesty, if I should not come with my pitcher to *Jacob's* [= James's] well, as others do.") He sagaciously took time by the fore-lock and sued in advance for the reversion of valuable and honorable appointments. Every step in his promotion was zealously recommended by himself. A sincere believer in royal prerogative, Bacon made himself the constant and generally trusted adviser of royalty. To this honest service was added that welcome adulation of the royal intellect and learning, of which specimens are furnished in the dedication of his principal philosophical writings to King James. That in all this Bacon was moved only by a base and narrow self-interest, is a preposterous supposition. He was conscious of rare powers. The circumstances of his birth and station would naturally incline him to seek, as a natural right, what others could not aspire to without being, perhaps justly, charged with unlawful ambition. While not in advance of his age (the rather behind it) in regard to some matters of constitutional policy and right, he had large views and generous aims with reference to the establishment of order and prosperity in church and state, and he earnestly and lawfully desired the opportunity to labor for their realization and attainment. Besides, we must remember, with reference not simply to this matter of the means and arts, by which Bacon rose, but also, and much more, to many portions of his official life which have been far more severely criticised, that while ethical standards may be and are in fact inherently invariable, yet the practical interpretation and application of them in the judgment of conduct is visibly subject to great variations. It was less than a half century before the birth of Bacon when Macchiavelli published his notorious book, *Il Principe*, in which political ethics was made to sanction the use of any means, no matter how foul, by which the purposes of the state, or what amounted to the same thing, of its sovereign ruler, could be most directly accomplished. Granting that the book of Macchiavelli is to be considered as exactly reflecting only the political methods prevalent in Italy, and during an exceptional and passing period, and granting, also, that political morality had, in Bacon's time, made greater advances in England than in any other civilized country, the fact still remains that, in substance, what we now term Macchiavelism, abounding as it does in heinous offenses against abstract morality, was by no means then considered as altogether and essentially immoral. At all events the necessity of the state was easily held to compel, and practically to justify, occasional, or even frequent, deviations from the path of simple, absolute, self-respecting, and self-consistent morality. Under those circumstances it would seem that the man who was set to serve the prince must not be one who would be guided by a principle of universal love ("Love thy neighbor as thyself," the principle of all social ethics), but rather one who could ignore the dictates of such a sentiment, or even allow himself to be guided by an opposite one, in the service of his sovereign's interests and of his own, indissolubly bound up with the former. Something like this view was obviously present to the mind of Bacon when, in his essay "Of Goodness and Goodness of Nature," mentioning that "there be that in their nature do not affect the good of others," he goes on to speak of those in this class whose "malignity" is of "the deeper sort" and "turneth to envy and mere mischief," adding: "Such dispositions are the very errours of human nature; and yet they are the fittest timber to make great politiques of; like to knee timber, that is good for ships, that are ordained to be tossed; but not for building houses that shall stand firm." Are we to consider this passage as a sort of confession — and indeed a sufficiently direct one — on the part of Bacon the practical philosopher, who certainly knew what were the "colours" of moral good and evil — that he as a "politique," or statesman, was such only in view of his at least partial possession of one of those warped natures — "knee timber" — which cannot enter into the building of a firm and steadfast moral character, but are ordained to be tossed? At all events, I have indicated the direction in which, as I believe, we must — as bound in charity — look for considerations sufficient to palliate the severity of our moral judgment concerning incidents in his public career otherwise absolutely indefensible (as, *e.g.* in connection with the celebrated Peacham affair).

But to return to the point whence this digression began. Bacon's own experience sufficiently illustrated the truth of the following observations, taken from his essay, entitled "Of Great Place": "The rising unto place is laborious; and by pains men come to greater pains; and it is base; and by indignities men come to dignities. The standing is slippery, and the regress is either a downfall, or at least an eclipse, which is a melancholy thing. *Cum non sis qui fueris, non esse cur velis vivere.*" Bacon's "regress" was a "downfall," sudden, precipitous, disastrous; it was also a final and total "eclipse" of his public, official, career; and had he not at the same time had and followed, all along, with the better half of his soul, another and serener and nobler career, as a man of letters, and philanthropic missionary of science, accompanied, as seems evident to me, with a devout, self-renouncing christian trust, he might, before his death, well have employed the language of the Latin apothegm above cited by him: "When you are no longer what you were, you have no reason for wishing to live." I refer, of course, to the charges of judicial corruption, which were, in parliament, in the spring of the year 1621, brought against Bacon, and which, being sustained by his own penitent confession, led, early in May, to his deposition, by the House of Lords, from the office of Lord Chancellor, to the imposition of an enormous fine (remitted by the king), to imprisonment in the Tower during the king's pleasure (he sat in the Tower four days), to his incapacitation forever "for any office, place or employment in the state or commonwealth," and to his exclusion from entrance within the verge of the court (a condition which was subsequently annulled). The spectacle of a conspicuous and honorable reputation blasted is, alas! one which, in all ages, occurs but too often. Unhappily, also, human nature too often takes an inhuman delight in witnessing the mournful spectacle, and proceeds at once, most fallaciously and ungenerously, to argue from the just downfall of reputation to the utter absence or ruin of any germ or basis of real character and moral worth in the unlucky victim. Profound truth is contained in that ethical psychology which may be discovered underlying the warnings of Jesus of Nazareth: "Judge not, that ye be not judged," and, "Let him that thinketh he standeth take heed lest he fall." Our judgment upon others *is* at once a judgment upon ourselves; for are not they of the same family as ourselves? are not we like unto them? Let us beware, then, of joining in the self-ignorant and self-condemning hue and cry, which customarily follows public disgrace, and which has been abundantly, and still is persistently raised by many about the memory of the fallen Lord Chancellor. We may admit and deplore and profitably take warning from his discovered fault, but we may not, in charity, magnify it beyond its real, or into preter-human, proportions, and, in particular, in the absence of convincing proofs to the contrary, we have no right to charge that it was greater or other than he himself admitted.

Bacon once alludes (in a letter to the king) to his own frailty and to "the abuse of the times," of which, he said, he might "partake." But he did not, for he could not, in the end seek to shelter himself behind this plea. "I do again confess," said he, in a letter to the House of Lords, "that on the points charged upon me, although they should be taken as myself have declared them, there is a great deal of corruption and neglect, for which I am heartily and penitently sorry, and submit myself to the judgment, mercy and grace of the court." The acts charged (twenty-eight cases were specified) were (in general) the taking of fees or bribes from suitors whose cases he was to decide. Bacon, admitting the general truth of the specifications, denied that any of them were cases of "bargain and contract for reward to prevent justice, *pendente lite.*" Indeed, the very first complaint against him was brought by one who alleged that Bacon had received from him a sum of money while a suit was still in progress, and had afterward decided against him. What this complainant and some others had to find fault with was precisely the incorruptibility of Bacon's judgment, and their own folly in bestowing their money for nought. Bacon's fault was a too great, but not wholly unnatural or inexplicable, readiness to receive the money offered. But while Bacon thus denied that he had ever received bribes as of express contract to pervert justice, he specifies two other ways in which bribes may be taken, and claims that they cover all the cases which could be charged against him: the one, "where the judge conceives the cause to be at an end, by the information of the party or otherwise, and useth not such diligence as he ought to inquire of it"; the other, "where the cause is really ended, and it is *sine fraude*, without relation to any precedent promise." As to the first of these cases he admits: "I doubt on some particulars I may be faulty. And for the last, I conceived it to be no fault, but therein I desire to be better informed, that I may be twice penitent, once for the fact and again for the error." Upon this statement of Bacon's let us suspend our judgment, and believe that he was conscious of complete purity in all his past judicial intentions when he declared, "I was the justest judge that was in England these fifty years," though he added, "it was the justest censure in parliament that was these two hundred years."

The story of the last five years of Bacon's life contains much to stir at once our pity and our admiration. We are reminded of a great ship, returning weather-beaten, storm-tossed, rent, from a long voyage, and compelled still to plow its proud way through the few leagues which yet separate it from the haven's rest, against winds of passion and waves of anxiety and distress. Wracked with mental agony and physical disease, we find Bacon suing piteously to have one after another of the ingredients in his cup of punishment removed from him, and then, when his request was granted, desiring and buoyantly hoping to be restored to the highest and most honorable positions of service near the person of his sovereign; at last, grievously disappointed, crying out in his bitterness, "The talent which God has given me I have misspent in things for which I was least fit." During all this time he maintains a wonderful activity of literary production and scientific research, and at last, childless and alienated from his wife, dies on the morning of the 9th of April, Easter Sunday, 1626.

Bacon, acknowledging to Sir Thomas Bodley his many errors, mentions, as the "great one which led the rest, that knowing myself by inward calling to be better fitted to hold a book than play a part, I have led my life in civil causes, for which I was not very fit by nature, and more unfit by preoccupation of mind." Had this preoccupation been less genuine and intense than it really was, Bacon's place in history would have been infinitely less important and interesting than it now is. It is by the fruits of his study, his reflection, his intellectual spirit and literary inspiration, that he still lives. I need not at length advert to the place which Bacon occupies in the history of English literature. He is well known as the facile master and the founder in English literature of that favorite style of composition, the didactic and reflective Essay. Montaigne, in France, had preceded him by twenty years in the use of this literary form, but in a different spirit. The essays of Bacon contain the classicalism of the Renaissance combined with the practical moral sense of the Englishman. His History of King Henry VII was written under the direction and supervision of

King James, by which it was not improved. Among the writings classed as "religious" is a "Confession of Faith," which Mr. Spedding terms a "*summa theologiæ* digested into ten pages of the finest English of the days when its tones were finest," and with reason. The characteristic of such English seems to me to be its *naïve dignity;*—I use the epithet *naïve* in the sense in which Schiller employs it, when he applies it, as opposed to "*sentimental*," to the works of *nature's* poets, Homer and Shakespeare. Two prayers of Bacon's, the Student's, and the Writer's, Prayer, give touching evidence, in noble form, of the author's religious spirit.

I mentioned in the former part of this chapter Bacon's own early declaration that he had "taken all knowledge to be his province." At a maturer age, in an account of the "Plan" of a great work contemplated by him, he affirms, with reference to this "province," his intention to be not like "an augur taking auspices, but . . . like a general who means to take possession." Such expressions denote great self-confidence, and this quality we are accustomed to look upon with mistrust, if not with positive aversion. And yet it is only an overweening self-confidence, where the self in which confidence is placed is only a spectral shadow, and not a living, solid substance, that is either morally reprehensible or dangerous. There is a self-confidence which is well-founded and noble, and in every relation in life, physical, intellectual, and moral, the advantage is with those who can and do possess it. *Possunt, quia posse videntur.* Besides, it must be remembered that we have not yet quitted the epoch of Renaissance hope, faith, and courage. Renaissance meant youth, and youth means a belief in the possibility even of the impossible. If the Renaissance corresponded in reality to its name, it could not be content (whether in this it showed its wisdom or not) simply to admire and to feed its fresh young life upon the restored riches of the past. Nay, it would argue, what man has once done why may he not do again?—and more, and better; for is not man older and more mature, hence wiser and stronger, than ever before? And so we discover two successive (but partly synchronous) streams of the Renaissance life, the one reproductive and assimilative, the other new-creative. And the representatives of the latter movement are scarcely less numerous than those of the former. Gradually we see them letting go the leading-strings of their ancient guides, and striking out, or professing to strike out, entirely *de novo*. Thus it is that we find Descartes, who shares with Bacon the honor (and to whom, technically and strictly speaking, belongs the principal share of the honor) of being termed the founder of modern philosophy, professedly breaking entirely the chain of connection with all foregoing philosophy, and seeking altogether independently and *de novo* a starting-point from which, Archimedes-like, he may, as with a lever, move and control the whole world of thought and of cognizable truth. Of the same mind, in general, is Bacon, and we are to consider that when he expresses himself in tones like those above repeated, he is the spokesman not more of himself than of his age; he is one of the heralds of the modern era of thought, and *must* speak in loud and confident tones.

Just as Descartes cleared the way for his own constructive speculations by first enforcing upon himself a methodical and universal doubt respecting all notions hitherto received, so Bacon requires, of the modern renascent mind, as a condition precedent to the entering upon the possession of the province of "all knowledge," that it rid itself of all its previously received ideas (*idola*, false, vain ideas). These are *Idola* of the Tribe, the Cave, the Market-place, and the Theatre, as he in his figurative language terms them, or false and ill-founded opinions resulting from an universal defect of the human mind, or peculiar to the individual, or due to the misleading use of language, or derived from the dogmas of earlier philosophers. The mind is not only, considering its own present possessions as prepossessions, to make a clean sweep of them, thus making itself like to a waxed tablet, as yet unwritten. It must also keep itself in this condition until, under the operation of a scientific method fitly framed to guide it to a knowledge of the truth and nothing but the truth, it is provided with its appropriate nourishment. To this end the flights of fancy must be checked. Men are called upon to refrain for a time from the highest generalizations. "The understanding must not be supplied with wings, but rather hung with weights, to keep it from leaping and flying." One of the marked characteristics of modern, and especially of British, thought since Bacon's time has been the resolute tendency to live up to this maxim.

But what is the true and lawful method, the only safe and successful method of human knowledge? It is the glory of having answered this question, which alone Bacon claims for himself. That province of all knowledge on which he had proposed to set his mark, he does not finally profess to have conquered, but only to have shown how, and how only, it can and must be conquered.

But his conception of the method of knowledge is determined by his conception of the nature, or rather the true object and goal, of knowledge, and hence our exposition may better proceed from the latter to the former.

The title which Bacon proposed for his great work contains a direct suggestion of that which he regarded as the true and lawful, and only attainable, goal of human cognition. That work was to be entitled *Magna Instauratio*, or Great Restoration (Renewal, Reparation). *Restoration*—but of what? Of nothing less than the *imperium naturae*—the empire of nature—to man. From this empire, as Bacon holds, man fell, when, seeking that knowledge of good and evil on which a curse was set, he lapsed from the favor of God. For the restoration of the latter, supernatural provision is made in the Christian plan of redemption. The former it is man's business to recover by his own exertions.

The empire of nature is mastered by knowing nature. This knowledge leads to useful arts, inventions, discoveries. By these the estate of man is relieved. They are "fruits and works," and "fruits and works," says Bacon, "are as it were sponsors and sureties for the truth of philosophies." "The true and lawful goal of the sciences is none other than this: that human life be endowed with new discoveries and powers." From this point of view Bacon finds it easy to declaim against earlier philosophers, and especially against the "professorial" and disputatious Greeks, whose "wisdom abounds in words but is barren of works."

That knowledge of nature which is available for the end just stated can, obviously, not relate to the highest generalities. It is not such knowledge as the metaphysical philosopher seeks, when he inquires concerning the ultimate essence and ground of physical existence. It is the knowledge of the proximate causes and observable laws of phenomena. It is this knowledge which, enabling us to "command nature in action," leads to the production of "effects."

What, now, is the method which can conduct to such knowledge? It will consist, first, in placing the mind in a purely receptive attitude with reference to nature. We are to "wait upon nature"—in agreement with the first member of Bacon's favorite (though not original) apothegm, "Man the servant and interpreter of nature." We are to receive and record the impressions which she produces with the unprejudiced simplicity of the little child. And then, further, our "interpretation" of her is to consist in our making ourselves her mouth-piece. She, duly questioned and listened to, will infallibly disclose to us all that it is needful or useful, or indeed strictly possible, for us to know respecting her secrets. To this end dissection of nature is better than abstraction. "My logic," says Bacon, "aims to teach and instruct the understanding, not that it may with the slender tendrils of the mind snatch at and lay hold of abstract notions (as the common logic does), but that it may in very truth dissect nature, and discover the virtues and actions of bodies, with their laws as determined in matter: so that this science flows not merely from the nature of the mind, but also from the nature of things; no wonder that it is everywhere sprinkled and illustrated with speculations and experiments in nature, as examples of the art I teach" (N. O. II, 52). "Starting directly from the simple sensuous perception" (I cite Bacon), the mind must "be from the very outset not left to take its own course, but guided at every step; and the business be done as if by machinery" (N. O., Pref.). Such a method "leaves but little to the acuteness and strength of wits, but places all wits and understandings nearly on a level. For, as in the drawing of a straight line, or a perfect circle, much depends on the steadiness and practice of the hand, if it be done by aim of hand only, but if with the aid of rule or compass, little or nothing; so it is exactly with my plan." This plan, this machine, the use of which was to ensure to all men substantially the same success in prosecuting natural investigation, is "induction." "Our whole hope lies in induction," cries Bacon; resting of course on experience (which, says he, "is by far the best demonstration"), or rather on experiment, which is experience methodically directed and digested. The preparation of a "Natural and Experimental History," or description of observed facts, is the first thing in order. Then we are to draw up three "Tables of Instances"—the first, of instances in which the phenomenon whose cause or nature is to be discovered is present; the second, of instances in which it is absent; and the third, of instances in which it is present in varying degrees. The third and last step is "Induction, true and legitimate induction, which is the very key of interpretation." The application of it rests upon a *supposition* concerning the essence of natural phenomena, which I cannot here fully explain. Suffice it to say that Bacon supposes nature to be made up of a limited number of simple natures or "forms," which are to the phenomena as the real to the apparent, or substance to accident, or, according to the Baconian theory of causation (compare Spinoza's), as cause to effect.

What we have to do, then, is to take our tables of instances and, examining the latter severally, to proceed by a "method of exclusions" to find out that nature which is always present when the phenomenon to be investigated is present. We exclude, namely, first those "natures," which being present, the phenomenon in question is invariably absent. Then those are excluded which are less present the more the phenomenon is present, and *vice versa*, and so on, proceeding by a mechanical process of sifting, which requires but a slight measure of intelligence, till there is left but that one nature which of course, and necessarily, will be held to account for the phenomenon, and, by being able to bring about or control which, we are able to bring about or control the phenomenon. A partial example, and the only one offered by Bacon, is given in the second book of the *Novum Organum*, where heat is investigated, and motion of a certain kind (namely, expansive, upward tending, acting on particles, not on whole bodies, and not sluggish, but rapid and violent) is concluded to be its ultimate "nature" or "form."

The *Magna Instauratio* was planned to consist of six parts. The *Novum Organum*, of the spirit and purpose of which I have just been giving some account, was to form the second part. Bacon has not given it to us in systematic, scholastic form, but rather in a series of aphorisms. The first part was to relate to the Divisions of the Sciences, and is measurably supplied in the Advancement of Learning, subsequently rewritten by Bacon in Latin, and enlarged, under the title *De Augmentis Scientiarum*. A few paragraphs near the beginning of the second book may be commended to any who would read liberal, large-minded views respecting the way in which institutions for the advancement of learning (*Universities*) should be conceived and endowed, and their professors selected and rewarded. Bacon's contributions to the third part, "The Phenomena of the Universe; or a Natural and Experimental History for the Foundation of Philosophy," are among the least successful portions of his work. In them he rather uncritically records as "phenomena of the universe" many alleged facts which existed only in the ignorant imaginations of him and his contemporaries. To the fourth and fifth parts, entitled, respectively, "Ladder of the Intellect," and "Forerunners; or, Anticipations of the New Philosophy," he contributed still less, and to the last, "The New Philosophy; or, Active Science," nothing at all; this latter, he confessed, lay "beyond his strength and his hopes," but he surely believed that, with his method, it would certainly follow as a "birth of time."

Bacon's place in the history of philosophy is easily stated. Of philosophy as such, in distinction from physical science, he had but slight conception and still slighter opinion. For the great truths of ethics, which it is one of the most important works of philosophy to investigate and demonstrate, Bacon was content simply (though honestly enough) to have recourse to "faith," or else to let "suffrages decide." The accurate distinction between philosophy and science was for him, practically, as for his and our own countrymen generally, lost in the distinction between religion and "philosophy" (or "science"). Bacon's tendency, however, is to make physical science and its method coextensive with the realm of all knowledge and all method. Physical science is in his view the mother and type of all sciences, and he expressly recommends the application of its method to all subjects—the best (or worst) result of which (as far as it concerns topics ordinarily deemed philosophical or akin to philosophy) is seen in modern descriptive, empirical psychology, and the mechanistic, eudæmonistic (or, in its last result, pessimistic) ethics, founded exclusively upon it. Hence the justice of Prof. Adamson's remark: "Into questions of metaphysics, as commonly understood, Bacon can hardly be said to have entered; but a long line of thinkers have drawn inspiration from him, and it is not without justice that he has been looked upon as the originator and guiding spirit of that empirical school which numbers among its adherents such names as Hobbes, Locke, Hume, Hartley, Mill, Condillac, the Encyclopedists, and many others of smaller note." (Article *Bacon*, Encyc. Brit., 9th ed.)

As to his scientific merits, strictly estimated, scarcely more can be said. The charge that he was at most only a *dilettante* in science is admitted by Prof. Fowler, of Oxford, the latest sympathetic editor of the *Novum Organum*, to be quite just. It is often charged, to the discredit of Bacon's scientific insight, that he steadily refused to admit the truth of the Copernican astronomy, notwithstanding that it was generally received in his time by the ablest men of science. Of the scientific merits of others who had preceded, or were contemporaneous with, him (*e.g.* Galileo, Harvey, etc.) he was either ignorant, or else purposely ignored them. Of some, as, for example, his countryman, Gilbert, founder of the theory of magnetism, he spoke in slighting terms. Bacon undoubtedly wrote of "philosophy," as Gilbert himself said, too much "as a Lord Chancellor." (Compare Cowley's lines:

> "Bacon, at last, a mighty man, arose,
> Whom a wise king and nature chose
> Lord Chancellour of both their laws.")

It was perhaps partly as the result of an innate tendency (and certainly, if we regard it abstractly, a very foolish one) to regard himself as (in the words of one of his contemporaries) the "great Secretary of Nature and all learning," that he fell occasionally into a tone of lordly contempt, calculated to render his positive errors and ignorances only so much the more conspicuous and ridiculous. And as regards his formerly oft-vaunted method, so far is he from having invented the inductive method of investigation, that he seems to have been ignorant of the real form of logical induction, which had been known and practiced long before his time. It is well known that as matter of fact different discoverers have gone to work in ways largely different, the differences being determined by peculiarities of personal temperament, or of circumstance, or of subject-matter, and the like. As a particular "way of getting at results," perfectly legitimate for Bacon, or for any one else who may think he can succeed by it, there is nothing to be said against Bacon's plan. Only it is not induction, and friends and foes of Bacon agree that scientific discovery never has, as matter of fact, resulted from its observance as such. And in as far as it depends on the presupposition that mental endowment is of slight consequence in the scientific investigator, and that, the method being supplied, it will work like a machine, no matter who handles it, it implies that which is radically, and by the history of scientific discovery is shown to be, false. Scientific discovery is like poetic creation, and creates and follows its own laws before they are technically drawn up, formulated, tabulated. It anticipates, often half unconsciously, its own conclusions. The divining idea, consciously and formally expressed as hypothesis, precedes and determines in large measure the method. In other words, there is a "scientific use of the imagination"; there is an organic, unforced mental activity, necessary as well for successful scientific work as for any other characteristic function of the living human mind.

But if these things be so, if, in the somewhat exaggerated language of the editor of "Mind," Prof. Geo. Croom Robertson, "science and philosophy . . . would be to all intents and purposes exactly where they are, though he had never been, or never written," if he was neither a philosopher nor a genuine man of science, what was Bacon? He was a missionary, a preacher, a scientific protestant, as Socrates was a philosophical one. Each was possessed with something, aye much, of the reformer's intense narrowness. To Socrates, speculations such as his predecessors had indulged in respecting physical things on earth, and in the "divine" economy of the heavens, were both useless and hopelessly vain. Man must know himself as a moral being, and in insisting upon this, Socrates started a stream of intellectual tendency which, more than any other in the history of pure thought, has enriched philosophy, and left fruits (which Bacon pretended not to see) in the life, the civilization, the character and destiny of the world's best races. Bacon, on the other hand, with equal pertinacity, insisted precisely on that which Socrates had rejected, and neglected that which for Socrates was of greatest worth, and there can be no question that the impulse to scientific inquiry which has been so fruitfully followed up during the last two centuries, owes an immense debt to Francis Bacon's eloquence. The consequence of Socrates' protest and mission was the relative neglect of physical inquiry, and a rich harvest of philosophical truth — of nourishment for the mind and heart of our best Occidental culture. The consequence of Bacon's protest and mission has been, in England (and considerably in France), where his influence was greatest, a comparative neglect of philosophical inquiry, and a rich harvest of material power through discoveries, inventions and technical arts. The immediate problem now is to hold both philosophy and science in due esteem, to recognize the fit place, as well as the complete mutual harmony of each, and to allow each to receive its proper culture. Only so can our culture be, not narrow and insular, but as generous as man, and as broad as the nature of things.

It is, therefore, equally wide of the mark for us to term Bacon, with Justus von Liebig, a coarse charlatan, a "scientific nut-cracker" to his royal master King James; he was too honest, and too much in earnest in his convictions for that; or to say, with Lord Campbell, that "he it was that first systematically showed the true object of *philosophical* inquiry, and the true means by which that object was to be attained"; for such a statement as this shows only the grossest ignorance on the part of him who makes it. We can only say, with Prof. Robertson, that he was "a preacher in a time of intellectual uprising," and as such "has never had an equal."

CHAPTER VI.

THOMAS HOBBES.

"Our Savior, God-man, had been born one thousand five hundred and eighty-eight years. In Spanish harbors lay anchored the famous hostile fleet soon to perish in our sea. It was early spring-time, and the fifth day of April was dawning. At this time I, a little worm, was born, at Malmesbury." Thus, at the age of eighty-four years, did he whom his followers and admirers termed the "Apostle of Malmesbury," Thomas Hobbes, begin a short metrical account (in Latin) of his own life. In the lines immediately following, the philosopher-poet grows circumstantial and sings the praises of that "no mean town," his birth-place, mentioning, among other things, that "here the Latin tongue had its first school" (in England). There was no reason to be ashamed of his native place. But, he continues, "I was the victim of unjust time, and along with me numerous ills were also born. For the report was spread abroad among our towns that with that fleet" (the Spanish Armada, termed "invincible") "the last day of our nation was at hand. And then my mother conceived such fear that she gave birth to twins, myself and Fear. Hence it is, as I believe, that I detest my country's enemies, and love peace, in the company of the muses and pleasant companions." If, as is the fact, temperament is congenital, and is often determined by ante-natal circumstances, we have, in this account which Hobbes gives of his birth, the physical or genetic key to one side, and that the least edifying one, of his whole life. Fear, his twin-brother, was, in the words of a friendly student of Hobbes' life and work, "the companion that never left him through life"—a veritable Siamese twin.

Let us stop here a moment on this point, and revert to the Virgilian motto prefixed (I know not whether by Hobbes or by his editor) to the metrical autobiography from which I began by quoting. It will enable me at once and at the outset to furnish the reader with the double guide to the interpretation of nearly everything in the recorded thought and actions of the thinker whom we have now before us. The motto consists of lines well known:

"Felix qui potuit rerum cognoscere causas,
   Atque metus omnes et inexorabile Fatum
   Subjecit pedibus, strepitumque Acherontis avari."

(Happy he who has been able to know the causes of things, and has cast beneath his feet all fears, and inexorable Fate, and the din of greedy Acheron.) You have here the moving principle of Hobbes' abstract thought, thirst for knowledge of causes, and, by sufficiently direct implication, that which the elder Disraeli (Quarrels of Authors) terms Hobbes' "solitary principle of action . . . self-preservation at any price": not so much the casting under his feet, as the eluding, as much and as long as possible, of "all fears" and of "inexorable Fate," and especially of the embrace of muttering, "greedy Acheron." And in this, compared with the usual measure of human life, it must be conceded that he managed to succeed reasonably well. For Hobbes had enjoyed the green fields of earth this side the Acheron ninety-one years, before the unwelcome but irrevocable order came to cross that river and explore whether beyond its din and darkness there might not be other and greener, namely, Elysian, fields to enjoy. But let us return to our narrative, taking, for the main facts, Hobbes himself for our guide.

His father was a minister of the Church of England, who gave to his son, at baptism, his own name. What became of the gentle, timorous mother, how long she was spared to be to him strength in his early weakness, to inflict wounds of correction and to bind up wounds of accident; or what share his father may have had in the history of his youthful life, as monitor, companion, or instructor; or whether, indeed, he ever was a real boy, with boy's delights and fancies, Hobbes does not inform us. What he remembers at the age of eighty-four is, that when he was four years old he learned to "talk, and read, and *count*, and also, though indifferently, to form letters." Note well, in this enumeration of early acquirements, the mention of counting (*numerare*), for, I doubt not, to Hobbes' mind it was the most important and interesting of all. For to him it would mark the real beginning of his life as a proper human being. The old logic had said, somewhat indefinitely, but more comprehensively, Man is a rational animal. Hobbes, defining less comprehensively, but more explicitly, said, in effect, Man is a *reasoning*, that is, a calculating, computing animal; for all reasoning (he maintained) is computation, *i.e.* a variety either of addition or of subtraction. And Hobbes was preëminently just such an animal. Moreover reasoning is, in the view of Hobbes, an addition or subtraction of *words*, as symbols of conceptions. When, therefore, the little Hobbes had begun to be able to speak, read, and write words, as well as to count, he was, obviously, at least a rudimentary reasoner. Then he was beginning to live. It was of little consequence that he learned to love and honor his parents and to fear God, if indeed he did learn all this. It mattered not that a spirit — a better Psyche — within him, making him perhaps then nearer heaven than ever afterward, without computative ratiocination might catch glimpses and so report direct evidence of a life and existence nobler than any known to flesh and blood. All this might be merely idle fancy. The main and sure thing was to be a calculating, computing, ratiocinative machine. This at the age of four years Hobbes expressly began to be. This therefore, and this only, it was important for him in his truthful autobiography to note, as being, to him, the first decisive step in living.

But Hobbes had enough of the humanistic spirit of the dying — or maturing — Renaissance to delight in classical studies. These occupied through life much of his time, and perhaps more than anything else were the object of his sincere love. He finds it therefore (and reasonably) of interest to note next, that at the age of six he was already immersed in the rudiments of Greek and Latin (or these in him). Verily, that clerical father of his — perhaps, as in Bacon's case, his mother, too — was a true child of the literary and intellectual regeneration. How often does it happen, I wonder (or does it ever happen?), in free America — where freedom, I fear, means too often anything but intellectual liberation from a fancied conceit of complete native self-sufficiency — that youth are thus early directed into the way of genuinely humane culture? How many among us, who repute ourselves liberally educated, have not been painfully conscious that, at the age of twenty-five or thirty, or even later, we were still painfully limping over ways in which, not simply the enthusiasts of learning in an earlier time, but the men who, in Europe, as thinkers and statesmen, now lead our civilization (in England the Mills and Gladstones, for example), and not only they, but thousands of their less distinguished, but classically educated, contemporaries, were already in early youth vigorous runners? We have yet to learn, as a nation, not to waste our time in disputing about the value of different styles of education, or indeed of any sound mental discipline whatever, but to go ahead and educate ourselves by early, persistent, thorough and never-ceasing training. We may claim that our national temperament is such that early and persevering mental application is dangerous for us. But patient thought and study are not half so perilous for our nerves and brains as the passionate fret and worry incident to the strife for the possession of the thousand now alleged necessaries of decent existence — comforts, luxuries, knick-knacks, places of honor, means of showing off, the not desiring which we are accustomed to regard as denoting lack of honorable ambition, or ignorance of that which makes life worth living. Genuinely patient thought and study are as much a sedative as an excitant; for they bring the repose of strength. And not simply this. Both classical and scientific studies are the mind's best recreation. Such Hobbes seems to have found the former, for we are told that before he left the school in which he was fitted for Oxford, his proficiency as a scholar had enabled him, for a "literary pastime," "elegantly to express the Medea of Euripides in Latin verses of the same metre as the original."

At the age of fourteen Hobbes was sent to Oxford, where he was received into Magdalen Hall and put in the lowest class in logic. Here, as Hobbes rather amusingly describes, he attended sedulously upon the prelector's readings, who proceeded with gravity to repeat to his beardless hearers the names of the various syllogistic modes, declaring which belonged, severally, to the different figures, and which of them could be legitimately used. "Which things," says Hobbes, "I learned, though slowly, and then cast off, and was permitted to prove some things according to my own mode." Obviously Hobbes was like many another of his age — Bacon, Descartes, Gassendi, Locke — in his inability to perceive the whole value and beauty of *Barbara, celarent, darii, ferio, baralypton;* and the student of his works finds that with him, as with them, a thing of capital importance is to endeavor to simplify logical method, to assimilate it to practice, and especially to cause the truth to be duly felt, that the knowledge of its formal precepts, being derived from analysis of the best practice, does not consciously precede and mechanically determine practice, but the rather exists only for its occasional correction and guidance, and cannot lawfully be severed from it. Next Hobbes was advanced to the class in physics, where his master seems at once to have treated him to such high philosophical generalities as that all things consist of matter and form, as parts, to the old, crude, early Greek doctrine of effluent images as causes of our visual and auditory sensations, and to alchemistic sympathies and antipathies as accounting for numerous physical effects; — to these and, says Hobbes, to "many other such things above my comprehension." But Hobbes, who, with so many men of his age, shared Descartes' passion for perfectly, mathematically, clear and distinct ideas, and who, notwithstanding that he was destined in his philosophy to assign so important a place to words, could never be dazzled, much less contented, with words to which he could attach no definite, palpable, calculable signification, was not the man to take, or pretend to take, satisfaction or even interest in things which he doubtless already considered as not simply above his comprehension, but probably above the comprehension of any one, because (in his view) all false and absurd. Whence he turned to things more agreeable. He read anew the books he had once studied but not learned. He took pleasure in looking at his old geographical and astronomical maps and seeking to realize to mind and imagination all that they represented.

Leaving Oxford, after a six years' residence there, in 1608, with the first degree (Bachelor of Arts), and fortified with a commendatory letter from the rector of Magdalen Hall, he was in the same year received into the family of William Cavendish, Baron of Hardwick, and subsequently Earl of Devonshire, as tutor for his eldest son. Connected with this family he remained not more (nay, less) on a footing of service than of friendship during the greater portion of his life. The first period of his connection with the house lasted twenty years, and was, according to Hobbes' own statement, by far the happiest of his life. It furnished him abundant leisure and means (in the form of books) for the prosecution of his studies. These he directed especially to ancient literature, particularly history and poetry. Of the historians, Thucydides pleased him most, showing him "how inept a form of government is Democracy, and how much wiser is one man than a crowd of men." The political troubles, which were destined to terminate in disaster for Charles I and royalty, were already brewing, and Hobbes, as a warning to his countrymen, translated the History of Thucydides into English, and in the year 1628 made, with this translation, his *début* as an author. In the meantime he had entered into near relations with English men of thought, among others Francis Bacon, who is said to have secured the aid of Hobbes for the translation of some of his works into Latin. It were interesting to know precisely what impression Bacon made upon Hobbes. That the latter must have been sympathetically affected by the general spirit and direction of Bacon's thought, there can be no question. It is true (and the fact is curiously symptomatic of the literary manners of the time,—it need not necessarily be attributed to what Disraeli terms Hobbes' "mighty egotism") that Hobbes mentions only once in his works "Lord Chancellor Bacon." It is also true that that side of scientific method for which Hobbes had the most marked predilection was the deductive, rather than the inductive, of which he makes only extremely rare and casual mention. But this has not hindered the world from perceiving the intellectual kinship of Bacon and Hobbes, and that the work of the latter was really to take up, and in some of its most important applications to expound, the parable of the former. Not to insist upon the keen relish which Hobbes felt for physical inquiries, and upon his thoroughly utilitarian conception of philosophy as existing "for the commodity of human life"— points of obvious but no less significant and fundamental resemblance to Bacon — the decisive consideration is that each of them makes sense, — or what is now termed *feeling*, in order the better to indicate the inclusion, in the principle, not only of so-called sensible perceptions of objects, but also of internal perceptions of conscious states, — the source of the whole material of philosophical knowledge. Philosophy is thus identified with what is now known as (in the widest sense) the physical science of phenomena. Bacon had conceived that the method of physical science was applicable to the moral and political sciences, as indeed it is, if you consider the facts, about which these sciences are concerned, only on their phenomenal, not on their real, or ontological (*i.e.* their ideal, and essential) side. Hobbes resolutely makes this application. Just as, germinantly and typically in the speculations of Bacon, more manifestly in the reasonings and investigations of such pioneers in science, contemporary with and personally known to Hobbes, as Galileo, and expressly in the mechanical physics of Descartes (with whose speculations, also, he became fully acquainted), the truth was coming into new and more vivid light, that all physical phenomena are modes of motion, so Hobbes, extending the generalization, declared that all mental phenomena were also such modes; and going on to treat of the facts of man's life in morality and society, he was led naturally to regard them purely as instances of a blindly mechanical play of sensation and passion — with what result we shall hereafter see. And note, I pray, again, and thoughtfully, the fact incidentally implied in a previous observation, that the method of deduction, emphasized and employed by Hobbes, is, if you consider the whole and complete method, whether of physical science or of metaphysical philosophy, not contradictory but complementary to induction. Narrowness and error are found only when the one is insisted upon to the exclusion of the other. One of Bacon's most serious deficiencies was, by universal admission, his relative failure to perceive the specifically scientific value and necessity of deduction, side by side with induction. And this failure has been seen to stand in direct connection with his unfamiliarity with the mathematical sciences, which furnish the model and indispensable organon of the natural sciences. Now, considering the history of English thought as a whole, we can see that Hobbes, while floating in the same general stream of intellectual tendency, and hence in sympathy, with Bacon, not so much contradicted, but rather supplemented, Bacon, by his insistance on deduction. And that which led him to see more clearly its nature and value was precisely the special acquaintance with mathematics, especially geometry, which Hobbes first formed, when already past forty years of age, in Paris.

Of Hobbes' repeated visits to the continent, the first had been made in the year 1610, when, in the company of his pupil, he travelled in France, Germany and Italy. The former having died in 1628, and his father, the Earl of Devonshire, two years earlier, Hobbes, in the same or the following year, repaired to Paris, but soon returned, to accompany a young nobleman of the name of Clifton to the continent. It was during this journey that Hobbes, whose studies had hitherto been so largely devoted to classical literature and to history, and whose career as an original writer, however active his thinking may have been, had not yet begun, applied himself, whether in the first instance through accident or intention, to the study of the elements of Euclid. From this time he was, at least by predilection, if not altogether in reality, nothing if not a geometrician. Henceforth he honored in geometry "the only science that it hath pleased God hitherto to bestow on mankind." It was, for him, the "mother of all natural science," and the source—through the arts which depend upon it—of "whatsoever assistance doth accrue to the life of man." All *that* was due to geometry, through which civilized Europeans differed from the savages of America. The writings of geometricians had increased science, while those of ethical philosophers had only served to multiply words, and this because geometry was "subservient to nothing but truth." Mathematics, especially geometry, was in Hobbes' view nothing but logic, the true method of reasoning, put in practice, and the best way to learn logic was to study the demonstrations of the mathematicians. Henceforth Hobbes was in possession of a method for the exposition and demonstration of the principles he desired to propagate. He would appeal to common experience for simple principles of axiomatic validity, and deduce from them, with the absolute necessity of a fate-directed mechanism of method, conclusions which, because resting on unquestioned demonstration, there could be no motive for resisting, and no possibility of resisting. In this fascination with geometrical method the student of the history of thought will recognize at once the relationship of Hobbes to his age, and especially to such contemporaries, of the first magnitude in the history of philosophy, as Descartes and Spinoza. It was for these men, proceeding in their reasonings from such widely different starting-points, yet having each (I class here Descartes and Spinoza as one) such absolute confidence in the applicability of mathematical method to the treatment of philosophical problems, to show to us who come after them, by the results of their endeavors, that their methodological presupposition is false. Philosophy in their hands gives place to an unduly extended generalization of physical science. The questions of philosophy proper, which are questions of life, are either misconceived or practically suppressed; they are not answered.

Of even greater consequence, for its influence upon the final crystallization of Hobbes' own views, was his fourth residence on the continent in the years 1634–1637. He was accompanied by a ward in the person of the young heir of the house of Cavendish, which he had already so long served. They travelled together through France, Savoy and Italy. Hobbes has given an interesting though compressed account of his mental history during this journey. Perpetually, he says, whether traveling by water, by coach, or on horseback, his thoughts were occupied with the nature of things. And it seemed to him that in the whole universe but one thing was real (*vera*), though disguised in various ways: one thing, but which was the basis of things which we falsely suppose to possess an independent nature and existence; — for the distinctions which we believe to exist among things are, ontologically considered, mere "ideas (*phantasiæ*), the progeny of our brains, and nothing else"; — intrinsically, there is nothing in things but motion (*Partibus internis nil nisi motus inest*). Add to motion "configuration" and you have the exact description of the world as it exists to-day in the view of physical science. Doubtless the development of this thought was helped on in the mind of Hobbes by the discussions concerning motion and its laws which were everywhere absorbing the attention of thoughtful minds and were nowhere more animated than in Italy, where the recent persecution of Galileo had lent to them a tragic interest. It was the good fortune of our hero to meet Galileo at Pisa, who received him kindly and conversed with him at length, and repeatedly, respecting his discoveries. Returning to Paris, Hobbes communicated to Mersenne, the mild priest and learned scholar who had been able to secure the confidence of minds so opposed as Descartes and Gassendi, the fruits of his meditations. Mersenne listened kindly, and in many things commended. "From that time," says Hobbes, "I, too, was numbered among the philosophers."

Returning to England in the year 1637, Hobbes, now but little short of fifty years old, set about developing and "connecting his ideas" with a view to their systematic exposition. But even the "execrable calamity" of civil war stood threatening at the doors, or rather in the heart, of the nation. Hobbes viewed the spectacle with constitutional horror (*Horreo spectans*, he says). Besides, he believed his own life to have been endangered through the publication and private circulation of a pamphlet containing views respecting the nature of civil authority, which were far from being adapted to the then temper of the English people. Accordingly, he retired again to the capital of France, his "loved Lutetia," where he remained, mostly, during the following eleven years, diligently engaged in the composition and publication of his most important works. Of these the first, "Philosophical Elements of a True Citizen" (generally cited, from the last two words of the Latin title, as the *De Cive*) was published, in a small edition, in 1642. In it he set forth, tersely, vigorously, boldly, the outlines of his celebrated — and notorious — theory of the state. In it he sought to deduce from an hypothesis concerning the nature of man without society and government, the necessity of a civil polity and its necessary and essential nature. The deduction proceeds, oddly enough, from the assumption that man is naturally not a social being, to the conclusion that he must necessarily live in society!

Man is, according to Hobbes, not what the Greeks termed him and what he everywhere practically shows himself to be, namely, a ζῶον πολιτικόν; he is not "a creature born fit for society." If, he assures us, we "shall more narrowly look into the causes for which men come together, and delight in each other's company, [we] shall easily find that this happens not because naturally it could happen no otherwise, but by accident"— which is tantamount to saying that it comes about by brute or blindly mechanical necessity. Hobbes regards men in a state of nature as so many individual depositaries of a certain amount of power, in the exercise of which they are guided solely by passion. Of passions, the strongest and hence dominant one is the passion for self-preservation, which is man's chief natural good, accompanied by the correlative fear of destruction, which is man's greatest natural evil.

All men are by nature equal. For each is able to inflict upon the other the greatest of evils, namely, death. Says Hobbes, making a curious application of his beloved mathematical style of reasoning, "They are equals who can do equal things the one against the other; but they who can do the greatest things, namely, kill, can do equal things. All men therefore among themselves are by nature equal; the inequality we now discern hath its spring from the civil law."

All men have by nature an equal right to all things. As a consequence, each man is fully authorized to do whatsoever will enable him, as far as possible, to assert this right. In the assertion of it he will justly be guided by his sense of his own advantage. "In the state of nature," affirms Hobbes, "to have all, and to do all, is lawful for all. . . . From whence we understand likewise, that in the state of nature profit is the measure of right."

In view of this state of things, and the circumstance that, whether from vain-glory and other selfish passions, or from the necessity of self-defense, all men are naturally inclined to hurt each other, it is obvious that the natural state of mankind must be, as Hobbes terms it, "a war of all men against all men." And from the same principles above mentioned it follows with equal clearness that if any one man can succeed in bringing all others under his power, he has a right to assert and maintain this power. In Hobbes' words, "A sure and irresistible power confers the right of dominion and ruling over those who cannot resist."

Such are the views laid down by Hobbes in the first chapter of the *De Cive*, and they contain the perfect key to his whole political theory. It is easy for Hobbes to show that this natural state of universal war, described by him, in which every man's hand is against every one, is not only not advantageous, but intolerable. And it is not difficult for him, at whatever cost of paradox, to argue that, although it is nature which has made men thus bellicose, yet (in Hobbes' own words) "the fundamental law of nature is to seek peace, where it may be had, and where not, to defend ourselves." He may go further and enumerate, as he does, nineteen other dictates of natural reason, which require the faithful performance of contracts, gratitude, mercy, humility, and so forth, all binding as well upon the superior as the inferior. He may go still further and describe the origin of (some) states in a compact into which men voluntarily enter. It remains none the less true that the right of him who (by whatever train of historic events) is once endowed with supreme political power, remains, in the representation of Hobbes, tinged with those attributes of absolute, arbitrary power, which in the state of nature belong to him who by brute force succeeds in bringing himself to the top of the heap and there maintaining himself. Although the ruler abstractly ought to, and presumably will, be guided by the laws of natural reason, and make the safety and welfare of the citizens, his subjects, his only and his intelligent care, yet the latter, in the matter of obedience, have no business to inquire aloud or to discuss whether he is thus guided or not. Indeed — and now prepare for another paradox — there can never be any possible room for such discussion, for Hobbes alleges that it is impossible for the ruler, through the civil law, which he alone dictates, to command aught contrary to the law of nature. For the first law of nature is the absolute and indefeasible right of him who is in power to command, without consulting his subjects; and this right, in the case of "political states" formed by compact, the subjects have in the beginning, and before they knew how it would be exercised, pledged themselves to respect; they are no longer masters of their own actions; it is theirs only to obey. Should the sovereign, in the exercise of the right and obligation, attributed by Hobbes to him, of determining what religious doctrines are to be professed and what ceremonies are to be observed, command anything opposed to the subject's conscience, he must yet defer outwardly to his monarch's will, using (as Hobbes remarks in the Leviathan) the liberty which God through Elisha accorded under similar circumstances to Naaman. And in general, "the law of nature," says Hobbes, "obligeth in the internal court, or that of conscience, but not always in the external court, but then only when it may be done with safety."

The sovereign, in short, is in Hobbes' view the soul of the state. "He that hath the supreme power is in order to the city, as the human soul in relation to the man." The citizens are simply his instruments — puppets in his hand. Only one thing, says Hobbes, he may not do, or at least may not command me to do, and that is to "prejudice my body." He may not order me to take my own life. Even though honor may not be preserved, yet physical life must be. "Death was the one subject about which Hobbes would not dispute," says Disraeli.

This political doctrine is the philosophy of absolutism, and well deserves to be placed side by side with the theological absolutism which we have encountered in Duns Scotus and especially in William of Occam. I cannot forbear to mention, in passing, that the best refutation of the initial principles or premises of both, in Hobbes' time, was furnished by the well-known Cambridge Platonist, Ralph Cudworth.

The details of philosophical criticism on this theory of the origin and nature of civil government must here be omitted. Such criticism will discover in it, as in nearly everything human, both reason and unreason. A more obvious and facile line of reflection is that which would trace a connection between Hobbes' pessimistic view of human nature and his own self-confessed constitutional timidity, breeding a general distrust of mankind. As to this point Disraeli is on the right track, although he doubtless exaggerates a little when he declares that Hobbes "never looked on human nature but in terror or in contempt." Of the importance of his work Hobbes was fully convinced. Just as, in his view, "natural philosophy" began its being with Galileo, so, he declared subsequently, "civil philosophy" had no existence in literature before the publication of *De Cive*. It "pleased the learned," he says in his metrical autobiography, "and was altogether new. I was translated with eulogium into various languages, and became known by name far and wide among the nations." To the extreme royalist party, at the epoch in history when it was published, a book could not but be acceptable which stoutly maintained, on alleged grounds of reason and scripture, theses like the following: "Monarchy is ever in the readiest capacity to exercise all those acts which are requisite to good government." "A monarch, retaining his right of government, cannot by any promise whatsoever be conceived to have parted with his right to the means necessary to the exercise of his authority." "The best state of a city is that where the subjects are the ruler's inheritance." At all events, soon after the flight from England, and arrival in Paris (in 1646), of the Prince of Wales, subsequently Charles II, Hobbes was selected to instruct him in mathematics.

During a serious illness, in the year 1646, Hobbes'

friend, Père Mersenne, called upon him and undertook to recommend to him the Roman Catholic church, as possessed of power to grant plenary pardon. Hobbes replied characteristically, "Father, I have examined, a long time ago, all these points; I should be sorry to dispute now; you can entertain me in a more agreeable manner. When did you see Mr. Gassendi?" A few days later an English clergyman was admitted to pray with Hobbes, who, it is related, "first stipulated that the prayers should be those authorized by the Church of England; and he also received the sacrament with reverence." Hobbes remained till his death an inflexible, if not a devout, churchman. And here it is right to say, in reference to the oft-repeated charge of atheism brought against Hobbes, that it is as unjust as such charges often are. There can be no question of the sincerity of Hobbes' churchmanship, or of his christianity (which he was wont to sum up in the one proposition, "Jesus is the Christ"), or of his theism. On the other hand, it is equally true that he was not a man of fervent piety, and that the direct support which he believed religion could receive from speculation was extremely slight. It is also certain that his philosophical principles, strictly and exclusively interpreted and developed, are inconsistent with the contemplation of man as a moral being, and are, as regards the recognition of God, in the direct line, if not of positive atheism, yet of theological agnosticism.

In the year 1650 Hobbes published in London his treatise on "Human Nature," and *De Corpore Politico*, and in the following year the "Leviathan," his *opus magnum*, which develops in detail all his philosophical views, and which became at once, and long continued, the object of numerous and violent attacks, but also, on the part of many, of enthusiastic applause. In it the mechanical theory of human nature, knowledge, and action, is systematically developed, and serves as a basis for a detailed exposition and reinforcement of the political doctrine previously expounded in the *De Cive*. The immediate effect of its publication upon his personal fortunes was, according to his own account, anything but propitious. The royalist clergy, and, still more, the Roman Catholics, could not brook the absolute dependence upon the civil head of the state into which Hobbes would reduce them. He was, he declares, falsely accused, to the fugitive king, of justifying the impious doings of Cromwell; — though not, certainly, without some color of reason; for had not parliament wrested to itself actual power, and hence (according to Hobbes' principles) right, and was not Cromwell its representative and soon to be its successor? At all events Hobbes was met with an order not to appear again in the presence of the prince. Thus accused, and deprived of royal protection, he saw only enemies all about him. He bethought him of the fatal end of Dorislaus and Ascham, parliamentary ambassadors to Spain and the Netherlands. And so, not sure of protection even in England, but knowing that in no place he could be safer, he resolved to return to his native country.

"Frigus erat, nix alta, senex ego, ventus acerbus;
Vexat equus sternax et salebrosa via."

(It was cold, the snow was deep, myself an old man, the wind bitter; to this was added the vexation of a stumbling horse and a rough road.) Arriving in London, he sent in his submission to the Council of State, and then retired to carry on his studies in peace.

This is Hobbes' version of his reasons for returning to England, written late in life, twelve years after the Restoration, when he was enjoying the royal bounty of Charles II, ten years after he had, in deference to ecclesiastical influence, partially recanted the doctrines of the Leviathan, and when, in the language of a Westminster reviewer, he was loudly professing a "new ultra-conservatism and ostentatious loyalty, the response of his fears to the exigencies of his situation." I will not now discuss the question to what extent Hobbes' account is truthful. I call attention to a curious assertion of his enemies. To the "Leviathan" was prefixed a frontispiece representing, not the sea-monster of that name mentioned in the Book of Job, but Hobbes' Leviathan, the Commonwealth, "which is but an artificial man," identified with the monarch or supreme ruler. The figure is that of a crowned giant, whose form towers above mountains and valleys, plains and cities, "entirely made up of little men from all the classes of society, bearing in the right hand the sword, and in the left the crosier." Of this figure it was asserted (though really, as far as I can learn, without sufficient apparent reason) that in the first edition the features were those of Oliver Cromwell, while in later editions they were changed to be the likeness of Charles II. Hobbes desired the doctrines of his book — which, in spite of all protestations to the contrary, he could not but regard as marking an epoch in the history of political philosophy — to be taught at the universities. On the contrary, it and himself were treated with obloquy. Let me cite a passage from Disraeli, showing, by a specimen, what treatment Hobbes had to endure from his own university of Oxford: " The ungenerous attack of Bishop Fell, who, in the Latin translation of Wood's 'History of the University of Oxford,' had converted eulogium into the most virulent abuse, ... was only an arrow snatched from a quiver which was every day emptying itself on the devoted head of our ambiguous philosopher. Fell only vindicated himself by a fresh invective on 'the most vain and waspish animal of Malmesbury,' and Hobbes was too frightened to reply. This," adds Disraeli, " was the Fell whom it was so difficult to assign a reason for not liking:

> I don't like thee, Dr. Fell,
> The reason why I cannot tell,
> But I don't like thee, Dr. Fell."

The Leviathan received the honor of being condemned by act of parliament in the year 1666.

The last twenty years or so of Hobbes' life were almost constantly filled up with "wars"—"quarrels of authors"—in which he was not less pleased than harassed; for he delighted to deliver blows, when it could be done without too imminent danger to himself. In allusion to his roaring pugnacity Charles II is reported to have remarked one day, when he saw Hobbes approaching. "Here comes the bear to be baited." Hobbes, namely, in his declining years, when his philosophical principles had been fairly launched into the stream of the world's thoughts, was greatly busied with physical and, especially, mathematical questions. He turned, as he says, to his "loved mathematics" (*amata mathemata*). Whatever he handled, he was not the man to confess himself second to any other. Accordingly, in addition to the aspersions of ecclesiastical and political enemies, he became involved in conflict, on physical questions, with the chemist Boyle and the Royal Society, and on mathematical questions notably with Dr. Wallis, professor at Oxford. It was this Dr. Wallis who victoriously defended the copiousness and capacity of the English tongue, by a literal translation of a French quatrain intended to illustrate the superiority of the French language—

"When a twister a twisting will twist him a twist," etc.,

and then, continuing upon the same theme, produced two other equally marvelous quantrains!

I shall not attempt to explain the mathematical principles involved in the "Peloponnesian War" of twenty years—including occasional truces—between Hobbes and Dr. Wallis. Hobbes has celebrated it in a few Latin lines, which recall Virgil's Æneid and the story of the contests, without which Rome could not have been founded. Hobbes classes his enemies as "algebrists"—of whom, as distinguished from geometricians, he had a fervent horror—and "theologians"; these constitute the "*exercitus Wallisianus*," or "army of Wallis." It is enough to know that he considers himself finally to have routed the hostile host. "In a point of time," he says, "I scatter, overthrow, put to flight, their well-nigh infinite number." The weapons used on each side were selected indiscriminately from the armory of argument and of objurgation. An amusing degree of irreverence is shown by all the combatants in the titles of their printed missiles. Hobbes, in the year 1656, publishes "Six Lessons to the Professors of the Mathematics" (Ward and Wallis) at Oxford. Wallis immediately returns the kind favor in a " Due Correction for Mr. Hobbes, or School-discipline for not saying his Lessons Right." Neither disputant is deterred by any consideration of false courtesy from expressing his whole mind concerning the other. Hobbes entitles his sixth "Lesson," "Of Manners," and prostrates his adversaries with the following parting shot (taking care to italicize the complimentary epithets employed—italics were in great requisition in those days): "So go your ways, you *Uncivil Ecclesiastics, Inhuman Divines, Dedoctors of morality, Unasinous Colleagues, Egregious pair of Issachars, most wretched Vindices and Indices Academiarum* [Hobbes' fire was frequently directed against the universities]; and remember Vespasian's law, that it is uncivil to give ill language first, but civil and lawful to return it." This should unquestionably have been a staggerer to poor Ward and Wallis, yet they rallied—strange to say!—and replied in this tone, accompanied by a frugal, yet sufficient, expenditure of italics: "It seems, Mr. Hobbes, that you have a mind to *say your lesson*, and that the mathematic professors of Oxford should *hear you*. You are too old to learn, though you have as much need as those that be younger, and yet will think much to be whipped. . . . You tell us, 'though the beasts that think our railing to be roaring have for a time admired us, yet now you have showed them our ears they will be less affrighted.' Sir, those persons (the professors themselves) needed not the sight of *your ears*, but could tell by the *voice* what kind of person *brayed* in your books," etc. But I need hardly continue to narrate such particulars of these bloodless encounters. It is enough to say that however fascinated Hobbes may have been with the mathematical method of demonstration, yet he was not a great mathematician.

Hobbes dreaded death, and a long life was measured

out to him. Dr. Wallis related of him that he once told the countess of Devonshire that were the whole world his, he would give it for one day of life. In his eighty-fourth year he wrote: "My life is not inconsistent with my writings: I teach justice, and I cultivate justice." His long life had indeed been, in his private relations, moderate and blameless. In the Cavendish family, where he was perhaps best known, he had found life-long friends. In their house he died, before completing the ninety-second year of his life, December 1679.

Hobbes was not a great philosopher, and yet he occupies an important place in the history of modern, and especially English, thought. His reduction of all phenomena, including those of mind in their physical relations, to modes of motion, was a rather remarkable declaration of a scientific view, now, at least, universally accredited. In his philosophy of man, the foundation of his political theory, he was the first one to follow the method, recommended by Bacon and since followed by Locke and his followers, of purely empirical observation, analysis, and description. If in man a distinction is to be made between man true to himself (*i.e.* man as he might be and ought to be, but never is, except approximately) and man as he actually appears — between man the *noumenon* and man the *phenomenon* — between man as a free, ideal, spiritual agency apprehended in philosophical self-consciousness, and man as a series of "mental states" which, however determined, follow each other in time, or a "bundle" of "mental processes" or "perceptions," it is to the latter exclusively that the attention of Hobbes and his celebrated successors is directed. This is identifying philosophy with empirical psychology, *i.e.*

substantially suppressing philosophy. The analogy with Locke is strikingly illustrated in the following incident of Hobbes' argument in the *De Cive*, and it well illustrates the impotently negative results which must follow the attempt to solve philosophical questions by the simple application of the genetic-descriptive method. Hobbes declares that man is "not born fit for society" because he is born a helpless infant, incapable of knowing what society is. In like manner, we shall find Locke arguing that man has no innate ideas, *i.e.* that he has not, independently of impressions made upon him, any mind or mental nature, because children and idiots are not conscious of possessing anything of the sort! From the premises afforded by the exclusive adoption of such a method, the denial of freedom and the reduction of civil society and government to a result of the brute necessity of blind mechanism (or, as Hobbes terms it, "accident") follow as a matter of course; and perhaps mankind owes Hobbes a debt of gratitude for having so bluntly and honestly drawn this conclusion. But every man is a man, after all, and cannot wholly divest himself of everything which belongs to the, not phenomenal, but real, inward, invisible essence of humanity. And so we find Hobbes, like so many others of his stripe of thought, still occasionally acknowledging, in glaring contradiction with his principles and disharmony with his system, an inner forum of conscience, attesting freedom and accountability to a divine, spiritual power, of which the true man is the offspring.

Such philosophy as that of Hobbes results from a disposition (historically grounded in and justified by a dread of scholastic subtleties, from which the light and power of reason had fled) to make things easy;* in other words, to treat as an affair of sensible demonstration an order of truths which lie back of, and indeed shine through, but are not absorbed in, sensible data. The knowledge of the data is to take the place of the knowledge and the power of that which they, rightly considered, do but reveal. Physical science of phenomena is to take the place of philosophical science of ideal and absolute reality.

* "At *De Principiis* alium tamen edo libellum,
Fecique ut posset clarius esse nihil."

CHAPTER VII.

JOHN LOCKE.

BACON, Hobbes, Locke — such are the names which we elect to consider among the English thinkers of the seventeenth century. Many others might be selected, which would furnish themes for interesting study. I might mention Lord Herbert of Cherbury, Hobbes' acquaintance and early contemporary — at once scholar and cavalier, diplomat and philosopher, brother of George Herbert, the favorite religious poet (who died, by the way, in the year in which John Locke was born), and author, among other things, of a work on Truth (*De Veritate*), defining, and defending the sufficiency of, natural religion, and proclaiming, somewhat in the way of the later common-sense philosophy of the Scotch school, the innate possession, by human reason, of certain notions or truths which antedate and govern our experimental knowledge and control our religious faith; the same who (as he himself relates in his charming autobiography, recently edited anew by W. D. Howells), having finished his book, fell on his knees and implored God to indicate to him, by a sign, whether he should give his work to the world or suppress it; whereupon, though surrounded by the absolute calm of a bright summer afternoon, he distinctly heard a peculiar sound which could proceed, he was sure, only from heaven, and which he interpreted as an intimation that he was to proceed, in peace, with the publication of his book. Or

I might ask you to enter with me upon the study of Ralph Cudworth, the greatest of the so-called "Cambridge Platonists"— a late but effective child of the philosophical Renaissance—and see him dealing weighty blows at hydra-headed "Atheism" with the sledge-hammer of his ponderous learning, or what were, perhaps, more attractive and edifying, drawing from the Platonic arsenal of argument to reinforce his own well-studied conviction of the immutable foundation of morality in that divine reason whence man's is borrowed (as opposed to the theory of the foundation of morality in the absolute but unreasoning sovereignty of a divine will), and urging, with clear and convincing insight, the evidence — destined, for whatever reason, to remain for so long a time unheeded by, or at least unconvincing to, so many of his countrymen — that, even in the matter of that which is termed sensible knowledge, sense knows nothing except as it is enlightened by implicit, active reason. Let any one open the ample volumes of M. De Rémusat's History of Philosophy in England, from Bacon to Locke (in French: Paris, 1875), and he will find an analysis and appreciation of the views of some fifty persons — a generous number, certainly — who participated in the philosophical discussions of a century and a half. Rémusat's work begins, it is interesting to note, with one Sir Thomas Wilson, who, about the middle of the sixteenth century, ventured upon the daring reformatory innovation of writing and publishing treatises on logic and rhetoric in English; for which crime, happening subsequently to make a journey to Rome, he was incarcerated. In the view of the Inquisitors, "nothing but heresy," remarks Rémusat, "could seek to make itself intelligible to every body." Run through the list, now, of these for the most part unhonored co-workers in the field of thought, and you find numbers who guard not simply the tradition, but also, according to the measure of their forces, the living well-spring of that truth which gives vitality to all worthy human existence, to civilization, nay, more, to the world itself. But you miss the *esprit de suite*, the power of sequent demonstration, the single-eyed devotion to a grand, definite purpose, the energetic, comprehensive grasp of principles, which have made the masters of philosophic thought. "Excellent views," indeed (to employ Rémusat's phrase), you find scattered among many of their writings, and I would add, far more than the germs of truths which it is the business of philosophy to-day, as in all days, to guard, to develop, to exhibit in all their many-sided and imperial power. But we must admit with the French historian (who is by no means unsympathetic) that if elevation is not wanting, there is a certain obvious defect of profundity. More especially is there a failure to separate philosophy from theology, and to recognize in the former a science at once distinct from all others, and universal, comprehending all others. Under these circumstances confusion and incompleteness, diffusion and discontinuity, are inevitable defects, and, in particular, philosophy is robbed of half its power through the inevitable suspicion that its dicta are inspired by dogmatic bias, and not by the logic of living, experimental fact. But, on the other hand, I deem it no discredit to the most of the unrenowned fifty on whom M. de Rémusat turns the light of nineteenth-century intelligence, that, in the judgment of a recent English critic, himself a duly baptized child of latter-day, positive light (who declares, for his part, that "scientific psychology seems to require us to renounce [such] entities [as understanding, reason, will, or the ego] and all their works ") — that, I say, these men, in this critic's judgment, "are for the most part in relation to philosophy not representative English writers. Their notions and methods are those of the men who do not swim in the stream, but in the eddies and backwater of English thought." It matters not that they do not swim in the stream of recent English thought, if loyalty to truth and reason requires them to resist or keep out of the current. It is not necessary to go with the multitude, or to follow a popular guide, in order to be in the right.

What the stream of English thought just referred to is, and whither it tends, is well known, and I have already expressed myself concerning it in these pages. Rather than repeat myself, I will cite respecting this subject the apposite and sympathetic utterances of accomplished navigators in the stream itself, quoting from publications of the past year. I call to the stand first Professor J. Croom Robertson, editor of *Mind*, who mentions (in the number for January, 1879) that "the most characteristically English movement within modern mental philosophy" is "the continuous pursuit of psychological inquiry in the spirit of positive science." This is empirical psychology, the analysis and classification of conscious phenomena, and is, strictly speaking, no more a portion of mental or any other *philosophy* than is the comparative psychology of the animal kingdom in general, or the physiology of nervous action, or the anatomy of the brain. It does not properly touch, or, if made to touch, it does not solve any philosophical question concerning cause, substance, and purpose. It is an extremely interesting, and in many ways practically useful, *science of phenomena*, and the knowledge of it is an essential prerequisite of philosophy — yet, radically considered, in no other sense than that in which a knowledge of the phenomenal universe in general is essential. Rational psychology, however, which treats of the soul as an entity, a variously self-manifesting power, and a purpose which it is itself to realize, is a portion of philosophy. Empirical psychology has to do with the phenomena, or appearances; rational psychology with noumena, or realities; or, if there be no psychological realities, as the critic before cited supposes, it has at least one function, that of demonstrating that there are none. Note, further, that just as psychology is seen to have two sides of the kind just noted, so every other philosophical discipline is similarly double-faced; as, for example, ethics, æsthetics, and those derivatives from ethics which refer to questions of education and the life of men in organized society. To each of these branches of philosophy there is a corresponding empirical side — a body of phenomena which may be collected, analyzed, described, classified, in short, subjected to treatment according to the recognized methods of "positive" science, without, nevertheless, touching upon the philosophical side of the questions involved. And it is to be observed that the characteristic bent of English thought in the direction of empirical psychology has been accompanied by the no less characteristic (and in principle identical) bent toward the empirical treatment of every department of philosophy, and this in accordance with the express recommendation of Francis Bacon himself.

Now it is obvious that if the empirical side of these

various lines of inquiry is pursued in the fancy that it is the only side, excluding consequently the investigation of strictly philosophical questions by the method peculiar to philosophy, and if then the answer to philosophical questions is sought among the data and results of empirical investigation — no matter how positive and scientific — only negative, not positive, answers can be received. Since, by hypothesis, the noumena are back of, and not absorbed in, the phenomena in which their power is manifested, since power is not identical with motion, or substance with observable state, it is evident that noumenon, power, and substance — all *realities* — are not to be learned from the exactest analysis of phenomena, motion, and state — all appearances. The end of the misguided and misnamed philosophy which thinks differently and persists in seeking among the latter alone, or principally the solution of the problems concerning the former, can only be denial, scepticism, or agnosticism. To this complexion the students of the subject will find British thought chronically arriving. Its latest conclusion, which is no new one, is (in the words of Prof. Huxley, Nineteenth Century, April 1879) that "our sensations, our pleasures, our pains, and the relations of these, make up the sum total of the elements of positive (*sic*), unquestionable knowledge." This statement is followed up by the favorite assurance of Prof. Huxley, that the "conclusion" stated makes neither for materialism nor for idealism, being equally consistent with either; whence the inference, as old in English philosophy (at least in part) as Locke, that we do not and cannot unquestionably know whether materialism or idealism is true, or whether there be any matter or mind at all. So much for those who love to handle philosophical phrases. Doubtless a still larger number of studious Englishmen have been led by the prevailing absorption in physical (including empirico-psychological) inquiries, to adopt the first of the alternatives mentioned by Prof. Fowler, in the Introduction to his edition of Bacon's Novum Organum, published in 1878. Speaking of "ontological or metaphysical questions," Prof. Fowler says: "A deep sense of the unprofitable character of these speculations has, indeed, been a characteristic, not of the Baconian philosophy only, but of British philosophy in general, which, with a healthy instinct, has *usually either avoided them altogether* or discussed them solely with a view of showing that they lie outside the limits of human knowledge." Doubtless, in manifold cases, the wisest thing for one to do is to "avoid" what one has neither inclination nor, possibly, ability to pursue.

As for Locke, with whom we have now to concern ourselves, he was one who, while practically settled in the possession of those ideal goods which philosophy defends, and which (in Hegelian phrase) incorporate themselves in the institutional life of man (church, society, state), devoting himself to the search after the *faculties* of the mind, initiated a movement which has resulted in losing out of sight the essential *truths* of mind.* J. S. Mill, who so severely censured his countrymen for their want of philosophy (see essay entitled "Prof. Sedgwick's Discourse"), and who yet went about, fruitlessly, to supply

---

* "Tel était l'état philosophique des esprits en Angleterre, lorsque Locke est venu les pousser dans la voie où ils avaient commencer à faire quelque pas, en les instruisant *à plus considérer les facultés que les vérités de l'esprit humain.*" Rémusat II, 255.

the deficiency by clinging to that national method which had proved so unfruitful, terms Locke the "unquestioned founder of the analytic philosophy of mind," and his essay the "beginning and foundation of the modern, analytical psychology." The national school of empirical psychology, which, as descriptive, analytical science of mental phenomena, but not as philosophy, may be justly vaunted, fairly begins with Locke.

But Locke was much more than an analyst of mind and of the elements of cognition. Let us first seek to see him in his life, and in his manifold, influential work.

He was born in the same year with the Jewish-Dutch philosopher Spinoza, 1632, on the 29th of August, at Wrington, in Somersetshire. His father, whose name was also John Locke, was a country lawyer. But he lived in troublous times, which tried men's souls and principles. The son — the subject of our present study — wrote in 1660, "I no sooner perceived myself in the world but I found myself in a storm which has lasted almost hitherto." It was the storm of political and religious dissension between Puritan and Cavalier, Parliament and King. It raged about the home of Locke's boyhood, and he was only ten years of age when his father announced his adhesion to the cause of parliament and people, and "took the field as captain of a troop of horse in the regiment of volunteers raised by his friend and employer, Alexander Popham, now Colonel Popham, in the parliamentary army" (Fox Bourne, Life of Locke, I, 7). After a year's service he left the army, and it was several years before he was able to repair the damage done meanwhile to his modest fortune.

Of Locke's mother little is known, except that she was

(as Locke is reported to have said) "a very pious woman and affectionate mother." She probably died too young to have great influence upon the development of her son's character. The father's influence was greater, and inspired in Locke deep respect and affection. I scarcely know with what ground Pallas Athene declared to Telemachus (in the Odyssey) that "few sons are like their fathers, the majority are inferior, few better." Perhaps this was intended to spur the ambition of Ulysses' son, or to furnish him, in case of his remaining hopelessly inferior, with the self-indulgent plea, "I could not help it." Locke certainly was an illustration of the greater truth there is in the maxim, "Like father, like son," at least in regard to moral qualities and practical sense. He always remembered with admiration and gratitude his father's treatment of him, his "being severe to him by keeping him in much awe and at a distance when he was a boy, but relaxing, still by degrees, of that severity as he grew up to be a man, till, he being become capable of it, he lived perfectly with him as a friend." That this early "severity" of the father was not the cruelty of unreasoning passion, but the kind wisdom of intelligent principle and conviction, is made manifest by the remark once made by Locke to a friend, "that his father, after he was a man, solemnly asked his pardon for having struck him once in a passion when he was a boy." If Locke were living in our day and in our land, where all the freedom there is, is by no means monopolized by the *elders* of the people, and where these latter, absorbed in money getting, are too busy or too unintelligent and unfaithful to train the juniors for freedom, can we doubt that he, with the notions of combined rigor, justice and affection imbibed from his own training, would find as much occasion to publish "Thoughts on Education" as there was in his own time?

At the age of fourteen Locke, through the influence of Col. Popham, was received into Westminster School, where he remained six years, and had for schoolfellows, among others, the subsequent poet, Dryden, and Robert South, the famous preacher. The school was then under the head-mastership of the renowned Dr. Richard Busby, who remained in his position from 1638 to 1695, and was able before he died to boast "that sixteen of the bishops who then occupied the bench had been birched with his 'little rod.'" Whether Locke was "birched," or whether his not being subjected to that form of torture had anything to do with his not becoming a bishop, is not related. Certain it is, as we shall see, that he subsequently came dangerously near to being a clergyman, and that at school he was a good boy and faithful student. Perhaps I should say, rather, a patient student; for at this stage his education properly consisted in undergoing a thorough course of prescribed *training*, to which he and his schoolfellows were held down by strict discipline. The topics of instruction were not greatly varied. It seems to have been little else than Greek and Latin, Latin and Greek, in a constant round of grammatical and rhetorical and declamatory exercitations, *viva voce* translations into Latin and Greek, compositions in the same languages in prose and verse, etc. etc., from the beginning to the end of the year, supplemented, near the end of the course, by some study of Hebrew and Arabic and "a little elementary geography." Such a course of training was doubtless, from some points of view, open to criticism; and Locke, later in life, openly criticised it. It is certainly not requisite that every person should receive a classical training, and now-a-days, surely, one is not shut up to the alternative of accepting this or remaining uneducated. But if one is to study the classical languages, just such patient, persistent work as was insisted on at Westminster (however modified in the details of method), and nothing less, is needed. I am free to say that I look back gratefully upon the two years of ante-collegiate drill in Latin and Greek, which most resembled the style above described, as among the most valuable in my early education. Locke profited by his school-work, and maintained to the end of his life that a thorough knowledge of Greek was an essential part of a gentleman's education. The experience of his countrymen seems largely to have proved the correctness of his opinion.

After his first year at Westminster Locke had become a "king's scholar"—a title which procured him residence and instruction free of charge, and certain sums in money in addition. At the expiration of his school-boy life there he was elected to a junior studentship in Christ Church, Oxford, then under the direction of Dr. Owen, an Independent preacher, as vice-chancellor. In little more than three years Locke was ready for his bachelor's degree, and in June, 1658, less than six years after going to Oxford, he received his second, or master's, degree. I do not find that Locke acquired any reputation for brilliant scholarship, though he was unquestionably not a negligent or heedless scholar. It is of most consequence for us to notice that, like Bacon and Hobbes before him, the fields of (so-called) peripatetic philosophy into which he was invited were not green fields for him. Filled with a genuine thirst for knowledge, his mind could not slake its thirst in such muddy waters. Molière's *Bourgeois* declared, after listening to the "Barbara, Celarent," etc., of his "*maître de philosophie*," "*voilá des mots qui sont trop rébarbatifs, cette logique là ne me revient point. Apprenons autre chose qui soit plus joli.*" Locke was likewise repelled by the "*mots rébarbatifs*" of the Oxford professors. In the "Epistle to the Reader," which precedes his "Essay concerning Human Understanding," he complains of the "frivolous use of uncouth, affected, or unintelligible terms, introduced into the sciences, and there made an art of, to that degree that philosophy, which is nothing but the true knowledge of things, was tho't unfit or incapable to be brought into well-bred company and polite conversation." In these last phrases we are let into the secret of one of the motives which must always be taken into account in estimating Locke's character and work. Locke was a wellbred man. Says a French writer, whose book on Locke was published in 1878, describing Locke's manners: "No other peculiarity [marked him] than an exquisite refinement and the rarest mixture of elegance and correctness, ease and gravity. . . . The only thing which he could not endure was bad breeding. Politeness was, in his view, more than an ornament, it was a christian duty." In particular, I add, Locke was possessed of that peculiar kind of breeding, which makes it almost a crime to know anything which cannot be communicated, and especially to make display of pretended knowledge with the use of an unintelligible jargon of "uncouth" words. Locke would have everything plain and popular, fit for "well-bred company," and he is to be looked upon as one of the first to illustrate the characteristic tendency of

English philosophic and scientific discussion to adopt a form, as far as possible, intelligible to the average intelligence. Locke was, it is true, also one of the first to illustrate the danger of this tendency — the danger of forgetting that after all it is results only, and not scientific processes of inquiry, which can always be popularized, and that for the latter a technical language or symbolism, and technical procedures, are necessary, which, it is true, need not be displayed in "polite conversation," but which have their due place, and must be mastered and employed by every one who would possess more than general knowledge. Locke's very desire, I mean to say, for plainness and intelligibility, has rendered his style, by universal admission, loose and inexact (not to mention the "colorless prolixity" which De Rémusat rightly blames in him and most other English philosophical writers), and has consequently made his reasoning obscure and his conclusions uncertain. About logic Locke felt as Hobbes had felt. Its technicalities, as insisted on, were more than useless; they were blinding and deadening. One should learn to think by thinking, as one learns the use of his limbs by walking. "God," said Locke subsequently, "has not been so sparing to men to make them barely two-legged creatures, and left it to Aristotle to make them rational, *i.e.* those few of them that he could get so to examine the grounds of syllogisms, as to see, that in above three-score ways that three propositions may be laid together, there are but about fourteen wherein one may be sure that the conclusion is right, and upon what grounds it is, that in these few the conclusion is certain, and in the others not." Above all the disputations, in due logical form, in which every student was obliged to take part, seemed to Locke better adapted to produce a contentious spirit and dishonest strife for verbal victories, than a habit of vigorous and just reasoning. In view of all which, one is inclined to regard as probably true the report that "Mr. Locke spent a good part of his first years at the University in reading romances, from his aversion to the disputations then in fashion there." Certain it is that he sought diversion and instruction in "the company of pleasant and witty men, with whom he likewise took great delight in corresponding by letters." It was at this time that he fell upon the philosophical works of Descartes, "the first books," as he told Lady Masham, "which gave him a relish of philosophical things." Lady Masham (daughter of the celebrated Ralph Cudworth, and friend of Locke's last years) adds, characteristically: "He was rejoiced in reading these, because, though he very often differed in opinion from this writer, he yet found that what he said was very intelligible; from whence he was encouraged to think that his not having understood others had possibly not proceeded from a defect in his understanding." The careful student of Locke's Essay discovers abundant evidence that it was Descartes who "set Locke to thinking," positively or negatively determining his thought on many of the most important points treated by him.

It is scarcely fair to call attention to Locke as a poet. The man who was destined to influence opinion in matters of government, education, and abstract thought, did not possess an exuberant poetic vein. Yet two or three times in his life he did try his hand at verse-making, and once, at least, when a student at Oxford. The Dutch having been defeated by the fleet of the Commonwealth in 1653, and an advantageous treaty of peace having been signed by the Lord Protector, in the following year, Dr. Owen procured the production of a string of complimentary poems by Oxford scholars, of which Locke contributed two — one in Latin, the other in English. I find in them neither adulation of Cromwell nor poetic fire, but a couple of lines which show that the future philosopher was capable of "gushing":

> "We've heaven in this peace: like souls above,
> We've naught to do now but admire and love";

and still more that disclose a philosophic vein, as *e.g.* the closing ones:

> "Nay, if to make a world's but to compose
> The difference of things, and make them close
> In mutual amity, and cause peace to creep
> Out of the jarring chaos of the deep,
> Our ships do this; so that, whilst others'
> Their course about the world, ours a world make."

After Locke had taken his second degree he was elected to a senior studentship in Christ Church, a sinecure which he held for nearly thirty years. For a number of years after his appointment he resided at Oxford, teaching and prosecuting various physical studies. For the year 1661 we are told that he was appointed "Greek lecturer or reader"; for 1663, lecturer on rhetoric, and for 1664, "censor of moral philosophy." He performed some services, also, as tutor to individual students. Locke had been intended by his father for the church, and at the time he held the above-named offices, which were "usually assigned to clergymen," it was probably expected that he would, before long, become a candidate for holy orders. Prospects of ecclesiastical preferment were held out to him, in case he should do so, but his thoughts and studies had taken largely another direction. He was already the friend of Boyle, the chemist, and had himself paid special attention to chemistry. He belonged, with Boyle, to a scientific club at Oxford, in which all sorts of physical subjects were discussed, and was laying the foundation of that general acquaintance with such topics which led to his subsequent election to membership in the newly-founded Royal Society. At all events, his decision was in favor of medicine as a profession. After unusual delays, owing in part to political ill-will, he received the degree of Bachelor of Medicine in 1674. The degree of doctor he never received, although in a private way, among his friends and patrons, he rendered important medical services and was known by the appellation of "Doctor."

In the autumn of 1665 Locke accompanied Sir Walter Vane, as secretary, on an embassy to Cleve, the capital of the Elector of Brandenburg. He was absent from England about three months. His letters give minute details of manners and customs, which he observed with characteristic curiosity. Occasionally he grows humorous. Referring to the heavy "brass" money of the Brandenburgers, he says, "I wondered at first why the market people brought their wares in little carts drawn by one horse, till I found it necessary to carry home the price of them; for a horse-load of turnips would be two horse-load of money." And then, referring to their slowness: "A pair of shoes cannot be got under half a year; I lately saw the cow killed out of whose hide I hope to have my next pair." Returning to England, the prospect of entering upon a diplomatic career was held out to him, but rejected. In the same year occurred his introduction to Lord Ashley, subsequently Earl of Shaftesbury, whose family he afterward entered, rendering important medical services (he performed a successful surgical operation on Lord Ashley himself), acting as tutor to his son, for whom he was trusted to seek a wife, and, as the confidential adviser of his patron, entering upon the study of various political and religious questions of weighty interest. It may be of special interest to us to recall the circumstance that it was Locke who, as secretary to Lord Ashley, the most active and influential of the proprietors of "Carolina," was called upon to draw up a scheme entitled "The Fundamental Constitutions for the Government of Carolina," in view of an attempt then making to plant a colony there. Although everything in this scheme is not to be ascribed to Locke, yet many of its provisions, as has been observed, are in characteristic agreement with the liberal views he was about that time expressing in an "Essay on Toleration," which he never finished. Among them are the following: That "any seven or more persons, agreeing in any religion, shall constitute a church or profession to which they shall give some name to distinguish it from others"; that "in the terms of communion of every church or profession these following shall be three . . . : 1. That there is a God; 2. That God is publicly to be worshipped; 3. That it is lawful, and the duty of every man, being thereunto called by those that govern, to bear witness to that truth"; "No person above seventeen years of age shall have any benefit or protection of the law, or be capable of any place of profit or honour, who is not a member of some church or profession, having his name recorded in some one, and but one, religious record at once"; "No person whatsoever shall disturb, molest, or persecute another for his speculative opinions in religion or his way of worship." Obviously we are here far removed from that governmental absolutism in matters of religious doctrine which Hobbes allowed, and far in advance of the intolerance of which Locke, in his own lifetime and country, was an impatient witness. I may as well answer right here the question which may naturally be asked concerning Locke's own religious views. I have only to say that he was, throughout his life, a sincere Christian, but one whose Christianity was of the most beneficent type, namely, practical. "The christian religion we profess is not a notional science," said he, "to furnish speculation to the brain or discourse to the tongue, but a rule of righteousness to influence our lives." He accepted the christian revelation, and wrote a work which he was subsequently called upon to defend, on "The Reasonableness of Christianity." But in the matter of dogmatic interpretation he claimed and allowed the largest liberty.

In 1672 Locke had some thought of visiting the American colonies for his health. Instead of this he made a short visit to France. Locke's health was never firm. Perhaps this was one thing that deterred him from marrying. At any rate, when at one time he was urged to marry, he replied playfully that his health was the only mistress whom he had for a long time courted — a mistress so reserved that it would likely require all that remained of his life to secure her good graces and keep her in good humor. In 1672 his relation to Shaftesbury, then lord chancellor, had procured him the salaried office of secretary of presentations, and in the following year the secretaryship of the council of trade and plantations. In 1675, having obtained a medical studentship at Christ

Church College, he was led by his ill health to make a second journey to France, where he remained, first in the south of France, afterward in Paris, nearly four years. During this absence he was a careful and extremely minute observer of manners and customs, seeking in every way to add to his knowledge, and to learn of facts which might be of value to his friend Boyle and the Royal Society. At Paris he formed valuable relations with men of science. Everywhere his note-book accompanied him, it being his custom to employ it not only for the registration of facts observed, but also for the noting down of thoughts as, and whenever, they occurred to him. For all the time his brain was busy with varied problems relating to religion and politics, medical science, and the nature and limitations of human knowledge. Returning to England, we find Locke engaged in the greatest variety of occupations. He is making trips into the country, corresponding among others with his French friends, counselling and assisting Lord Shaftesbury in his political duties, superintending the education of the latter's grandson, destined to become so well known as a philosophical writer, writing verses to a young lady to convince her that she should "gad no more" and that (in his words, again)

"Home's the heaven where you are ador'd,"

declaiming in very sensible prose — as a physician — against the destructive absurdity of strait lacing, forming the acquaintance of Damaris Cudworth, subsequently Lady Masham, whom we have already met, and finally, at the age of fifty, his political patron having died in voluntary exile at Amsterdam, and himself being suspected and denounced on account of his personal relations to him, retiring for safety to Holland. During his stay here, a demand having been made for his extradition, he lives for some time in concealment. Pardon being subsequently offered him, he indignantly rejects it, averring that he was not a guilty man. He forms intimate relations with men of learning in Holland, publishes in one of the first learned periodicals ever issued an abridgment or sketch of his still unpublished Essay concerning Human Understanding, travels through the Low Countries, becomes the valued friend of William of Orange and assists in preparing for the revolution which placed William on the English throne. In the month of February, 1689, Locke, in the company of the Princess of Orange, who was to grace the English throne as Queen Mary, and bringing with him the manuscript of his famous Essay, landed again on English soil. He had spent nearly five years and a half in Holland.

The following and last portion of Locke's life was filled with the most varied and honorable activity. King William was so impressed with the sterling quality of his political wisdom that he insisted with great urgency on being allowed to avail himself of it in his diplomatic service. He pressed Locke to accept first an important embassy to Cleve and Berlin. Locke declined on account of his inexperience in diplomatic labors and perhaps still more on account of his health. It was then proposed to him to go to Vienna, where the milder climate would be more favorable to his impaired constitution. But he persisted in remaining in England where he believed he could be of greater service to the government and the country than abroad. And indeed weighty questions of immediate and far-reaching practical consequence were awaiting solution, to which Locke, with earnest zeal and very influential success, devoted himself. These were questions relating to religious toleration, political rights, finance, the encouragement of trade, and, as Locke's biographer rather surprisingly expresses it, the *improvement of the temper of politicians*. What may have been his success in the last point, I cannot say. Certain it is that (as one of the most recent foreign biographers of Locke perceives, in substance) he was one of the first to procure, for independent, reasoned *opinion*, recognition and weight in the determination of public affairs. A Letter concerning Toleration, which Locke had written in Latin, while in Holland, having been published there anonymously, and apparently without Locke's knowledge, and an English translation being soon afterward printed, Locke presently found occasion to write "second" and "third" "Letters" to defend the first one against the illiberal attacks made upon it. The religious liberty and comprehensiveness, for which he here contended, was in advance of the measures actually adopted by the government, which therefore in so far disappointed Locke's hopes. It is worthy of notice, however, that Locke himself did not think it politically safe to grant political privileges to Romanists, who acknowledge in all things the supremacy of a foreign Pontiff, or to Atheists, since, as Locke argued, promises, covenants and oaths can have no hold upon those who deny God's existence.

Locke rendered a more important service to the Revolution, and to the theory of political liberty, by his "Two Treatises of Government" (1690). The object of the first one was to "detect and overthrow" the monarchical absolutism, defended, on scriptural grounds, in the published works of Sir Robert Filmer (and in obvious agreement with Thomas Hobbes); the second was an "Essay Concerning the True Original, Extent, and End of Civil Government." In these treatises we find the contract-theory of the origin of political society, as in Hooker and Hobbes, before Locke, and Rousseau, and so many others, after him, but applied in a broader spirit and with a more comprehensive regard to facts than is discoverable in the works of either Hobbes or Rousseau. Hobbes made men, by the contract through which they entered into a civil state, delegate and abandon all rights, except that of preserving one's life. Locke interpreted the contract as the very means by which the people, the sole original source of all government, guaranteed the preservation of all their rights. They established government, not because they were originally unfriendly equals (though this, he held, was partly true), but, obviously, in order that they might the better repress infractions of the natural law of right which all men confess, and secure their individual and mutual good. Accordingly the supreme law of government, Locke maintains, is the law of the people's good, or happiness, "the preservation of their goods, the protection of their persons and their rights." In opposition to Sir Robert Filmer (and virtually to Hobbes, who, however, is not mentioned), Locke is led to insist upon what we should now term "constitutional limitations" of the sovereign's power. Another point which is also noted, as bearing in the same direction, is his development of the theory of property — the right to *possess* — as the exclusive result of *labor*. That this falls far short of an adequate philosophy of civil society, I should be among the first to urge. But, I repeat, it is not the philosophical spirit which prompts Locke's inquiries in general. He would keep close to immediate, practical facts, to the leadings of a broad, common (non-speculative) sense. Prof. Marion remarks of Locke: "*Il a la superstition des faits,*" which is certainly an excellent superstition for any one who is concerned for the practical direction of affairs. And from this point of view it must be admitted that Locke, with excellent judgment, animated by regard for human rights and human duties, for the radical and for the conservative side of justice, labored to shape the unwritten law of his country. But not only its unwritten law. Though not sitting in parliament, it is related that his opinions on subjects of approaching legislation were commonly sought, and communicated, printed, and circulated among members in advance of discussion, and with important results. Locke held also, for a few years, offices of administrative trust, as commissioner of appeals, and of trade and plantations. He published views on money and interest, which seem not to have descended to several of our own financial Solons; for a foreign critic remarks that "his arguments acted slowly but surely on opinion, and when the reforms which he demanded were finally effected in legislation, no one dared again propose as a serious, and especially as an honorable, remedy [for financial distress] the attribution to existing coins of a nominal value superior to their real value." That instruction in political science, which has of late been so intelligently urged by some of our leading educators, would, it is obvious, find some of its most valuable and practical texts in Locke's writings; and I hope all will agree with me in wishing that two or three hundred of our national legislators could take a few lessons from him in the ethics of finance. It is interesting in this connection to note in passing, painful as the thought may be to the advocates of the "people's money," that Locke was one of the original proprietors of the Bank of England, founded in 1694.

It is of interest to remember that among the friends with whom Locke at periods was in active correspondence, was Sir Isaac Newton. Their acquaintance may have begun through their common membership in the Royal Society. Sir Isaac communicated with Locke concerning his mathematico-physical speculations, and also respecting the interpretation of passages in scripture. Locke assisted Newton to obtain certain valuable positions under the government, which the inadequacy of his stipend as a Cambridge professor made him desire, and having received from the famous chemist, Boyle, as his executor (Boyle died in 1691), a recipe for transmuting a certain kind of red earth into gold, had some correspondence with Newton concerning the application of it. Science, we see, was then still capable of pursuing occasionally an *ignis fatuus*, especially if it glittered with gold. It is fair to say that Newton had his doubts, and Locke himself is not known ever to have attempted, or to have caused others to attempt, to prove the value of Boyle's recipe.

In the year 1690 the first edition of the Essay Concerning Human Understanding had been published. Four editions were published before Locke's death, together with translations into Latin and French. Others defended and attacked it, and Locke himself entered the lists, in his own defense, against the criticisms of the Bishop of Worcester. The occasion of the composition of the essay had been the circumstance that at a gathering of a few friends, assembled to discuss subjects of common interest, the interlocutors, of whom Locke was one, were hopelessly puzzled, and it occurred to Locke that an inquiry as to "what objects our understandings were or were not fitted to deal with," must be made before they could profitably proceed further with their discussion. A person who was present at the famous gathering has told us that the conversation turned upon questions of morals and revealed religion. For twenty years Locke was occupied with the reflections which issued in the essay, and during this time, as we know, his life had been so unsettled, and his occupations so various, that the opportunities for continued thought and literary labor must have been rare. In view of the disconnected way in which it was brought to completion, Locke himself claims the reader's pardon if he discover in it a degree both of prolixity and apparent incoherence.

Fox Bourne, Locke's recent biographer, declares that Locke's conscious purpose was "not to build up a metaphysical theory, but to ascertain by actual observation what were the means and methods by which ordinary people acquired knowledge and developed their thinking faculties." In other words, Locke would furnish so much of descriptive psychology as relates to the cognitive functions. He would ascertain what are the exact historical facts respecting the growth of intelligence in the individual. Had this really been Locke's only purpose, and had he strictly adhered to it, I doubt if his name would ever have been mentioned but with the respect and gratitude due to every one who explores and describes a portion of the field of phenomena with more accuracy than any predecessor.

But this was not the case. In general, those who most scout metaphysics are the most dogmatic in their metaphysical assumptions. Every man must have, and does have, consciously or virtually, his philosophy, and if from prejudice or indolence he will not take it from philosophers, or seek it by appropriate philosophical methods, he is sure to take it from some other source, and the chances are ten to one that he will be led astray. The empirical psychologist is rarely content to be that and nothing else, but is prone to seek in his science the answer to philosophical questions. This is what Locke intentionally did. But for this very reason, in the language of an extremely able English critic, he "took description for explanation"—and incomplete description at that. The "facts" described, the *phenomena* of mind, were held (and were expressly employed) to disprove a famous pyschological hypothesis of metaphysical bearings, and to contain the only possible answer to important philosophical questions. Instead of rising to the height of a commanding principle, he fed in the valleys and shadows of minute facts of appearance. Of his honest purpose and sincere conviction there cannot be the slightest question. But then something more than this is requisite to establish one's claim to adequate philosophical insight.

The hypothesis upon which Locke made war, and to the refutation of which the first book of his Essay is devoted, was the hypothesis of so-called Innate Ideas. This book was the one last written, and the polemics it contains cannot be fully appreciated without a knowledge of the positive views set forth in the following books. In these Locke sets out with a fiction—the fiction that the mind is "like a piece of white paper," on which "experience" is the only writer. This fiction is a thoroughly natural and even necessary one for purely descriptive, historical psychology. The object-matter of such psychology is made up of appearances, mental "*phenomena*," and these present themselves in the form of so-called mental "images," or "impressions," which, from the analogy of sensible experience, naturally suggest the notion of a colorless mirror in which the so-called images are reflected, or of a "piece of white paper" on which the impressions are stamped. All science of phenomena proceeds on the basis of similar fictions. Thus physical science assumes atoms and blind or mechanical forces, which are never given in sensible experience, cannot be construed in sensible imagination, and are for science at most symbols of the unknown. The important thing to notice is that such working hypotheses or "auxiliary conceptions" have, and can have, no absolute validity until interpreted and, if need be, corrected in the light of a philosophical principle.

The mind, now, being assumed (not observed or demonstrated) to resemble a piece of white paper, or, in other words, to possess originally no nature nor any power of its own, is supposed to be provided with all the "materials" of its knowledge by processes which are essentially independent of its own activity, and of which involuntary sensation is the all-inclusive "original." Moreover, nothing belongs to mind, or to its nature, except what *comes into* it and remains there in the form of a conscious possession or *state*, *i.e.* in the form of an observable image or "idea." This latter position constitutes the nerve of Locke's argument against innate ideas. Holding this essentially *static* view of mind and of knowledge, the doctrine of innate ideas could mean for Locke nothing but the doctrine that certain ideas are clearly and necessarily in the mind of every individual from the beginning of his conscious life. But nothing is plainer than that "children, savages, idiots," and the greater number of persons arrived at the "age of reason," are not explicitly conscious of any such "necessary" or "innate" truth as that "Whatever is, is," or of any such "innate ideas" as God, soul, substance, etc. Hence, Locke concludes, there are no such ideas.

It is hardly necessary to state that Locke, as was quite natural for one starting from the point of view of purely descriptive psychology, wholly misapprehended the import of the doctrine of innate ideas or the intention of its supporters. That doctrine rests on a view of the nature of mind, far more comprehensive and true to all the facts of the case than the view with which Locke sets out. It implies that mind has a nature and an activity peculiar to itself, for the development of which exciting conditions — be these sensible "impressions" or something else — may be needed, but which are distinguished in reality, and must be carefully kept distinct in theory, from the conditions as such. It implies that mind is not simply and characteristically what it *has*, but what it *does*, not a state, but an activity. "Innate ideas" (an unfortunate phrase, it must be confessed) are the inherent, independent, rational fibres of the mind's own activity (as distinguished from that side of mind by which, as in sensation, it is relatively passive), and it is by no means necessary that they should become visible, and be explicitly and universally and constantly recognized as threads or states of empirical consciousness (or as "ideas"), in order to prove their reality. They are present still, if only virtually and unconsciously, determining the direction and shaping the results of thought, and without them no rational consciousness whatever would be possible.

This is implicitly allowed by Locke, when, proceeding with his work, he finds it impossible to carry out his first fancy of the mind as a purely neutral tint, or as a mere faculty of passive receptivity. He sets out to determine, by reflective analysis and observation, whence we have the "materials of our knowledge" or of "all our thinking," and proceeds as if the descriptive account of the "materials" were to explain the "knowledge" or the "thinking." He quickly perceives that consciousness is not explained when the objects of consciousness ("ideas of sensation and reflection") have been enumerated. The *activity* is not explained by the *objects* with which it is casually or chiefly concerned. Mind, for Locke, is like a mirror, conscious of the images reflected on its surface. The images do not explain the consciousness. Accordingly, the "white paper" theory, so far as it seemed to imply that mind was blankly passive and receptive, and only that, is practically modified in the progress of Locke's inquiries. The "white paper" turns out to be capable of "operations" and to possess "powers." Here Locke is immediately on the track of a conception of mind as an ideal value, a living power, an energy of intelligence, containing implicitly in its nature that of which innate ideas (in their true purport) are the explicit and developed expression. Such a conception furnishes the only true key to man's characteristic nature, and is indeed the door by which (and not by any mere classification or registration of phenomena) man is permitted, if at all, to enter into the knowledge of real being universally. Locke does not follow up this cue very far, and yet he does follow it so far, and the language which he employs in his discussions is so indeterminate, that it has been possible for some to find in his Essay quite the opposite of the pure empiricism and sensationalism which he seems to teach, and to which (as we shall see in subsequent chapters) the historical development of his ideas distinctly led, namely, a so-called "intellectualism," virtually tantamount to Aristotle's "active reason" or Kant's "*reiner Verstand*." Locke's prevailing tendency, however, is certainly not in this direction. Mind continues to be conceived by him, after sensible analogies, as an unknown and inconceivable something, an attributeless and hence indefinable substratum, or "substance," on which "ideas" may be spread and to which they adhere. Matter, on the other hand, is for him the name of another form of apparent "substance," of which our knowledge is equally indefinite. Hence Locke's admission — so startling to his contemporaries — that the substance of the soul might be material. Since nothing was known either of immaterial or material substance, it might obviously be the case, for aught that he could tell, that both were intrinsically identical.

Locke sought, in his general tendency, to reduce the intelligible to the sensible, and to explain the former through the analogy or on the basis of the latter. The ontological agnosticism to which he was led was the same which, in the whole history of thought, has resulted — as it must necessarily result — from similar attempts. That Locke did not rigorously deduce and apply all the consequences of this result and proclaim a universal philosophical scepticism, was due to the confusion of his own thought, and to the practical hold which the vital, synthetic truths by which alone man, as man, in the true sense lives, through which the universe subsists, and which all positive, affirmative philosophy defends, had upon him. It remained for David Hume, as the spokesman of a later generation, to complete Locke's destructive work.

On ethics Locke wrote nothing, though repeatedly urged to do so and having it for a time in mind. His final conclusion was that there was no occasion for such a work; the Gospel, as he alleged, containing "so perfect a body of ethics that reason may be excused from that inquiry, since she may find man's duty clearer and easier in revelation than in herself" (cf. Bacon). But whenever Locke finds occasion, incidentally, to express himself concerning a question of ethical inquiry, he falls at once into the hedonistic or utilitarian vein, guided by such principles as that "It is a man's proper business to seek happiness and avoid misery" (which Kant would term, with justice, a *rule of prudence*, and not a *law of morality*), and that that is "always the greatest vice whose consequences draw after it the greatest harm." It is the failure to raise himself above this point of view of the "arithmetic of pleasures" which, better than anything else, marks the theoretical deficiency of his political ethics. Perhaps the most charitable and just thing which can be said with reference to Locke's general deficiencies as a thinker, is that he was but one of the millions who are — for whatever reason — unable to rise in *theory* to the heights which, in the temper of their lives and substance of their characters — *i.e.* in their vital manhood — they practically occupy.

I have already once mentioned the title of a modest little work ("Some Thoughts Concerning Education"), first published in 1693, and often reprinted. I have not left myself the requisite space for reporting with any detail its contents, though I know of no work of his in which the author appears to better advantage. One of the most attractive traits in Locke's character was his sympathy with children. One feels that, childless though he was, yet in writing these counsels concerning their proper education, he is performing a labor of love. The work is remarkable for the due and catholic regard evinced for every means of education necessary for a perfect manhood, in body as well as in knowledge and character. But there is in it no false sentimentalism. The truest love is the firmest. The main point is to teach the child "to get a mastery over his inclinations, and submit his appetite to reason." It was more important that a firm foundation should be provided for character than that the memory and intellect should be stocked with the knowledge of abstract facts. This latter was the last and "least part of education" (Bourne). With regard to which Locke remarked, very sensibly, that the tutor of a boy "should remember that his business is not so much to teach him all that is knowable, as to raise in him a love and esteem of knowledge, and to put him in the right way of knowing and improving himself when he has a mind to it."

In the year 1691 Locke became an inmate of the Masham family at Oates, Essex. He did this upon invitation, but not without stipulating that he should bear his fixed proportion of the family expenses. He still retained, however, for a number of years, lodgings in London, where he was required to be from time to time.

In his very last years he became quite infirm, the difficulty with his lungs increasing, and partial deafness overtaking him. Lady Masham attended him with the affection of a daughter. As for Locke, he saw his end approaching with contented resignation, though not without a delicate tinge of gentle melancholy. On the whole, I know of no scene in the literature of biography more touching in its innocence and simplicity than that which relates to the last year of Locke's life. In his letters he is overflowing with love and gratitude to his friends, seeking to give evidence of the same by every token of generosity and cheerful interest. The last letter which he is known ever to have written (addressed to his cousin Peter King) ends with these words: "I wish you all manner of prosperity in this world, and the everlasting happiness of the world to come. That I loved you I think you are convinced. God send us a happy meeting in the resurrection of the just. Adieu!" A few days before his death he received, in private, the holy communion, and said after it, "I am in perfect charity with all men, and in sincere communion with the whole church of Christ, by whatever names Christ's followers name themselves." The day before his death he said, "As for me, I have lived long enough, and I thank God I have enjoyed a happy life;" but, he added, with an old man's life-weariness, "after all, this life is nothing but vanity." He added words of christian counsel to those around him, such as, however, he had not waited till that hour of weakness and approaching dissolution to give. On the 28th of October, 1704, while sitting in his chair in his room, where Lady Masham had "cheered him" by reading from the psalms of David, death came upon him naturally, without a struggle, as sleep upon a child. A fittingly peaceful end to a life of quiet dignity and of the most sincere devotion to the cause of truth, wherever and as far as Locke recognized it, and of mankind.

CHAPTER VIII.

GEORGE BERKELEY.

WE are ourselves living, as a recent German writer has remarked, in a Renaissance age, which, if less impassioned than the first Renaissance, is more intelligent, more comprehensive, having broader sympathies, and animated by a more just historic sense. It has also a more extensive historic range of view than its earlier prototype, since this range includes the first Renaissance itself, together with all its fruits hitherto developed. It is this new movement which has found expression in the remarkable tendency of the last quarter of a century in the direction, not simply of a careful restoration of the monuments of all of the important thought and work of our predecessors, ancient and modern, but also of a vital, organic comprehension of their significance. The labors undertaken in this view have their counterpart, and in some degree their complement, in the fruitful ethnological investigations which distinguish our time. As a result of all, man bids fair in due time to comprehend himself in and through the aid of his history. Himself and his thought are no longer viewed as isolable, independent units, to be explained solely or most readily by exclusive reference to themselves, but rather by reference to their places in an historic, organic development (or at least in organic relations which become most distinctly visible when viewed historically) from which they are inseparable. One of the happy effects of this movement in the history of speculative opinion is the growing perception of a single purpose, a tendency, sometimes obvious and pronounced, sometimes indicated by negative signs, toward a uniform result, in all the products of philosophical inquiry. If the line of progress is zigzag, it is perceived that there is, nevertheless, a progress, at least in this sense, that what the earliest thinkers were led to hold as true is also found true by their latest successors, varied, and, it may be, corrected in expression, but unchangeable, as becomes the truth, in its essence.

We shall possibly find these last observations in some degree illustrated in our examination of Berkeley's life and work. That, however, to which I purposed here more particularly to direct attention was the rich tangible fruits which historical scholarship has borne for English philosophy. Within the last fifteen years complete editions of the philosophical works of Bacon, Berkeley and Hume have been given to the world. These are not mere reprints, but critical editions, in which ripe scholarship has been employed to furnish a correct text, and to provide the means for the proper understanding of the same. We need scarcely go back more than another fifteen years to meet with the first complete edition of Hobbes, and a special collection of the philosophical works of Locke. Nor has the biography of the philosophers been neglected, without a knowledge of which no one now thinks it possible fully to appreciate a thinker's motives and intentions. Bacon, Locke and Berkeley have been particularly fortunate in this respect, through the attention they have received. If for the sketch of Locke's life, which was presented in the last chapter, I was principally indebted to the full and comprehensive biography lately published by Mr. H. R. Fox Bourne, I must now acknowledge beforehand a similar indebtedness to Prof. Fraser's Life and Letters of Berkeley, for the biographical details employed in the present chapter.

Locke was contained in germ in Bacon and Hobbes. That germ, watered perhaps by Gassendi, and certainly stimulated by Descartes, explains, in its way, Locke. But Locke does not in any such sense explain Berkeley; the latter is far from being simply a natural development of the former. Locke is emphatically Berkeley's starting-point, and explains his most glaring deficiencies. For the rest, the relation between the two philosophers is better illustrated if we compare Locke to a slow-burning wick, and Berkeley to an electric light, quickly-blazing and intense, and suppose the latter to be kindled (though, obviously, not otherwise explained) by the former. If Locke was a common soldier, modest, but rendering, on the whole, a rather mechanical service, Berkeley is a bold and dashing general, bent on conquest. If with Locke truth is a thing to be minutely sought, and, as far as it is discoverable, to be undiscriminatingly and passively *accepted*, with Berkeley it is a kingdom to be seized upon by force. If the one is calmly and myopically analytical, observant, the other is warmly enthusiastic and assertorical — not satisfied with demurrers, pleas of necessary ignorance, limitation, and the like; nay, indignant at them. Berkeley professes, with his more energetic vision to penetrate the clouds which bounded Locke's mental horizon, and lo! they become for him celestial forms of light.

To his contemporaries Berkeley was a man possessing

all the charms which can arise from unaffected virtue, unusual brightness of intellect, and sweetness of speech. The reader will recall at once Pope's line, ascribing

" To Berkeley every virtue under heaven."

Add to this his varied life, his travels, his odd and his noble enthusiasms, and one has the elements of one of the most interesting and attractive biographical pictures, of which our literature can boast. Let us briefly contemplate it.

It has long been known that no gentleman is so charming as the cultivated Irishman. We ascribe to him quiet, unostentatious breeding, a graceful mastery of intelligence, and that quickness and minuteness of perception which is essential to humor. Shall we ascribe Berkeley's possession of any of these qualities to his Irish birth? For George Berkeley was born in the county of Kilkenny, Ireland, at Dysert castle or tower, now a ruin, near Thomastown, and in the valley of the Nore, March 12, 1685. He was the eldest of six sons born to William Berkeley, "gentleman," a person of English descent, and connected — just how it is impossible to make out — with the noble family of Berkeley, in England. His mother seems to have been an Irish lady; according to one account she was an aunt of General Wolfe, the hero of Quebec. On the whole, little — strangely little — is known of Berkeley's immediate family. His grandfather is said to have received from Charles II the collectorship of Belfast, in reward for services rendered to the royal cause. There is evidence that his father, in mature life, was connected with the army, where he rose at least to the rank of " captain of horse" (like Locke's father). All of the brothers of George Berkeley received a liberal training, and one of them, like our hero, entered into holy orders. We can infer, with sufficient certainty, that the gentle blood of the family brought with it the tradition of liberal culture, along with determined loyalty to the national dynasty and church. For the rest, nothing is reported concerning the special home influences under which the boy Berkeley grew up. But we know that the dogs of war, let loose after the dethronement of James II, must have passed within sound of the youth as they rushed down the valley of the Nore; even as Locke, too, was, almost, born amid the turmoil of civil strife, and Hobbes first saw the light when all England was quaking through fear of foreign invasion. Is the sensational shock produced by such near experience of war's alarms one of the proximate causes which may occasion that deeper, more active and fervid energy of aggressive thought, whence philosophy arises? If so, some one or more of our colleges may now number among its undergraduates a predestined philosopher. However this may be, we know from Berkeley's own statement in his recently recovered Commonplace Book, that from his "childhood" he "had an unaccountable turn of thought"—presumably in the direction of those philosophical speculations for which he was subsequently famous. He was "distrustful," he notes, somewhat mysteriously, "at eight years old, and consequently by nature disposed to these new doctrines." The student who is familiar beforehand with Berkeley's character and philosophy will feel that he may, without violence to essential truth, call Wordsworth to aid in the interpretation of this "memorandum," and declare that he who was destined to be "Nature's priest" was distrustful of the "shades of the prison-house" that "begin to close about the growing boy." He dreaded instinctively the fetters which earth, sense, matter — fate, brute necessity — were preparing to lay upon him. Through and above them all he saw the "vision splendid," which was a constant and brilliant testimony against the necessity or substantial reality of the fetters mentioned, and already he was in unconscious germ and spirit that earnest, valiant thinker, the whole power of whose rare eloquence was to be exerted in order to convince mankind that the physical, as such, is insubstantial and powerless, that its whole value and significance are exhaustively apprehended and explained, when it is viewed as the visible symbol and language of Mind, — as a *word*, or *logos*, which God is always speaking to us, and nothing else. Who will not reverence boyhood, on seeing it big with a thought of such sublimity and simplicity — a thought which sums up in brief the essence of all positive philosophy of physical existence? And the rays of this truth, I imagine, illuminate the naïve, unprejudiced perceptions of childhood far oftener than we suspect. I note further, before accompanying Berkeley away from his childhood home, that he was here face to face with lovely natural scenery. Away from the bustle of the town, he was enfolded in the quiet of "grassy meadows," kept green by the "gray waters" of the "stubborn Newre" (as Spenser calls it) and surrounded by "wooded hills." Nature here wore a friendly aspect, and Berkeley's biographer is doubtless right in supposing that these familiar childhood scenes may have had much to do with the development of that fresh and hearty appreciation of outward nature which always characterized him and more than once appears in his writings.

At the age of eleven years Berkeley was sent to "His Grace the Duke of Ormonde's School," in Kilkenny, where he was prepared to enter at once not the lowest, or fifth, class, but the second. This school, "the Eton of Ireland," boasts many illustrious names upon its roll of honor. Jonathan Swift, with whose fortunes Berkeley was destined to be singularly connected, had preceded him here by a number of years. Here Berkeley may be supposed to have received the usual training in the classical languages and in mathematics.

In the year 1700, Berkeley was entered at Trinity College, Dublin, with which, as Scholar or Fellow, he was destined to remain nominally connected during a quarter of a century. The external history of his life as a student is soon told, and I adopt for this purpose the words of Prof. Fraser:

"He pursued his studies, in those first years at Trinity, according to report, with extraordinary ardour, 'full of simplicity and enthusiasm.' He was made a Scholar in 1702. In the spring of 1704 (the year of Locke's death) he became Bachelor of Arts. He took his Master's degree in the spring of 1707. After the customary arduous examination of that University, conducted in presence of nobility, gentry, and high officials, he passed with unprecedented applause, and was admitted to a Fellowship June 9, 1707, 'the only reward of learning that kingdom has to bestow,' as one of his biographers curtly says."

Some characteristic incidents are related of the time of his student life. The story told of Giotto (but which, it seems, was also told of the Greek painter Parrhasius, and afterward of Michael Angelo and Guido), to the effect that, having occasion to depict the agonies of death by crucifixion, he actually induced a poor man to be bound to a cross, and then stabbed him, is well known. Had the requirements of his art made it necessary for Giotto to endanger or sacrifice his own life, even legend would, assuredly, have hesitated to represent him as going about it so jauntily and recklessly as in this case, where it was only another's feelings and life that were at stake. But a tale told of Berkeley's early college life represents him — whether authentically or not — as almost suffering death of his own accord, that he might know what were the sensations experienced in death by hanging. He had, as we are told, been led by curiosity to witness a public execution. Returning to his room, he allowed himself to be tied to the ceiling, after which the chair on which he was standing was removed, it having been previously agreed that, on a signal to be given by the experimenter, he should be relieved. His companion, however, waited in vain for the signal, and when he let Berkeley down, the latter fell motionless to the ground. On returning to consciousness his first words are said to have been (addressing his companion): "Bless my heart, Conterini, you have rumpled my bands." Conterini (the same who became subsequently, through marriage, Oliver Goldsmith's uncle) withdrew, not unnaturally, from the engagement he had made to repeat the experiment in his own person. To the same period in his life is ascribed the visit which Berkeley made to the famous Cave of Dunmore, and the detailed description which he afterward wrote out of this natural curiosity. In these acts and incidents are prefigured traits characteristic of Berkeley throughout his life — untiring zeal and utter forgetfulness of danger in the investigation of facts of every kind.

Referring to the hanging experiment, Prof. Fraser continues:

"This, among other eccentric actions, we are told, made Berkeley a mystery. Ordinary people did not understand him, and laughed at him. Soon after his entrance he began to be looked at as either the greatest genius or the greatest dunce in College. Those who were slightly acquainted with him took him for a fool; but those who shared his intimate friendship thought him a prodigy of learning and goodness of heart. When he walked about, which was seldom, he was surrounded by the idlers, who came to enjoy a laugh at his expense. Of this, it is said, he sometimes complained, but there was no redress; the more he fretted, the more he amused them."

All this has the air of the tales usually circulated concerning genius—tales which are always readily believed, if not for their literal truth, at least for their truth to character. The reader may feel already the sharp contrast between Berkeley's individuality and Locke's; the latter a perfect pattern of common sense and propriety, too well bred, if not too common-place, to attract attention, turning, as a gentleman should, about a pivot determined and steadied by society, feeling and independently expressing a dissatisfaction with the substance and method of the philosophy taught him, but turning, for his immediate relief, to personal and epistolary intercourse with "pleasant and witty men," and to the reading of romances, and not prepared till forty years later to speak out plainly to the world; Berkeley, on the other hand, finding the axis about which his whole nature turned, in his own teeming brain, positive, enthusiastic, energetically subtle, self-forgetting, and forgetting equally the world, at first, doubtless, surprised at his own eccentricities, then annoyed at their consequences, but very soon, as his genius rapidly crystallized in the definite form of an organic, commanding thought, which was ultimately reckoned to him for his chief eccentricity, recognizing in this very thought, not the freak of an erratic and abortive genius, but the marks of a genuine *revelation*, such as in all times it belongs to real genius to bring into the world; proceeding, therefore, at once, while yet only a student, in very throes of thought, to struggle with and seek to master this revelation, and finally, as we shall see, when only twenty-five years of age, proclaiming it with all the impetuosity of youth and of fervent conviction, to what he conceived as a waiting and expectant, a needy and a desirous, world.

From about the year 1705 to 1710 the biography of Berkeley is almost exclusively the biography of his thought. Of the individual, in his external or miscellaneous history, we learn next to nothing. We know indeed that "early in 1705" he was active in promoting the formation of a philosophical society for the discussion of the "New Philosophy"; for it is necessary not to forget that we are now well past the Renaissance time; the modern mind has been making some of its most memorable endeavors to go alone; on the continent Descartes and Spinoza and Malebranche have lived and written, and their words have resounded in Great Britain (not to mention, also, Leibnitz, whose thought, however, was less known and less influential there); and in England Bacon had preached, Hobbes had dogmatized, and Locke had analyzed and reasoned; the Essay of Locke had been published ten years before Berkeley entered Trinity, and Newton's Principia thirteen years, and these works were the subject of active discussion, and were rapidly displacing the traditional Aristotelianism of schools and universities. The new society consisted, besides Berkeley, of seven persons whose names are not known. It appears from the "statutes" that attention was to be given, not only to abstract philosophy, but also to experimental and descriptive science. A "museum" was contemplated, and the officers were to include a "keeper of the rarities," who was required, either in person or by deputy, to "attend at the museum from two to four on Friday," the day of the meeting. The proceedings were to be kept secret, but we learn that they were to include the discussion, in "solemn discourses," of some subject previously agreed upon, followed by free debate, which being concluded, members were free to "propose to the assembly their inventions, new thoughts, or observations, in any of the sciences." Obviously no exclusiveness of scientific or speculative interest was intended. But of the fortunes of the society we are not informed. We only know that the new philosophy intensely exercised and interested Berkeley, that it set him vigorously to thinking, and that there soon flashed upon him the light of a "new principle," as he termed it, a principle which presented itself to him with the clearest light of self-evidence, and which, once generally perceived and accepted, was, according to his unhesitating conviction, destined to be fraught with consequences of incalculable value for the relief of man's intellectual and moral estate. This "principle" now took complete possession of Berkeley. It identified him with itself. He became wholly its devoted servant. He viewed himself as irresistibly called to be its mouthpiece, its apostle, its protagonist. In his Commonplace Book we are privileged to see Berkeley putting himself, as it were, in training, morally and intellectually, to enter the arena of opinion with his priceless principle. We see him balancing, swinging, poising himself, seeking to strip himself of dead weights of prejudice or incautious error, strengthening his intellectual joints, minutely examining all the parts of his mental harness, encouraging and cautioning himself. His new principle is a philosophical one, it is a theory of the nature, the definition, the explanation of existence. Accordingly we find him testing the application of *his* definition to all the leading forms and attributes of existence, to matter and spirit, time and space, cause and substance, understanding and will. Of course, among these thoughts jotted down from day to day during a period of two or three or more years, and relating to some of the most arduous topics of human reflection, there are uncertainties, hesitations, contradictions even. They are, in fact, only chips from the intellectual workshop, irregular, unformed, or like flashings of an early morning sun, which casts long shadows. But in spite of all abatements, the record of this metaphysical travail possesses a very fascinating interest, and as an evidence of speculative precocity has scarcely a parallel. Especially touching are the passages where Berkeley, contemplating the resistance, the manifold criticism, he is bound to encounter, braces himself up to meet it. "I am young," he imagines the unkind objector charging, "I am an upstart, I am a pretender, I am vain. Very well. I shall endeavor to bear up under the most lessening, vilifying appellations the pride and rage of man can devise. But one thing I know I am not guilty of: I do not pin my faith on the sleeve of any great man. I act not out of prejudice or prepossession. I do not adhere to any opinion because it is an old one, a reviv'd one, a fashionable one, or one that I have spent much time in the study and cultivation of. . . . If in some things I differ from a philosopher [Locke] I profess to admire, 'tis for that very thing on account whereof I admire him, namely, the love of truth."

At another time he expostulates with an imagined adversary. "In short, be not angry. You lose nothing, whether real or chimerical. Whatever you can in any wise conceive or imagine, be it never so wild, so extravagant, and absurd, much good may it do you. You may enjoy it for me. I'll never deprive you of it." No, indeed! for all this belongs to the sphere of that metaphysical prejudice, which, along with all other vanities, Berkeley has renounced. And, accordingly, we find Berkeley, on another page, reminding himself in a "Mem." "to be eternally banishing Metaphisics, etc., and recalling men to Common Sense." To his own absolute conviction, his "new principle" appears like the simplest common sense, almost truismatic, and he reflects, with satisfaction, that the "*sillyness* of the current doctrine makes much for" him. "Whenever my reader finds me talk very positively, I desire he'd not take it ill. I see no reason why *certainty* should be confined to the mathematicians." "What I lay before you are undoubted theorems, not plausible conjectures of my own, nor learned opinions of other men." "What I say is demonstration — perfect demonstration." Still Berkeley specially cautions himself "upon all occasions to use the utmost modesty — to confute the mathematicians with the utmost civility and respect, not to style them Nihilarians, etc.," followed by a characteristic monition to self-restraint, in these words:

"N. B. To rein in ye satirical nature."

Now and then there is a touch of Irish humor. "There

are men who say there are insensible substances. There are others who say the wall is not white, the fire is not hot, etc. We Irishmen cannot attain to these truths. The mathematicians think there are insensible lines. . . . We Irishmen can conceive of no such lines. The mathematicians talk of what they call a point. This, they say, is not altogether nothing, nor is it downright something. Now we Irishmen are apt to think something and nothing are next neighbours." You perceive Berkeley is preparing for a serious and determined tilt with the mathematicians. He adds: "I publish not this so much for anything else as to know whether other men have the same ideas as we Irishmen. This is my end, and not to be inform'd as to my own particular." Certainly not! Berkeley was thoroughly assured as to the nature of his own ideas. Finally, the whole contemplated work, the incalculably important philosophical revolution, was not to stop with an abstract speculative victory, but was to be "directed to practice and morality — as appears, first, from making manifest the nearness and omnipresence of God; secondly, from cutting off the useless labour of sciences, and so forth."

But the reader will now be ready to ask what was this new and weighty principle (which, I should here mention, Berkeley first laid before the public in the "Treatise concerning the Principles of Human Knowledge," first printed in the year 1710, when Berkeley was only twenty-five years old)? I have mentioned beforehand that it is a theory of the nature of existence, and before stating definitely *what* theory it is, I wish to remind the reader that Berkeley perfectly perceived the folly, so fashionable in all times among a certain order of thinkers, of affecting to regard it as a matter of practical indifference what view is held concerning the radical question of philosophy, to wit, what is the ultimate nature of being. He saw perfectly well that it makes a world-wide difference whether, as a so-called idealist, you find the absolute radicle and essence of universal being in living, knowable spirit, or in an unliving and intrinsically unknowable something, conventionally termed — for convenience, and for the sake of having a word to designate the object of our absolutely blind, and obstinate, faith — Matter. In the former is given a vital principle, possessed of a faculty, to wit, Reason, capable of accounting for the visible order and invariable law of concrete phenomena, and of a power, namely, Will, competent to be the source of the incessant motion of phenomena, or of their miscalled forces. The latter is without these advantages, and its defenders must rely on chance or irrational, unintelligible necessity, in their necessarily abortive attempts to comprehend existence. With the former, too, alone, is consistent the development of those practical disciplines which have direct reference to human life and practice, ethics, æsthetics, social philosophy. Moreover, any doubt in reference to the mentioned question of ontological principle will reflect itself in, and to that extent weaken and warp, the subordinate parts of philosophy, theoretical and practical, which depend on it, and any partial concessions to the negative, hypothetical principle, Matter (in the sense above explained, all alleged philosophy founded on which is always, and necessarily, and exclusively negative — philosophy of denial), any such concessions, I say, serve but to introduce confusion and disharmony, where light is demanded. In other words, philosophy must have a principle, and it can have only one principle. I add — what is so obvious that it were a gratuitous insult to the reader's intelligence expressly to mention it, but that it is so often and on the authority of such influential names denied — this principle must be positive and knowable. Further, this principle can be nothing but Spirit, Mind, Personality — Spirit Supreme and, in the universal language of mankind, Divine, when speaking absolutely and concerning questions of primary explanation, and spirit in its various derivative and relatively dependent potencies, when it is a question of secondary explanation. This is the lesson which the history of philosophy (far from being a jumble of contradictions or a progress in an endless circle) teaches with impressive and authoritative clearness, and which with equal evidence, in my opinion, results from an unprejudiced contemplation of the nature of thought and of things (or from the theory of knowledge and the theory of being). This is that comprehensive idealism, which has found varied expression in the greatest systems of ancient and modern philosophy, and to which the life of man in morality, the workings of artistic genius, the philosophical impotencies of physical *speculation* (as distinguished from physical *science*), and a thousand other tongues bear witness.

Thus much I have deemed it necessary to premise with a view to putting the reader in immediate position to see in what direction we must look for the positive and valuable meaning, the tendency, the real bearings, the explanation, the justification (so far as justification is possible) of the "new principle" which, when propounded to Berkeley's contemporaries, for the most part struck them, as it does others to-day, as only a curious paradox. Berkeley's doctrine, in other words, is to be understood in its affirmative import, and judged in its relation to the general doctrine of philosophical idealism, as just now broadly defined. The peculiar form which it assumed in his early works, and by which it is (I think, unfortunately) most, and almost exclusively, known, was immediately occasioned by Berkeley's study of Locke; of ancient philosophy Berkeley does not appear at this time to have possessed any special knowledge. The metaphysical outcome of Locke's Essay had been comparatively negative. Strict knowledge, according to Locke, we could be said only to have concerning our own individual ideas and their obvious relations. Of substantial existence, or being, considered absolutely, we could have no knowledge. We were surrounded — of this Locke made no doubt — by various material existences, of which, however, we could never know the essential and conditioning nature, or substance (matter), but only the conditioned qualities, and these only indirectly, through the impressions which objects made upon us. We possessed also an intuitive certainty of our own existence as so-called spiritual or thinking beings, but knew not what the substance of our spiritual being was. It was possible, Locke affirmed, that this substance might be material; we knew, and could know, nothing positively to the contrary; and if it were otherwise impossible, God might, in the exercise of his brute omnipotence, have annexed to matter the power to exercise spiritual functions. These negative conclusions, the very paralysis of philosophy and, as such, pure philosophical absurdities, rather than principles, were violently repugnant to Berkeley's mind, and seemed to him unnecessary and irrational, even on Locke's principles. Why assert, or assume, or admit the reality of that, of which, it is admitted, we can know nothing, of which no conception is possible, which nothing requires us to believe, and which, were it possible and existent, could neither effectuate nor explain anything? Why pretend that matter, as a form of substantial being, exists? Do you say that through the senses impressions of material substances are received, and it must be that they exist so as to cause these impressions? But the very conception of material substance, so far as it has any positive import, means something absolutely dead, inert, unchangeable, a purely passive, unperceived substratum, in which, it is fancied, perceived qualities may inhere and by which they may be held together. But the inert is no cause. Where there is causation there is life, not inertia; and where there is life there is spirit. Unliving matter can neither cause impressions, nor ideas, nor anything else. Besides, the supposition that the perceptible inheres, in any way, in the imperceptible, is a contradictory supposition, void of sense. But do you argue that your ideas of sensible objects are representative images, which inform you concerning the objects in question through their likeness to them? The answer is that no power in heaven or earth can make an idea to be like anything but an idea. Besides, were such likeness possible, there would be no means of proving its accuracy. The assumed material object is known only through the idea, and an independent comparison of the two is forever impossible. But, again, do space and time, as unthinking, unideal entities, so permeate all your conceptions that you cannot but look upon them as irresistibly evidencing their own reality and that of all the things which they seem to contain? The reply is that you are virtually begging, not solving, the question at issue. Time and space, and the sensible world which they condition, are not given as unthinking, unideal entities, but, on the contrary, precisely and only as living functions of thinking mind. They are given only as sensations, perceptions, conceptions, and in no other form can they be felt, perceived, conceived, or known; not, for instance, as possessing being independent of thought, or mind, or spirit. Do you appeal, finally, to the common sense of the non-philosophical portion of mankind in defense of your belief in unthinking and unthinkable matter? Berkeley will show you that this appeal is, technically, a decided blunder. Your notion of matter is exactly an artificial product of scholastic subtlety, of which the vulgar know nothing. Common sense believes in what it perceives and knows — in that which is livingly and clearly experienced in sensitive perception — and not in an imperceptible, inconceivable, indefinable something, which is neither given nor can be given in any possible experience. Material substance is nothing but an abstract idea, and this is enough, in Berkeley's eyes, to condemn it; for all purely abstract ideas are, in his view, empty, utterly meaningless ideas. So, then, Berkeley concludes — in his own eloquent statement of the famous "principle":

"Some truths there are so near and obvious to the mind that a man need only open his eyes to see them. Such I take this important one to be, namely, that all the choir of heaven and furniture of the earth, in a word, all those bodies which compose the mighty frame of the world, have not any subsistence without a mind, that their *being* is to be perceived or known; that consequently so long as they are not actually perceived by me, or do not exist in my mind or that of any other created spirit, they must have either no existence at all, or else subsist in the mind of some Eternal Spirit — it being perfectly unintelligible, and involving all the absurdity of abstraction, to attribute to any single part of them an existence independent of a spirit."

This is Berkeley's famous doctrine of immaterialism. It is the negative side of his philosophy, to which — unfortunately, but naturally — he was led in his early works to give the greatest relative consideration. It is by this side that he is chiefly known and judged; and yet wrongly and absurdly, for this is but the obverse of a principle, the other and positive side of which is a truth of unsurpassed grandeur and simplicity, profundity and weight, and by which Berkeley appears as occupying a worthy place in the long line of representatives of the world's best thought and faith. This truth is, that Being is, proximately, or in the first analysis, simply, active, causative power, and that since there is no power but the power of spirit, Being, absolutely and in the last analysis, is Spirit: whatever exists or appears to exist can and must only be philosophically, or ontologically (not phenomenally or, in the technical sense of the term, *scientifically*), explained through the power and qualities of spirit. The application which Berkeley makes of this truth to the case of our sensible perceptions is, that, since they must be caused, and since they cannot be caused by non-causative, and hence non-existent, matter, they must be ascribed to the agency of God, the Supreme Spirit. The world is God's voice, his language, a set of symbols or signs. Physical science, neglecting the questions of essential being and causation, has but to ascertain and record these symbols in their observable order of coëxistence and sequence. Philosophy shows that through them we are in communion with, and gracious dependence on, an omnipresent Deity.

I will not here enter into a minute and critical account of the deficiencies or possible exaggerations of Berkeley's youthful speculations. It is enough if I have made it evident that it was no idle delight in paradox that led him on, but a soul-absorbing, intellectual and moral interest; and that the philosophical principles which were the more or less clearly conscious motive and goal of his thought were worthy to fix his attention and employ for the time being the whole service of his eager mind. Obviously, those "coxcombs" who "vanquish Berkeley with a grin," seek their victory in too easy a manner. Nor did Dr. Johnson show a deeper intelligence respecting the "new principle," when he sought to overthrow it by kicking his foot against a post; or Dean Swift, when, as Berkeley on a rainy day stood waiting for admission at his door, he left the door unopened, on the plea that if Berkeley's body, a sensible object, was only an idea, it could enter just as well with the door shut as open.

It is interesting to note, as a curious coincidence, the circumstance that in the neighboring island of England a country curate, Arthur Collier by name, was contemporaneously reasoning in his solitude with results strikingly similar to those which Berkeley reached; which results, soon after the publication of Berkeley's views, he gave to the world—expressed in a style inferior to Berkeley's—in a work entitled "Clavis Universalis: or, a new

Inquiry after Truth, being a Demonstration of the Nonexistence, or Impossibility, of an External World." The echoes of Berkeley's doctrine, emasculated, unfortunately, by superficial interpretation, will be met with in some of the most noteworthy passages of the history of later and recent British thought.

The remaining portion of Berkeley's biography must be summarized more briefly than I could have wished. The Essay toward a new Theory of Vision had been published in 1709, the year before the full announcement of the "new principle" in the "Treatise concerning the Principles of Human Knowledge." In the Essay the principle was, in effect, applied beforehand to the case of one variety of sensible knowledge — that received through sight. It was argued that through this sense no knowledge of externality is given, there is no direct perception of distance, but only of a system of signs, which, rapidly and unconsciously interpreted, inform us indirectly concerning that which we fancy we see.

Admitted into holy orders soon after the acquisition of his second Academic degree, Berkeley remained at Trinity College under various appointments, as lecturer and preacher, till the year 1713. In the year preceding, however, he had paid his first visit to England, on leave of absence granted for ill health. In the year 1713 he published "Three Dialogues between Hylas and Philonous" (*i.e.* being interpreted, between the Friend of Matter and the Friend of Mind), intended to popularize his doctrines. This work Prof. Fraser terms the "gem of British metaphysical literature," having in mind, among other things, the author's "easy, graceful, and transparent style." Early in the same year Berkeley crossed again to England, and appeared with Dean Swift at the court of Queen Anne, where he was presented to his kinsman, Lord Berkeley, of Stratton. Soon after he was writing thoughtful essays for Steele's "Guardian," against the Free-thinkers. The same summer he made the acquaintance, destined to be lasting and cordial, of the poet Pope. To the same season belongs his introduction to Addison, and also to Bishop Atterbury, who is remembered for the following testimony to our philosopher's qualities. Being asked, shortly after his introduction to him, for his opinion concerning Berkeley, he is said to have replied, "So much understanding, so much knowledge, so much innocence, and such humility, I did not think had been the portion of any but angels till I saw this gentleman." In the autumn, still, of the same year, the Earl of Peterborough, on Swift's recommendation, selected Berkeley to accompany him as chaplain and secretary on a special mission to the court of the King of Sicily. Returning the following year, he went again shortly after to the continent as companion and tutor to a young man placed in his charge. This time he remained abroad nearly five years. A great portion of this period was passed in Italy and Sicily. The journal of his Tour in Italy is very minute, and represents him as giving the most careful attention to all sorts of things, to art, to manuscripts in the Vatican, to places and objects of historic interest, and also to natural phenomena, great and small. In one of the memoranda of his Commonplace Book, Berkeley had, years before, cautioned himself "always to make much of experimental philosophy." The memorials of this journey, as indeed of his whole life, show that his bent in this direction was not an artificial one. He exposed himself to great danger and fatigue in observing the eruptions of Mount Vesuvius, as appears from the account of his observations sent to England and published in the Philosophical Transactions of the Royal Society. On his passage through Paris Berkeley had, according to the common account, an interview with Father Malebranche, the French philosopher, in his cell at the Oratoire. A lively metaphysical discussion ensued, in the course of which Malebranche became so heated with excitement that he fell immediately ill and in a few days was dead. (Nothing of this appears in the biographies of Malebranche.) On his homeward journey Berkeley composed at Lyons a Latin essay on Motion (*De Motu*), a subject proposed by the Royal Academy of Sciences at Paris in the year 1720. Berkeley's essay is supposed to have been presented to the Academy, but the prize was awarded to a French competitor.

Arriving in England, Berkeley's attention was forcibly called to the subject of social economy by the widespread agitation and distress which followed the bursting of one of the earliest bubbles of modern commercial speculation, the famous South Sea scheme, and by the apparent decline in social morality, of which he regarded it as at once effect and cause. He prepared, accordingly, and published in the following year, an *Essay Toward Preventing the Ruin of Great Britain*, in which, contrary to the prevalent method of modern socialists, he sought the grounds of national safety and strength less in legislation than in the individual cultivation of morality, religion, and a generous public spirit.

We may pass rapidly over the record of Berkeley's return to Dublin, his services as Divinity and Hebrew lecturer at his Alma Mater, and his earliest ecclesiastical preferments, to see him again acting as the devoted and enthusiastic knight-errant, not of a new philosophical principle, but of a scheme for the promotion of education and virtue, which occupied his thoughts and absorbed his unwearied labors for years, and finally brought him to the American continent. On the occasion of his first visit to Italy, Berkeley, passing through France, had received perhaps his first impressions of the widespread misery and social decay of the old world. At all events, writing to friends at home, to whom he recommended an Italian tour, he said: "Your best way is to come through France; but make no long stay there; for the air is too cold, and there are instances enough of poverty and distress to spoil the mirth of any one who feels the sufferings of his fellow creatures. . . . The king indeed looks as he neither wanted meat nor drink, and his palaces are in good repair; but throughout the land there is a different face of things." And we have just had occasion to refer to the low state of public morals which depressed and alarmed Berkeley on his return to England. He began, therefore, at once, like so many before him, to dream of a happier society in the uncorrupted wilds of the new world, amid the smiles of a luxuriant and beneficent nature, and where the human elements to be educated and taken up into the social organism were at least untainted by contact with European immorality. In the year 1724 the flame refused longer to be contained, and Berkeley began to labor and plan for the realization of the dream. In the preceding year a comfortable portion of wealth had strangely fallen upon him through the death of the "Vanessa," celebrated through her unhappy relation to

Swift, and who, after learning of Swift's marriage to Stella, made Berkeley, whom she had never met but once, the heir to half her fortune. In May, 1724, Berkeley had been made Dean of Derry, a living which possessed an annual value of some eleven hundred pounds. But Berkeley was, as Swift truly described him, "an absolute philosopher with regard to money, titles and power," and having "seduced several of the hopefullest young clergymen and others" to enter into his scheme, he left a few months later for England, bent on resigning his deanery and founding on an island in American waters a college for Indian scholars and missionaries, "where," continues Swift, "he most exorbitantly proposes a whole hundred pounds a year for himself, fifty pounds for a fellow, and ten for a student." In furtherance of his scheme he had written a tract, which he proceeded at once, on his arrival in England, to publish, with the title, "A Proposal for the Better Supplying Churches in our Foreign Plantations, and for Converting the Savage Americans to Christianity, by a College to be erected in the Summer Islands, otherwise called the Isles of Bermuda." Perhaps to the same period belongs the composition of the "Verses on the Prospect of Planting Learning and Arts in America," which well sum up the motives and hopes that animated Berkeley at this time:

> "The Muse, disgusted with an age and clime
>   Barren of every glorious theme,
> In distant lands now waits a better time,
>   Producing subjects worthy fame:
>
> In happy climes, where from the genial sun
>   And virgin earth such scenes ensue,
> The force of art by nature seems outdone,
>   And fancied beauties by the true:

In happy climes, the seat of innocence,
　　Where nature guides and virtue rules,
Where men shall not impose for truth and sense
　　The pedantry of courts and schools:

There shall be sung another golden age,
　　The rise of empire and of arts,
The good and great inspiring epic rage,
　　The wisest heads and noblest hearts.

Not such as Europe breeds in her decay;
　　Such as she bred when fresh and young,
When heavenly flame did animate her clay,
　　By future poets shall be sung.

Westward the course of empire takes its way;
　　The four first acts already past,
A fifth shall close the drama with the day;
　　Time's noblest offspring is the last."

With unflagging zeal Berkeley labored to secure favor and means for the execution of his project. His persuasive eloquence astonished and converted the most incredulous. In his own handwriting there is extant a list of private subscriptions secured by him, amounting to over five thousand pounds. From the government he obtained the promise of twenty thousand pounds. He fed his imagination and that of his friends by laying out the plans for the future city, as well as college of Bermuda, in which his unusual knowledge and taste in architecture were of signal advantage to him. At last, after four years of exertions, all things seemed sufficiently ready, and in September, 1728, Berkeley, a few years after his marriage with one " whose humour and turn of mind," as he gallantly and affectionately said, " pleases me beyond anything that I know in her whole sex," set sail, in the company of a few devoted friends, for Rhode Island. There, according to an account given in a contemporary periodical publication, the dean intended "to winter, and to purchase an estate, in order to settle a correspondence between that island and Bermudas, particularly for supplying Bermudas with black cattle and sheep." His grant of money was payable in two years' time, "and the Dean (we read, further) has a year and a half allowed him afterward to consider whether he will stick to his college in Bermudas, or return to his deanery in Derry."

Berkeley landed at Newport in January, 1729. "He was ushered into the town," said the New England Weekly Courant, in one of its next issues, "with a great number of gentlemen, to whom he behaved himself in a very complaisant manner." The story is that the news of his arrival having been received in the midst of a holiday service in the Episcopal church at Newport, "the church was dismissed with the blessing, and Mr. Honeyman [the missionary rector], with the wardens, vestry, church and congregation, male and female, repaired immediately to the ferry-wharf, where they arrived a little before the Dean, his family and friends." In Newport and its vicinity Berkeley was destined to remain nearly three years. It were delightful could we go back in imagination and recall all the incidents of the Christian Philosopher's American residence. On Sundays we should see Quakers and Moravians, Jews and Congregationalists, "sixth principle and seventh principle Baptists," and numbers of many other sects which flourished in Rhode Island's tolerant air, crowding the Episcopal church and standing in the aisles, to listen to the charitable counsels of the benevolent philosopher and philanthropist. We should witness him founding a philosophical society in Newport, which has left as a legacy to the present day a valuable public library. We should follow him to his farm, three miles from Newport, and in close proximity to the ocean, where he built a house that is still standing, and where for the first time he enjoyed the quiet and comfort of a home. We might sit with him in his "Alcove"—a "favorite retreat below a projecting rock, commanding a view of the beach and the ocean, with some shady elms not far off"—where Berkeley is supposed to have meditated much of his "Alciphron; or, The Minute Philosopher," a series of dialogues against free-thinking, written in Rhode Island, whence their scenery is taken, and published subsequently in England. There he received his guests with "manly courtesy," gave counsel to the missionaries of the Church of England, and sought to elucidate his philosophical doctrine, for the benefit of one of its early disciples, Dr. S. Johnson, of Connecticut, a graduate of Yale College, and himself a philosophical author of more than ordinary repute. Berkeley did not travel about in the colonies. He preferred the lovely quiet of his country home. It is pleasant to know that he was so much pleased with Rhode Island that he would have been glad to plant his college there rather than in the Bermudas. But the king's bounty never reached him, and he was compelled to return to the old world, disappointed, near the end of the year 1731. But his interest in America did not cease with his departure from our shores. On the contrary, it continued, and in his correspondence with Americans was constantly attested until his death. To Yale College he gave lasting proofs of his enlightened interest. His Rhode Island farm he conveyed to the trustees of the college that the proceeds might be used to maintain three scholars "during the time between their first and second degrees." Among the number of persons — over two hundred — who have enjoyed the fruits of this endowment, are two college presidents — President Wheelock, the founder, more than a century ago, of Dartmouth College, and Timothy Dwight, president of Yale College from 1795 to 1817. Soon after his return to Ireland Berkeley sent a library of nearly one thousand well-selected volumes to Yale College, and made a similar gift to the library of Harvard College. Trinity church, Newport, still contains an organ sent back to it by Berkeley, from Europe, in 1733. "His offer of an organ to a church in the town of Berkeley, Mass.," remarks Prof. Fraser, "is said to have been too much for the puritanical rigour of the inhabitants, who unanimously voted it an invention of the devil to entrap the souls of men."

Yale College is fortunate in the possession of a portrait of Berkeley, painted in this country by Smibert, an English artist, who accompanied Berkeley to this country. The Berkeley Divinity School honors him in its name. The seat of the University of California, at the extreme limit of that westward course of empire to which Berkeley's eyes were turned, is, owing to the happy suggestion of the present President of the Johns Hopkins University, most appropriately named Berkeley, and the portrait of the philosopher adorns its walls. There will be academic shrines to his memory in this country as long as our land shall endure.

More than twenty years of life remained to Berkeley after his return from America. The most of this period was passed in the bishopric of Cloyne, to the honors and labors of which Berkeley was raised in 1734. His life here was one of active benevolence. His Roman Catholic neighbors bore public testimony to his liberality and worth. To the bodies as well as the souls of the sick he devotedly ministered. To this period belongs the third great enthusiasm of his life, that concerning the remedial value of tar-water in all cases of bodily ailment. In hours systematically rescued for study Berkeley conversed much with the ancient philosophers. Siris, a work of his later years, which begins with the praises of tar-water and ends with speculations deeply tinctured with Platonism and other ancient doctrines, is a characteristic monument of his ardent convictions concerning topics apparently the most diverse. The peculiar idealism of his youth is here not abandoned, but merged in a broader, deeper, more comprehensive idealism, the fruit of riper thought and wider knowledge. The condition of Ireland attracted his attention again to questions of social economy, concerning which he suggested wise and independent views in a periodical, "The Querist," founded by him.

Berkeley resisted all temptations to seek or accept further ecclesiastical promotion, valuing his time and quiet more than he would a diadem. He gave careful and affectionate attention to the education of his children. Music and painting were cultivated in his house with results in which he took especial delight.

In 1752 he removed to Oxford, where his son George was matriculated at Christ Church College. He was already infirm and had long been ailing. Death came to him in the following year as easily and gently as, before him, to the predecessor who had given the impulse to his early thought, John Locke. On a quiet Sunday evening, as he rests on a couch, his wife reads to him the lesson in the Burial Service, taken from the fifteenth chapter of the first Epistle to the Corinthians. Thereupon he makes some remarks upon this wonderful lesson of Christian faith. His daughter soon afterward offers him a cup of tea, and he makes no sign. Already the world of the senses was for him no more: he saw God face to face.

Thus ended the life of the truest, acutest philosopher that Great Britain has ever known.

CHAPTER IX.

DAVID HUME.

In Locke, Berkeley, and Hume, the three classic names in the history of British speculation, we have brought before us three very distinctly marked individualities. Characterized with reference to their philosophic tendencies, Locke is the serious, or, rather, the jejunely sober, inquirer; Berkeley, the philosophic seer and positivist, and Hume the academic sceptic. In their personal lives all three are, although in different ways, almost equally admirable. Locke combines gaiety and gravity in the good-breeding of the gentleman. Berkeley unites transparent purity of nature with the eloquent defense of ideals and unflagging labor for their realization. Hume applies the brakes—always an ungrateful labor—to the precipitous train of human speculation; he is the sworn enemy of all enthusiasms; he is the Mephistopheles, or "spirit of denial," in British thought. As such he is pelted with objurgations from all sides; he possesses, as he himself playfully puts it, the love of all men except "all the Whigs, all the Tories, and all the Christians"; and yet he is personally beloved by men of all parties, by believers and unbelievers, being blameless in conduct, benevolent in disposition, persistent in purpose, cheerful and serene in temper. Hume is a phenomenon, not inexplicable, but certainly very striking.*

---

* It is curious further to note that with Locke, having his birthplace and home in England, Berkeley, in Ireland, and Hume, in Scotland, philosophy completes the circuit of the British Isles. If it does not lose its insular character, it thus absorbs something from each of the elements composing that character.

David Hume was born in the Scottish capital, Edinburgh, on the 26th of April, 1711, old style. His father, Joseph Hume, a member of the Faculty of Advocates, was proprietor of a small landed estate, known as Ninewells, in Berwickshire, not far from the English border, and was connected with the family of the Earl of Home, or Hume. His mother was the daughter of Sir David Falconer, President of the College of Justice; the title of Lord Halkerton fell to her brother. I quote a passage from Hume's brief autobiography, written in the last year of his life:

"My family, however, was not rich, and being myself a younger brother, my patrimony, according to the mode of my country, was of course very slender. My father, who passed for a man of parts, died when I was an infant, leaving me, with an elder brother and sister, under the care of our mother, a woman of singular merit, who, though young and handsome, devoted herself entirely to the rearing and educating of her children. I passed through the ordinary course of education with success, and was seized very early with a passion for literature, which has been the ruling passion of my life, and the great source of my enjoyments. My studious disposition, my sobriety, and my industry, gave my family a notion that the law was a proper profession for me, but I found an unsurmountable aversion to everything but the pursuits of philosophy and general learning; and while they fancied I was poring upon Voet and Vinnius, Cicero and Virgil were the authors which I was secretly devouring."

We have above the words of Hume's tribute to his mother's memory. Here now is what she is reported to have said of him: "Our Davie's a fine, good-natured crater, but uncommon wake-minded." Not the first time, indeed, that a youthful "passion for literature" and preference for "the pursuits of philosophy and general learning," has been mistaken for weakness of mind and, indeed, for a sign of general good-for-nothingness. What that "ordinary course of education" was, through which Hume says he passed "with success," is scarcely known in detail. He appears to have pursued some studies between the age of twelve and sixteen at the University of Edinburgh, but took no degree. We have just read his declaration that the study of the law, which it was desired he should pursue, did not long engage his attention, and that Cicero and Virgil, who remained his favorite authors throughout his life, commanded his more absorbing interest. Did Cicero, even then, as the elegant writer and critic of philosophical opinions, furnish Hume with the ideal of his own future life and work? It were easy to trace the parallel, in more than one important particular, between the place of the ancient Roman and that of his modern Scotch admirer in the general history of literature. If it was due to the influence of Cicero that Hume was enabled to introduce into the style of philosophic discussion that masterly grace and perspicuity for which he is noted, we may be thankful to him, even though we may regret that Hume was not the man to receive inspiration, philosophic and literary, immediately from the broad-browed founder of the Greek Academy, rather than from the Roman senator, his far-off imitator and admirer. But what? Hume's philosophic inspiration, in the most fundamental points, was not of ancient origin, whether Grecian or Roman. It was recent, and British. It came from Locke and Berkeley, whose works he began early to study, with independent zeal, pen in hand, writing out, as he went along, volumes of manuscript notes upon the subjects and conclusions of their reasonings. Just how early he began to do this is unknown. But he could not have been far advanced in his 'teens, for his earliest and most extensive philosophical work, which, in its speculative principles, is wholly founded on the "new philosophy," was, he tells us, projected before he left college.

After quitting the project of studying law, Hume remained in Scotland for several years, employed in literary and philosophical studies. His "ardent application," in comparative solitude, to reflective pursuits finally told upon his health. He suffered a "decline of soul," which very naturally suggests to Prof. Huxley a comparison with the similar period of moral discouragement through which John Stuart Mill, in his Autobiography, represents himself as having passed at about the same time in life. The immediate occasion of it all seems to have been lack of exercise, followed, naturally, by a torpid liver. This episode of impaired health, through depletion of vital energy, led finally to the determination to try the effect of an absolute change of life. He "went to Bristol, with some recommendations to eminent merchants," and entered an office. "But in a few months," he says, "I found that scene wholly unsuitable to me." He was fully possessed with the thought of his "philosophical discoveries," and with his literary ambition. "I went over to France," he continues, "with a view of prosecuting my studies in a country retreat, and I there laid that plan of life which I have steadily and successfully pursued. I resolved to make a very rigid frugality supply my deficiency of fortune, to maintain unimpaired my independency, and to regard every object as contemptible, except the improvement of my talents in literature." One may trace here distinctly the influence on Hume of those models of practical philosophy held up by Cicero, and in which the favorite stoic conceptions of independence and perseverance are prominent. One is also impressed, through the absence of any reference to philosophical inquiry, and the mention only of "literature" as the object of his devotion, with a sense of the fact, elsewhere in Hume's life abundantly illustrated, that in his speculative productions the scientific and literary interests are inseparably intertwined, the philosophical work is not simply to produce — or, as the case may be, to destroy — conviction; it is also intended to gain applause as a specimen of literary art. We shall see presently how the failure to gain such applause led Hume at an early age to abandon the appearance of any attempt at pure philosophizing.

It was at Reims, but chiefly at La Flèche, in Anjou, that Hume sought and found the desired retreat for study. The latter place, the seat of a Jesuit college, is famous in the biographical history of philosophy as the scene of Descartes's youthful studies and incipient questionings. There is no evidence, and it is scarcely probable, that a knowledge of this circumstance directed Hume's steps to this place; Hume was too unsentimental to be affected by such motives; besides, Hume neither admired nor possessed accurate knowledge of the philosophy of Descartes. We may therefore perceive something of the irony of fate in the circumstance that to the same locality whence, more than one hundred years before, the youth had gone forth who was to raise provisional doubt to the first place in the method of philosophy — but only with the view of preparing the way for certain, positive affirmation — to this locality Hume also, himself comparatively still a mere youth, repaired to complete for publication a work in which doubt is set forth as the last word of theoretical philosophy; a work, too, of which the first historic germs are to be found, in part, back of Locke and British speculation, in the very doctrines of the French philosopher himself. A similar tone of reflection is suggested by the further circumstance, related by Hume himself, that it was while "walking in the cloisters of the Jesuits' College of La Flèche, . . . and engaged," says he, "in a conversation with a Jesuit of some parts and learning, who was relating to me, and urging some nonsensical miracles performed lately in their convent," that he first hit upon and employed the famous argument against miracles, subsequently developed in a famous essay, which has taxed the speculative ingenuity of nearly every theological writer since Hume's time. Hume says—he is addressing his Presbyterian friend and theological opponent, Principal Campbell:—"I believe that you will allow that the freedom, at least, of this reasoning makes it somewhat extraordinary to have been the produce of a convent of Jesuits, though perhaps you may think the sophistry of it savours plainly of the place of its birth."

The work which, on the basis of studies made and reflections recorded during previous years, Hume was making ready, while in France, for publication, was a bulky "Treatise on Human Nature." He returned in 1737 to England with his manuscript, applied to it once more the pruning-knife, and in September, 1738, sold the copyright of the first edition of his book for fifty pounds, "and twelve bound copies of the book." In January, 1739, when Hume was not yet twenty-eight years of age, the first two volumes of the Treatise (treating, respectively, of the Understanding, and of the Passions) were ready for sale. Vol. III, "Of Morals," appeared in the following year. To the results of this venture Hume looked forward with anxious interest. He had doubtless expected to startle the world into attention and to gain applause as an "ingenious author." His latest editor mentions — what there are none among Hume's admirers to contradict, and what is also sufficiently borne out by the facts of his biography — that "few men of letters have been at heart so vain and greedy of fame as was Hume." One extended notice the first part of his work did indeed receive, in "The Works of the Learned," in which the anonymous critic commented at length upon the egotism and dogmatism of the unknown author, upon the fragmentary nature of his argument and his close dependence on his forerunners, Locke and Berkeley, and upon other circumstances ill calculated to flatter his vanity. True, the critic thought it probable that "time and use" might ripen in "our Author" the qualities in which he now seemed deficient; we shall, he said, "probably have reason to consider this, compared with his later productions, in the same light as we view the Juvenile Works of Milton, or the first Manner of a Raphael, or other celebrated painters." But the tone of this prophecy was too plainly susceptible of an ironical interpretation, and Hume termed it "somewhat abusive." (There is an anecdote, deemed apocryphal, of Hume's having fallen into "violent rage on occasion of it, and . . . attacking the unlucky publisher sword in hand.") In his autobiography Hume says: "Never literary attempt was more unfortunate than my Treatise of Human Nature. It fell dead-born from the press, without reaching such distinction as even to excite a murmur among the zealots." Hume never recovered from the disgust with which its lack of literary success made him regard this first rather weighty birth of his brain and pen. "So vast an undertaking," he wrote later, "planned before I was one-and-twenty, and composed before twenty-five, must necessarily be very defective. I have repented my haste a hundred and a hundred times." "Above all, the positive air which prevails in that book, and which may be imputed to the ardour of youth, so much displeases me that I have not patience to review it." "I give you my advice against reading" it. Accordingly, in 1747, Hume, who had meanwhile met with more encouraging success in the publication of the first installment of his "Essays Moral and Political," recast the principal substance of the "Treatise" in the form of "Philosophical Essays," otherwise termed an "Inquiry Concerning Human Understanding," disowning the former and desiring the latter to be henceforth alone regarded "as containing his philosophical sentiments and principles." Of course no scholar will pay attention to this literary whim of a mortified author. Hume's Treatise belongs irrevocably to the history of British thought, where it must ever stand as the most complete document in evidence of the logical consequence of a certain method applied to certain data, all of which were delivered to Hume from the previous history of British speculation. Besides, it is not claimed that the later work contains an important improvement, or modification even, in point of doctrine, as compared with its predecessor. Prof. Huxley, while allowing that, in style, the Inquiry "exhibits a great improvement on the Treatise," seems inclined to ascribe to the substance rather deterioration than improvement. Mr. Grose, one of Hume's editors, is therefore justified in saying that "Hume's contributions to metaphysics were written by 1736, when he was five-and-twenty." Mr. Grose adds: "His contribution to the philosophy of religion [was completed] by 1750, when he was thirty-nine: and after this date he added nothing." The works on religious philosophy are the "Natural History of Religion" and the "Dialogues Concerning Natural Religion," the latter published posthumously by direction of the author.

Before going on to contemplate Hume in the remainder of his life and work, let us stop for a moment to consider the general import of the philosophical message which he, thus early in life, was impelled to deliver to the world. For a message it was, containing a lesson that stands written for our instruction, and we shall be wise if we heed and inwardly digest it.

The attempts of genuine philosophers are attempts to reduce to logical, intelligible expression truth of living, experimental, essential reality. But it is only given to philosophic genius to penetrate and grasp and formulate philosophic truths of being, which, in their essential simplicity and universality, are implicitly held by all men, since they are the life of all, but which it is given to but few to hold explicitly with the cool grasp and mastery of clear reason. The power of philosophy, or its destiny, if it has any in the world, is a power or destiny to lift men, slowly, it may be, but surely and irresistibly, up to that plane of philosophic insight on which genius stands. Such, for example, has been historically and still is the power of Platonism. But the very elevation of genius is one reason for its not being immediately appreciated. In the immediate followers of Plato there was an immense falling away of the essential thing, namely, the Platonic spirit, or the *vital knowledge* of Plato. Again, this very conception, just expressed, of *vital knowledge*, without which I cannot admit that philosophy has any existence except in name, is a thing, between which and such abstract definition of it, as philosophy, in view of its scientific character and aim, must seek to furnish, there exists such a disparity that a philosopher may at times well despair of giving to his thought, and the truth to which his thought relates, perfect, irrefutable, all-convincing verbal expression. Philosophic truth, relating as it does to living power, intelligence, act, is dynamic, fluent; the formulæ of language are static, rigid. The former takes hold on every side of the infinite and universal, so that while there are no significant words which do not express it, there are none which exhaust it. The insight of philosophic genius is then anterior and superior to verbal, systematic expression. And yet the only way by which this insight communicates itself lies, and must lie, through such expression. We learn first the letter. It is well known that, and for what reasons, the study and criticism of the letter blinds the vision and hinders the reception of the spirit. Were I now to attempt to illustrate this theme from the history of philosophy, I might produce a dissertation of interminable length, but full, I think, of instruction. The history of the Platonic or Aristotelian philosophy would furnish the most ample materials. The point I wish to make in the present connection is this, that the relation between Berkeley and Hume is strikingly like that to which I have just adverted between the spirit and the letter, between constructive insight and destructive literal criticism. Berkeley, doubtless, fell further short than many another of complete systematic expression of his positive thought. Nay, more, in addition to the needless and inexcusable inadequacy of his systematic exposition, we must recognize that Berkeley, in the inexperience of youth and owing to circumstances in the philosophical history of his times which need not be recapitulated, started out on a track, with a method, with a terminology and a set of philosophical conceptions, either absolutely false or misleading; that whatever greatness he exhibited as a philosopher was principally in spite of them; and that, following and employing them, he was led, in the famous immaterialism of his youthful works, to enunciate, as the doctrine by which he has been chiefly known, a theory equivocal in statement and partly questionable in substance. I find in Berkeley, then, a singular and unusual disparateness between his virtual thought and the mechanism of statement and argument by which, more or less unintelligently, he sought to communicate it. The true continuator of Berkeley, to my thinking, would be he who, neglecting or correcting this mechanism, should go about to apprehend and develop the thought into a comprehensive, reasonable idealism, such as is suggested or (of course always imperfectly) expressed in the leading forms of philosophic thought, of religious feeling, of artistic creation, and in the universal life of man. The "continuation" of Berkeley, through a process of literal criticism and drawing of verbal inferences, would lead to a very different result — to what result we shall presently see in contemplating Hume's conclusions.

All are aware of Sydney Smith's witty saying: "Bishop Berkeley destroyed the world in one volume octavo, and nothing remained after his time but mind, which experienced a similar fate from Mr. Hume in 1739." This is a verbal statement — only that — of what Berkeley did, and a literal statement of what Hume verbally accomplished. Locke's presuppositions and methods, developed and applied by Berkeley, led to an apparently literal annihilation, in theory, of the physical universe, but really, or in tendency (namely, having regard to Berkeley's intention and spirit), to the retention of it, with a new and profounder significance substituted for the older and vulgar one. Proceeding on different presuppositions and by a different method, this *appearance* of literal annihilation might have been avoided. Hume, adopting the literal, and nominally destructive, conclusion of Berkeley, and proceeding on the basis of the same Lockian data or principles, went on to prove that the word Mind, as well as Matter, had no cognizable or conceivable significance. Berkeley's partial negation was in the interest of a grander affirmation. Hume's comprehensive negation was, as far as he was concerned, final; it proclaimed virtually, but effectively, the impotency and incompetency of a certain method in philosophy, which is, nevertheless, still cherished and lauded and followed with astonishing pertinacity on the part of many; it pointed to no transcending affirmation, capable of explaining and giving sense to the negation; it admitted no ray of a light capable of piercing and expelling the darkness.

Of course nothing but a general statement of the reasonings and conclusions of Hume, and of the manner in which they are affiliated to the premises and results of his predecessors, Locke and Berkeley, is to be here attempted. The following summary indications may suffice. Locke, having inaugurated the application of the analytic and descriptive method in psychology — the method which seeks to trace the phenomenal growth of "mind" in the life of the individual, and so to determine what mind is and what are the nature and value of its operations — had drawn the speculative conclusion that all our knowledge is of ideas and of their relations, whether of agreement or of "repugnancy." Ideas were looked on as possessions of the mind, objects contained in it as a receptacle, images which might or might not have a representative significance, as revelatory of existences independent of themselves. One thing was certain: they gave no information concerning the essential nature of either matter or mind, of the real existence, however, of which two alleged forms of substances Locke, in agreement with a prevalent speculative opinion of his age, and with the vulgar opinion of all ages, made no serious doubt. Berkeley admitted Locke's negative conclusion as it regarded matter, and went further, alleging that not only do our ideas bring us no *knowledge* concerning matter, but that, accurately understood, they also bring us not even the suggestion of its existence: the conception of matter is, on the one hand, inherently unthinkable and absurd, like "wooden iron"; and, on the other, ideas are works or functions of mind, to which, therefore, and to which alone they can and do bear witness. We can, however — in this Berkeley agrees with Locke — have no *idea*, strictly speaking, of mind, as though, namely, through any given idea were *represented* to us the substantive nature of mind. But we have a *notion* of mind, as a power to cause and receive ideas, as also to will and to feel. But this latter and essential portion of Berkeley's doctrine was unaccountably, and we may, with practical truth, say fatally, neglected by him (especially in his earliest and best-known works).

Now Hume, taking up Locke's maxim of the restriction of knowledge to ideas and their relations, applied it in its full rigor. With a change of terminology, partly suggested by Berkeley, he declares that "nothing is ever present to the mind but its perceptions"; and "all the perceptions of the human mind resolve themselves into two distinct kinds," namely, Impressions and Ideas. Essentially, however, these are not distinct, for ideas are only "faint images" of impressions. The word impression sufficiently explains itself; it implies, notably, that the mind with reference to them is wholly passive. All our knowledge of "existence," Hume, then, is moved to affirm, is a knowledge of impressions or "perceptions"; and by the same reasoning by which you prove that the perception furnishes no cognition of matter, I prove (he declares) that it furnishes no knowledge of mind. There is not a peculiar form of knowledge, such as Berkeley had distinguished from perception under the name of notion, and whereby we have cognizance of the mind as a spiritual power. We have no knowledge but of perceptions; these only are "present to the mind"; and perceptions are perceptions, and nothing else, they are not powers: contemplate your perceptions (by the method of empirical psycology, Hume's method, and the favorite one in so much of English speculation) eternally, and you will hit upon no perception of power; you see no power, you can find a representative idea or image of, no power; therefore you know no power, whether spiritual or material: the mind, says Hume, reveals itself only as a "bundle or collection of different perceptions, which succeed each other with an inconceivable rapidity, and are in a perpetual flux or movement." And again, "the true idea of the human mind is to consider it as a system of *different perceptions* or *different existences.*" Each perception is a separate unit, numerically and absolutely independent of all others. The mind may, therefore, in agreement with Hume's intention, be compared to a row of beads without a string. They do indeed arrange themselves in a certain order, according to certain laws of mechanical association which Hume states but professes his utter inability to explain. The fundamental fact remains that they are — so empirical psychology declares, which, looking at appearances, reports the dynamical as statical, the continuous as discrete — "distinct existences," and that between such the mind "never perceives any real connexion." From hence follow two weighty, but negative, conclusions, openly avowed and strongly enforced by Hume, namely, that, so far as we are scientifically authorized to affirm, there is no such thing as personal identity, and that the relation of cause and effect, which we are accustomed to regard as necessary, is not necessary, but casual : " anything can be the cause of [*i.e.* can be followed by] anything." Our belief in causation or real connection is due only to habit or association, on observing, experimentally, that certain perceptions are frequently or, as far as we can judge, always followed by certain others. All belief is due only to original vividness or acquired intensity of impression. " When I am convinced of any principle, 'tis only an idea, which strikes more strongly upon me." The source of all logical persuasion is "feeling."

If the attention excited by Hume's Treatise, in which the foregoing views are set forth with great detail, fell mortifyingly short of the author's eager hope and expectation, the student of the subsequent history of philosophy is aware that in later times Hume's reasonings have had a most influential effect upon the course both of British and of continental speculation. His views, somewhat differently dressed and argued, have given tone to the utterances of many of the most brilliant (or at least loquacious) leaders of English thought, and it is well known that, before Hume's death, his criticism of the common conception of causation struck in the mind of Kant a spark which set the whole thinking world in flames, and fixed an indelible impression upon the whole bearing of the philosophy of our times. Just what Hume thought of his own performance it were perhaps difficult to determine, though he doubtless would have said of much of his reasoning, what he declared concerning Berkeley's, that it admitted of no reply, and produced no conviction. Of this there is no doubt, that he was firm in the determination, whatever might be the worth or fate of his philosophy, to establish his reputation as a literary artist, and the concluding section of the first book of the Treatise ("Of the Understanding") affords a striking example of such art. Here Hume strikes an attitude. He contemplates the unhopeful result of his investigations. "When I turn my eye inward, I find nothing but doubt and ignorance." "The understanding, when it acts alone, and according to its most general principles, entirely subverts itself, and leaves not the lowest degree of evidence in any proposition, either in philosophy or common life." "We have, therefore, no choice left but betwixt a false reason and none at all." These are Hume's words, whereupon he affects to find his brain heated, his mind confounded, and to "fancy" himself "in the most deplorable condition imaginable, environ'd with the deepest darkness, and utterly depriv'd of the use of every member and faculty." A "splenetic humour" is induced. "I dine, I play a game of backgammon, I converse and am merry with my friends; and when, after three or four hours' amusement, I wou'd return to these speculations, they appear so cold, and strain'd, and ridiculous that I cannot find in my heart to enter into them any further." On the whole, he concludes, "nature" (an obscure entity, Hume's *Deus ex machina*, which he often calls to the rescue, but never is able to define or explain), prompting to relaxation after the common manner of mankind, must be indulged. Let "good humour," above all, be maintained. If the impulse to speculation, to investigation of the "science of man," shall return, let it be obeyed; if not, well and good. To study "philosophy in this careless manner" is, he judges, the most philosophical way of studying it, because it is the most sceptical. Whatever conclusions are reached, and however absurd, they are innocent. "Generally speaking," says Hume, "the errors in religion are dangerous, those in philosophy only ridiculous."

The remaining two books of Hume's Treatise correspond to the foregoing beginning. In the one of them the mechanism of passion is illustrated. In the other the attempt is made to set forth morality as exclusively a phenomenon of the passional side of our nature. Moral distinctions are not founded in reason. The theory "that vice and virtue consist in relations susceptible of certainty and demonstrations" is combated. "Reason," says Hume, "is, and ought to be, the slave of the passions, and can never pretend to any other office but to serve and obey them." Moral distinctions are affairs of sentiment, or impression, or feeling, alone. Virtue is known by its generally producing pleasure (more particulary the pleasure of "love or pride"), and vice by its giving rise to a feeling of "uneasiness" ("humility or hatred"). Virtuous actions may also be recognized by their utility. The ground of our approbation of them is found by Hume largely in sympathy. Though Hume inveighs in the loudest terms against the notion that self-love is the dominant passion in human nature, and the key to all moral distinctions, yet the general kinship of his ethics, in principle, to the ethics of selfishness becomes instantly obvious on reflection. We are confronted with an analysis of the mechanism of passion, and not with an ideal of duty and privilege, dictated both by reason and feeling, and addressed to free and rational and responsible agents.

A word may be in place concerning a couple of famous points in Hume's religious philosophy. The well-known argument against miracles—namely, their opposition to uniform experience—follows, irrespective of other nonessential considerations developed by Hume, from exactly the same premises which disprove, in Hume's view, the personal identity and essential, creative freedom of man. If the premises are false, the conclusion—whether, for other reasons, correct or incorrect—cannot be properly derived from and supported on them. A miracle (so-called) implies spiritual, free, *i.e.* real, causation, the act, immediate or mediate, of intelligent power. Now Hume, on general grounds, denies such causation and such, or any other, power, or, at least, the possibility of our having any knowledge or conception of them. Hence he must deny or explain away any alleged evidence of real causative power, as well on the part of divine as of human beings. From Hume's doctrine concerning causation follows, with like necessity, his noted objection to the argument for God's existence, drawn from the alleged necessity of finding a cause for the existence of the world considered as a whole. We are authorized, according to Hume, to affirm causation only in cases of sequence habitually observed. An event which we generally find following after another is termed the effect of the latter. We must see the nominal effect following the nominal cause many times before we can conclude (by what is even then at best only an arbitrary "determination of the mind," in Hume's phrase) that a causal relation subsists between the two. But now we have had no experience of the creation of worlds. Besides, the world is, by hypothesis, one. If caused, it was only caused once. It is an "unique effect," if indeed it is an effect at all. Had we seen the world *once* come into existence upon the utterance of the creative word, we should not be entitled by our (Hume's) principles to conclude that it was the effect of such word. We must witness this habitually in order to infer that it is a case of (at least probable) causation. The argument is easy for Hume, his premises, *i.e.* his views concerning causation being granted; its conclusiveness is as questionable as is the soundness of the premises. Nay, more, its obvious, even laughable, absurdity makes of it a glaringly typical illustration of the disparateness between the method of empirical, sensational psychology and philosophical speculation and insight. We have seen this method, under Baconian inspiration, coming into use as an instrument of ostensibly philosophical investigation in the hands of Hobbes and Locke, and partially and, so to speak, incidentally applied by Berkeley. Hume now applies it with exclusive and absolute rigor.

What is the essence of this method? It is professedly a method of "pure observation." What is to be observed? Consciousness. What is consciousness in the light of such observation? It is a moving panorama, from the observer's personal participation in moving or perceiving which abstraction is made. This is a *possible*, but abstract and fatally incomplete, conception of consciousness. It is just such a conception as that which physical science, following its mathematico-mechanical ideal of method, forms of its objects. It, too, looks upon the world as a panorama, a moving spectacle, and its highest theoretical aim is to ascertain just what appears (*i.e.* just what is or may imaginably be presented to sensible observation). It does not, therefore, nor, when conscious of its true aim and real limitations, does it seek to determine aught concerning that which lies behind and is the final explanation of appearance. It knows observable motions, but not unseen forces, and sensible "configuration," but not real (whether material or spiritual) substance.

Now, British empirical psychology, deriving its model of method from physical "inductive" science, naturally arrives by it at results analogous to those reached by physical science. It furnishes a more or less admirable description of the field of conscious phenomena, with their rules of coexistence and sequence. But it does not go behind them, objectively or subjectively. Naturally, as physical science finds no "force" among the subjects of its analytic observation, so empirical psychology "hits upon" no "power" among conscious phenomena. As, for the former, the word causation has only the secondary, emasculated meaning of sensible *succession* of phenomena (or, in the last resort, mathematical equivalence of successive phenomena, excluding the notion of *efficiency*), so it has the same meaning for the latter. And as, from the point of view of the former, the terms matter, mind, substance, have no definable signification, so also from the point of view of the latter.

Hume, then, was perfectly right in drawing these negative conclusions. The *notion* of power, which strictly and ultimately is ideal or spiritual, and not sensible or physical (see above, chapter on Shakespeare), is not given as an idea, image, or phenomenon of sensible or panoramic consciousness, nor, consequently, is the notion of personal identity or self, which is indissolubly bound up therewith. The like observations, and on similar grounds, may be made concerning causation and substance. Any attempt to find answers to the questions relating to all these subjects (and these are all strictly philosophical questions, relating, as they do, to subjects of vital and ultimate reality), among the phenomena of sensible, imaginative consciousness, necessarily fails, since the subjects of such inquiry are utterly incommensurate with, and, from the very nature of things, absent from, such consciousness. Hume's defect lay, therefore, not in the erroneousness of his negative or "sceptical" conclusions, thus viewed with reference to the premises of presupposition and method on which they were founded, but in fancying that these premises were in the slightest degree germane to philosophical questions, and that no others were to be found. His merit is that, inheriting this fancy — or, rather, this prejudice — from his predecessors, he was more thorough-going and consistent than others in developing its theoretical consequences.

The consciousness contemplated by empirical psychology is static, spectacular, sensible. This is the inanimate hull, not the living kernel of real consciousness, which is dynamic, dramatic, rational. The former is and must be contemplated essentially as a succession of lifeless images or pictures; the latter is vital, self-illuminating, rational activity. The elements of the former are "*states of consciousness*," passive "feelings," while those of the latter are *acts*. The former are opaque "impressions" which reveal no objective reality that produces and no subjective reality that receives or perceives them. The latter are translucent with the light of self-conscious, active reason. The former are sensible, the latter intelligible. The former are observed, the latter are, in the fullest, deepest sense of the word, experienced; for here act and self-conscious agent are inseparable. It is in the self-revealing and self-possessing spiritual ego, as the type, given to the most immediate consciousness, of ideal (*i.e.* genuine) power and reality — or, in other words, it is in dynamic self-consciousness, where phenomenon is merged in reality — that the key is furnished for the solution of strictly philosophic questions, or questions of vital reality. It is here that the notions of power, cause, unity, substance, are illustrated, not in appearance merely, but in reality. And here, it is needless to state, they appear in their true light, utterly separated from sensible analogies. Causation, in particular, appears not as sensible succession, but as the realization of rational will.

To return, now, to the question of the "creation" or causation of the world, from the passing consideration of Hume's arguments concerning which this long expository digression set out, it is obvious that, if the question has any relevancy or pertinency at all, it is a rational and not a physical question, philosophical and not "scientific." Physical causation is succession within the limits of the sensible universe as already existing and presented to empirical consciousness. The causation of the world can be no such process, unless "God" be conceived after sensible analogies and so made a part (an unique part, it is true) of the universe, the "origin" of which is in question. In this case, God, a phenomenal existence, is conceived as uttering his word, which phenomenon is then followed by another phenomenon, namely, the appearance of the whole universe except God. Hume's argument (as we saw) is, that we must witness this literal succession repeatedly, "habitually," before we can regard it as a case of causation. His premises and his arguments are good, if physical conceptions are to dominate philosophical inquiry, or, in other words, if physical conceptions are ultimate conceptions. But, I repeat, the obvious absurdity of both premise and argument shows that the question at issue is not a subject of "scientific" consideration at all, but of rational or philosophical inquiry. The question, how to account for the sensible universe is wholly irrespective of time or succession. It concerns no more one moment of its existence (the "beginning") than any other (the present, for example). It is purely a timeless question of *nature* and *dependence*, and is answered when it is shown that the sensible side of the universe is purely dependent and relatively unreal; that the universe has also an *intelligible* side, by which alone it takes hold on power and life and reality; that, regarded on this side, it is the scene of order and ministrant to goodness and beauty; and that these elements in its life, which alone mark it as, and render it, intelligible, are unthinkable except as ever-present tokens, products, "effects," of ever-present, ever-active, spiritual, divine power. (Compare, again, chapter on Shakespeare.)

In 1742 Hume published the first installment of his Essays, Moral and Political. "The work," says Hume, "was favorably received, and soon made me entirely forget my former disappointment." In 1744 he was an applicant, through his friends, for an appointment as professor of "ethics and pneumatic philosophy" in the University of Edinburgh, but unsuccessfully. In 1745 he went to be a sort of moral guardian ("bear-leader," as Prof. Huxley happily phrases it) to the marquis of Annandale, a young nobleman infirm in mind and body. At the expiration of a year the situation became unendurable, and Hume retired, improved in fortune if not in temper. In May, 1746, Hume accepted an appointment, which he termed a "very genteel" one, as secretary to General St. Clair, in command of an expedition intended for Canada, but subsequently diverted to the coast of France. To this appointment was added the office of judge-advocate. The expedition soon ended in disaster. Hume, however, had made new friends, not the least among whom was General St. Clair himself, who in the following year invited him to attend him upon a military embassy to the courts of Vienna and Turin. Hume accepted with the more readiness because he had for some time had it in mind to apply himself to historical writing, and judged that the acquaintance with men and courts and countries, which he should thus acquire, would further him in this aim. Dressed as an aide-de-camp, in the uniform of an officer, Hume, who was fat and burly, cut an odd and amusing figure, which he himself good-naturedly recognized. Two years were passed on this mission, on returning from which Hume exulted in being "master of near a thousand pounds." He returned to Ninewells and busied himself with literary labors, some of which have been already referred to, but the most immediately successful of which resulted in his Political Discourses—the second installment of his Essays. These Discourses were very favorably received and gave Hume at once a European reputation, being twice translated, within a year, into French. In consequence of them Hume has been ranked as a pioneer in political science. They are marked by the application of strong matter-of-fact sense to the facts of politics. But they do not and were not intended to constitute a system.

In 1751 Hume removed to Edinburgh, and in the following year set himself up in house-keeping, and "completed," says he, in a letter written about this time, "a regular family; consisting of a head, namely, myself, and two inferior members, a maid and a cat. My sister has ... joined me, and keeps me company." Hume continues, characteristically: "With frugality I can reach, I find, cleanliness, warmth, light, plenty, and contentment.

What would you have more? Independence? I have it in a supreme degree. Honour? that is not altogether wanting. Grace? that will come in time. A wife? that is none of the indispensable requisites of life. Books? that *is* one of them; and I have more than I can use." Hume had, namely, though unsuccessful in his pursuit, a second time, of a University professorship (this time the professorship of logic in the University of Glasgow), secured his election to the office of librarian to the Faculty of Advocates, a position of little pecuniary value, but which placed a library of thirty thousand volumes at his disposal. His election was contested on the ground of his religious opinions. His success elated him greatly, and he ascribed it (in a characteristic and playfully jubilant letter) in great measure to the violent advocacy of his cause by the ladies. He was now in a position to devote himself to his project of historical composition. In this, as in all the work of his pen, a motive of literary ambition held a strong place. English literature had no great historian, combining "style, impartiality, judgment, care," and he would supply the deficiency. Accordingly he set himself about writing the history of England (as has been said) "backwards." In the fall of 1754 he had ready for the world the first volume, "containing the reign of James I and Charles I." His purpose to achieve an artistic triumph Hume undoubtedly accomplished. In order to do this he chose, with correct artistic perception, the rôle of the defender and eulogist of unfortunate royalty, although his professed political principles would more naturally have inclined him to the opposite side. Accurate and prolonged investigation was not necessary for his end, and he allowed but little time for it. But on the work of composition he bestowed the utmost care. In the published specimens of portions of the extant manuscript of his historical and other works the chips of the literary sculptor lie all along the route, in the form of words and phrases erased and changed, and sometimes changed again and again, until the expression finally satisfied him. Lord Brougham, in his life of Hume, accordingly denies to Hume the possession of the "cardinal virtues" of the historian, "fidelity, research, and accuracy," but considers that if we "turn to the secondary accomplishments of the historian, we can hardly find expressions too strong to delineate" his merit. His History abounds in the "strokes of a master's pencil, and beauties such as . . . would make this the first of histories, if the grace of form could atone for the defect of substance." The reception of the first volume of the History of England by the public was far from gratifying to Hume. His "disappointment" was "miserable." Scarcely any one, of whatever party in church or state, could endure it. Only the primate of England and the primate of Ireland, "two odd exceptions," as Hume observes, signified to him their satisfaction. "These dignified prelates separately sent me messages not to be discouraged." Hume was not discouraged, but continued at work, still residing mostly at Edinburgh, and published the remaining (for the most part, chronologically earlier) portions of his history in 1756, 1759, and 1761. He found time also in 1757 to superintend the publication of his Natural History of Religion.

By this time Hume, through his books, "was become," as he with a pardonable sense of satisfaction mentions, "not only independent but opulent," and was about determining to pass the remainder of his life in philosophical contentment, in Scotland, when, in 1763, he accepted the urgent invitation of Lord Hertford to accompany him on his embassy to Paris. Hume's reception on the part of men of letters and the fashionable society at Paris was overwhelming. He became the *manie dominante* in fashionable circles. "The 'Honest David Hume' of Dr. Carlyle and the Edinburgh club was the '*bon David*' of the French *salons*." The presence of the "*gros et grand philosophe*" was indispensable at every *fête*, at all the "*soupers fins*." Hume received all these attentions with much complacency, and was chiefly pleased "to find," says he, "that most of the eulogiums bestowed on me turned on my personal character, my *naïveté* and simplicity of manners, the candour and mildness of my disposition, etc." Perhaps also his hatred of the English, which became in the end quite unutterable, had something to do with his popularity. London was, in his view, the precise opposite of Paris, where, he says, "a man that distinguishes himself in letters meets immediately with regard and attention." Paris, in his judgment, abounded in "sensible, knowing and polite company" "above all places in the universe," and he felt strongly tempted to settle there for life. It is important to note concerning Hume, and the observation may pertinently be introduced in this connection, that, somewhat as in morals he viewed virtue and vice in their quality as "artificial" products (Treatise III, 1, 2), so in affairs of taste it was the overdressed art of rule and reflection which attracted him. The wild beauty of Gothic architecture was to him a monument of mediæval rudeness. In writing of his visit to Cologne he made no mention of the cathedral. The incomparable native force, and art above all arts, of Shakespeare, was for him (as for Voltaire) barbarism. Shakespeare, though a prodigy in his time, would not be so considered in the eighteenth century, when a poet must be "capable of furnishing a proper entertainment to a refined, intelligent audience." Sophocles, and Racine, whom he agreed with the French in regarding as the modern successor of the Greek dramatist, were the only proper models of taste. Hume was therefore at home in the artificial overculture of the Paris of the eighteenth century. He enjoyed here the friendship, especially, of such men of letters as "D'Alembert, Buffon, Marmontel, Diderot, Duclos, Helvétius, old President Hénault," although, sceptic and free thinker as he was, some of them laughed at him for his comparative "narrowness." But, early in 1766, he returned to London and subsequently to his Presbyterian and other friends in Edinburgh, with whom during his absence he had kept up a constant correspondence. He brought with him to England, Rousseau, his subsequent dispute with whom is famous in the "quarrels of authors." There was, indeed, little in common between the morbidly sensitive temperament of Rousseau, whom Hume compared to a man "stript not only of his clothes but of his skin, and turned out in that situation to combat with the rude and boisterous elements, such as perpetually disturb this lower world," and the phlegmatic, even-tempered good-nature and practical sense of the Scotch philosopher.

Again, in 1767, Hume was called away from his home by an invitation, which he deemed it impossible to decline, to act as Under Secretary of State to Mr. Conway, at London. In 1769 he returned to Edinburgh, "very opulent," says he "(for I possessed a revenue of one thousand pounds a year), healthy, and though somewhat stricken in years, with the prospect of enjoying long my ease, and of seeing the increase of my reputation." Hume's literary labors were ended. He had accomplished, with steady, patient purpose, all his ambitions. Henceforth he could live at ease, surrounded by friends and giving them pleasure, among other ways, by generous exhibitions of his "great talent for cooking, the science," as he says in a playful letter, "to which I intend to addict the remaining years of my life." His quarters being too contracted for this purpose, he built in the following year, 1770, the first house in a new street, which rather oddly was called, after him, "St. David's street."

In spring, 1775, he was attacked by a disease which at first gave him no alarm, but which, several months before his death, he recognized as "mortal and incurable." He made his will, settled up all his affairs, made a journey to London and Bath without receiving, permanently, the hoped-for improvement of his health, and returned to Edinburgh. Here he looked forward to his approaching dissolution apparently with the most absolute calmness and cheerfulness, never impatient, except, perhaps, at the delay of the painful close of his life's drama, and always affectionate and tender. Thus testifies the physician in attendance on him at his death, who adds, "When he became very weak it cost him an effort to speak, and he died in such a happy composure of mind that nothing could exceed it." This event occurred on the 25th of August, 1776.

Hume ends his short autobiography with the following estimate of his own character:

"To conclude historically with my own character. I am, or rather was (for that is the style I must now use in speaking of myself, which emboldens me the more to speak my sentiments), I was, I say, a man of mild dispositions, of command of temper, of an open, social and cheerful humour, capable of attachment, but little susceptible of enmity, and of great moderation in all my passions. Even my love of literary fame, my ruling passion, never soured my temper, notwithstanding my frequent disappointments. My company was not unacceptable to the young and careless, as well as to the studious and literary; and as I took a particular pleasure in the company of modest women, I had no reason to be displeased with the reception I met with from them. In a word, though most men anywise eminent have found reason to complain of calumny, I never was touched or even attacked by her baleful tooth, and though I wantonly exposed myself to the rage of both civil and religious factions, they seemed to be disarmed in my behalf of their wonted fury. My friends never had occasion to vindicate any one circumstance of my character and conduct; not but that the zealots, we may well suppose, would have been glad to invent and propagate any story to my disadvantage, but they could never find any which they thought would wear the face of probability. I cannot say there is no vanity in making this funeral oration of myself, but I hope it is not a misplaced one; and this is a matter of fact which is easily cleared and ascertained."

From this, charity, the very bond of perfectness, has nothing to subtract. Silent concerning errors, it has nothing to add to it, unless it be the tribute of a grateful recognition of the fact, which blinds to all errors, that David Hume was a man whom the friends that knew him heartily loved.

His tombstone bears this inscription:

DAVID HUME.

BORN 1711. DIED 1766.

LEAVING IT TO POSTERITY TO ADD THE REST.

CHAPTER X.

SIR WILLIAM HAMILTON.

THE most influential current of British speculation in the eighteenth century and in the first half of the nineteenth flowed through Scotch minds. One of these, David Hume, a fascinating puzzle to his contemporaries, and a kindling spark to subsequent European thought, we contemplated in the last chapter. Another of them, than whom, according to the testimony of his adversary and critic, John Stuart Mill, "among the philosophical writers of the present century in [the British] islands, no one occupies a higher position," presents himself for our present consideration — Sir William Hamilton. Among the names of Scotch thinkers omitted from this review of "British Thought and Thinkers," are several whom it were well worth the while to contemplate separately. I name, for example, Francis Hutcheson, Adam Smith and Thomas Reid, all successively professors of moral philosophy in the university at Glasgow; the first, Hume's early and respected and (in ethical philosophy) not uninfluential correspondent, the second Hume's trusted friend and enthusiastic eulogist, and the last the courteous and friendly adversary of the great doubter: Smith, too, as the author of "The Wealth of Nations," famous in the history of political economy, and Reid, as the effective enunciator of the "philosophy of common sense," the acknowledged father of the brilliant reaction which, in the early part of the present century, and under the leading of such men as Royer-Collard, Maine de Biran, Jouffroy and Victor Cousin, asserted itself in France in opposition to the prevalent materialism and sensationalism, which, on its part, also claimed (through Condillac) a British origin in the philosophy of the Englishman, John Locke. Along with these, the list of Scotland's philosophic worthies contains such names as Carmichael, Turnbull, Home (Lord Kames), Oswald, Beattie, Fergusson, Burnett (Lord Monboddo), Stewart, Alison, Brown, Abercrombie, and forty others, all honorable, and some possessing a degree of eminence. But to none of all those whom I have named was given Hume's faculty of startling and awakening paradox or his artistic cunning, and Hamilton was superior to all in a certain and remarkably athletic agility of intellect and breadth of learning.

It is interesting to note, as in contrast with the state of things in England, that the most eminent leaders of speculation in Scotland have nearly all held university chairs. That philosophy and the philosophical sciences (as they are termed), with the spirit of living inquiry which they presuppose and the all-inclusive range of their problems, should be at home in an university, if anywhere, is sufficiently obvious. The greatest philosophers of antiquity were teachers. The influence and renown of mediæval and modern universities have been more strictly proportioned to the ability and prestige of their teachers of philosophy than to anything else. A notable example is furnished in the German universities during the past century, rendered illustrious, as they have been, and centres of an inexhaustible intellectual and moral power, through the lives and teaching of such men as Kant, Fichte, Schelling, Hegel, and many others scarcely less worthy of mention. Nothing of this kind has been true of the English universities for hundreds of years past. We have seen how Bacon, and Hobbes, and Locke, instead of receiving from that which was offered — or, rather, forced upon — them at Oxford and Cambridge, under the name of philosophy, a fascinating, winning, quickening, awakening stimulus, such as is always and necessarily produced when questions of vital and commanding interest are exhibited in all their amplitude of significance and discussed with living power and conviction, or, in other words, when philosophical instruction is not mere repetition, but rational persuasion (or, in the Socratic and Platonic sense, intellectual midwifery),— that these men, I say, who certainly could not be charged with a total lack of philosophical interest or capacity, were simply repelled and bored. In like manner Hamilton, as a student at Oxford, wrote in 1807, the first year of his residence there, to his mother: "I am so plagued by these foolish lectures of the College tutors that I have little time to do anything else. Aristotle to-day, ditto to-morrow; and I believe that if the ideas furnished by Aristotle to these numskulls were taken away, it would be doubtful whether there remained a single notion." Accordingly Hamilton soon abandoned lectures and classes, and pursued his studies wholly by himself, the university simply furnishing him an academical residence, and, in due time, on examination, his degrees. Doubtless, a sufficient, if not the only or ultimate cause of this state of things in the English universities is to be found in the circumstance pointed out by Hamilton in his discussions of university education, that at Oxford and Cambridge the universities had become merged in the colleges. University professors did not exist, or else were deprived of their proper function. Instruction was practically confined to a numerous body of college beneficiaries, who were not and could not all be eminent as students and thinkers, and were prepared only to teach in a very elementary manner, by repeating unintelligently the words of a text-book. The higher education in this country — I remark in passing — is only of late beginning to rise above the college or gymnasial grade. The immense majority of our college professors (there are of course notable exceptions) have of necessity been and still are mere drill-masters, though, it is true, often capable, by native endowment, and desirous of being much more than mere drill-masters. Neither philosophy nor the humane and positive sciences can be or are carried by them much beyond their respective alphabets, and a Bacon or Hamilton, who should repair to them, hoping to acquire the developed insight and power of an independent intellectual worker or thinker, by coming in contact with such workers or thinkers, would almost certainly be doomed to disappointment. The moral of all this is, that the need of philosophy and all sciences in this country, the need of the best intellects among our youth, the imperative need for the solidification and broadening of our national character is, not that the colleges, which lay the necessary foundation, should be done away, but that the system of our higher education should be capped by the addition of the true university, where thought and investigation are free and active, unrestricted by lack of time and means, and always and intelligently and independently working upon the outskirts of the domain of the known to conquer more and more the limitless field of the unknown. One of the brightest hopes of America may well be founded on the circumstance that the directors of our higher education are distinctly recognizing the university ideal, and are here and there taking effective steps for its realization.

In Scotland, then, I repeat, the most distinguished leaders of thought were nearly all university men. Hutcheson, Smith, and Reid held successively the chair of moral philosophy at Glasgow. Stewart and Brown occupied the same chair at Edinburgh. In the Professors' court of the University of Glasgow William Stirling Hamilton was born on the 8th day of March, 1788. His father, Dr. William Hamilton, was Professor of Anatomy and Botany in the Faculty of Medicine, a position worthily held before him by his own father and his uncle. The subject of our present study was thus born, so to speak, in and to university life. In the same sense it could be said that he was born in and for the life of the student of medicine — a circumstance which, indeed, as we shall see, had an important bearing on the tenor and direction of his own studies.

His father, Dr. and Prof. Hamilton, died at the early age of thirty-one, when William, his eldest son, was but two years old. A younger son, Thomas, subsequently Captain, Hamilton, an author of repute, was at the time only two months old. To the mother's only care, supported by limited pecuniary resources, the training and education of these two children were thus early left. She, the daughter of an influential Glasgow merchant, Stirling by name, carefully solicitous respecting the physical and moral welfare, and the whole education of her children, combined affection with a certain and unmistakable Scotch strictness in her treatment of them, but secured their hearty respect and devotion. There was needed a considerable strength of will and purpose rightly to curb and direct the overflowing vitality of the elder son. For if the expression may be allowed, young William was an intense boy, "fond," says his biographer, "of active outdoor sports; given decidedly to practical jokes and fun; ... a youth, in fine, with an untold and ever-increasing amount of vital force about him." And in such force, I affirm — all theories of human automatism to the contrary notwithstanding, and in agreement, I am sure, with what Mrs. Hamilton found true in her son's case — there is always a great deal of spontaneity. It is apt to invent a way of its own, and to insist on having it, without reference to the unpleasant maxims of elderly people, and to show a very vexatious indifference to the performance of tasks set by those who are wiser than its possessors. So one of William's early teachers was compelled to report to his mother that he was "very anxious to become his own master," rendering it necessary "to be excessively pointed and strict" in dealing with him, and he was, it is added, "very much inclined to be idle, although more studious than at first." I think we may infer that Mrs. Hamilton, as an anxious and faithful mother, had her hands sufficiently full.

With his abundant vitality and powerful physical frame, Hamilton early developed an unusual fondness and ability for athletic sports, which followed him all through his youth and early manhood. He was an enthusiast about bathing, in which he would fain have indulged every day in the year, an extraordinary swimmer, an excellent skater and boatsman and gunner, and superior to others in leaping and running. As a young man, he would take a boy of ten or twelve years of age on his right hand, and allow him to "stand on it as he held it out." An amusing incident is related of his leaping with a pole over a very high wall, which effectually separated his companions from the forbidden fruit in a professor's garden, and landing in the astonished presence of the dignified proprietor of the temptation. But with all this physical vigor went a generous and gentle spirit of helpfulness and protection toward those who needed it.

At the age of twelve Hamilton had so far progressed with his studies, under private teachers and at the Glasgow public schools, that he was admitted to attend the junior Greek and Latin classes of the University or College of Glasgow. But in the following year (1801), much (and naturally) to his disappointment and indignation, he was withdrawn from college by the "judicious and inexorable" authority of his mother and sent away to a private school in England. After chafing there a couple of years he returned, in 1803, to Glasgow, joining the senior classes in Latin and Greek and the classes in logic and moral philosophy. In each of the two latter he won the highest honors of the year, awarded by the votes of the class. The three following years were devoted to the study of medicine, the first two at Glasgow and the last at Edinburgh. That in the intervals of summer leisure his education might still be visibly progressing, his mother provided by placing him, along with his brother, in the summer of 1803, which preceded his reëntrance at the University of Glasgow, in charge of a country clergyman, a few miles from Edinburgh. Thither he returned in the two following summers, while the season before his year at Edinburgh was passed in medical studies in connection with the Infirmary at Glasgow.

The correspondence of the year at Edinburgh reveals Hamilton's mother lecturing her son on his expenditures for books and physical apparatus, and the latter justifying himself with the plea that his purchases were mostly of medical and classical books immediately needed, and that the most of them were bought at a third or half of their shop price. At another time he argues (in a letter to his mother) that his "money has only changed its shape. What was little ago bank-notes, is now metamorphosed into the more respectable appearance of rare and cheap works; and from the monotonous repetitions, 'The Bank of Scot. promise to pay to the bearer on demand,' etc., they have now suffered the glorious metamorphosis of being converted into historians, and philosophers, and poets, and orators, and though last not least, into physicians." Prof. Veitch (on whose memoir of Hamilton this biographical sketch is chiefly founded) gives a partial list of the books which Hamilton had procured in his sixteenth, seventeenth and eighteenth years, indicating a wide and intelligent range of taste. He rapidly developed into a famous book-hunter. The correspondence of subsequent years abounds in enthusiastic references to treasures secured at second-hand bookstores: manuscripts, Commentaries on Aristotle, editions of mediæval and later scholars. etc. He communicated his enthusiasm to others. one of whom, Scott's biographer, Lockhart, and Hamilton's friend and companion at Oxford, declares, in a letter to his father, "Hamilton is a famous adviser in the purchasing of books." The result of this taste of Hamilton's — which, of course, at once stimulated and was stimulated by his extraordinary love of learning — was the final accumulation of one of the largest and choicest philosophical libraries in Great Britain, containing some ten thousand volumes.

Before the period of his studies at the Scotch universities was over, Hamilton had already developed that daemonic — and, especially, nocturnal — energy as a student, which attended him through life, hindered, as I am convinced, his intellectual productivity, and occasioned the illness which, protracted through many weary years, resulted in his death. From Edinburgh he wrote to his mother, " From nine in the morning till three in the afternoon, I have not a single moment to spare — out of one class into another." "I . . . have been so busy that I have not been in bed before two or half-past it for these six weeks, and am up every morning by a quarter-past eight." Later in life, as we shall see, he abused his body, in this way, even more unreasonably.

Finally, two of the Edinburgh letters contain amusing evidence of a trait which one may connect with Hamilton's subsequent successful defense of his right to a baronial title. In the earlier of these letters Hamilton says to his mother, " I wish you would give me a genteeler appellation on the back of your next letter," and ends with

"Your affectionate son,
W. S. HAMILTON, *Esq.* Remember that.'

The other one shows that Mrs. Hamilton did not "remember that," and the son threatens, in case the neglect be continued, to direct his letters to her, " Elizabeth Hamilton, without any ceremony."

In the year 1677 Robert Snell, a Scotchman, and graduate of Glasgow, dying in England, left a sum of money, the proceeds of which were to be used for the education of Scottish students at Oxford. It was through participation in the benefit of this foundation that Adam Smith was enabled to pursue his studies at this English university. Owing to his own excellent and successful career as a student at Glasgow, one of the "Snell exhibitions," as they were called, was offered to Hamilton.

It was while residing at Oxford that the decided bent of Hamilton's mind toward abstract studies and exhaustive learning was clearly developed. He entered upon residence there, at Balliol College, in May 1807. His studies now were mainly literary and philosophical, in preparation for the examination for the Bachelor's degree; though medicine was not wholly forgotten. The acquisition of the Bachelor's degree was conditioned upon the presentation of a series of books, selected by the candidate, and relating to various specified departments of learning, on the subject-matter of which a public examination was held. Hamilton sought the aid, as instructor, of one of the fellows of Balliol College, but soon discovered that this was unnecessary. "The tutors," in his own language, "whistled to their pupils the old tunes which, as pupils, had been piped to them." Accordingly it happened, according to the later testimony of one of his Oxford friends, that "Hamilton had no teacher, and was strictly a solitary student." He applied himself to work with extraordinary and characteristic energy. The range of his reading and knowledge far surpassed any that had long been known at Oxford. He had a remarkable facility at "tearing out the entrails" of a book, as he termed it. Says a fellow-student, "A perusal of the preface, table of contents, and index, and a glance at those parts which were new to him (which were few), were all that was necessary." He thus as an undergraduate acquired the reputation of being the "most learned Aristotelian at Oxford." Nor was his reading confined to Aristotle, but included all his commentators, Greek classics, Cicero, and the learning of the fourteenth and fifteenth centuries. Nor was he a mere retired book-worm. He was always ready for sports, and excursions, full of joyous humor, kindly, cordial, and possessed of unusual manly beauty.* At his examination, which "was continued for the exceptional period of two days, and occupied in all twelve hours," he was prepared, says a fellow-student, "to be examined in more than four times the number of philosophical and didactic books ever wont to be taken up even for the highest honors; and those, likewise, authors far more abstruse than had previously been attempted in the schools; while at the same time he was examined in more than any ordinary complement of merely classical works." "In fourteen of his books on the abstruser subjects of Greek philosophy," we are told that "he was not questioned, the greater part of these being declared by the masters to be too purely metaphysical for public examination." He won "the highest distinction the examiners could bestow" (said Dr. Jenkyns, subsequent master of Balliol). Dr. Parsons, at that time master of Balliol, said of Hamilton, in the year following his examination (Hamilton took his degree in 1810, after little

---

* One who heard Hamilton lecture, later in life, tells me that he was "gloriously handsome."

more than three years of residence), "He is one of those, and they are rare, who are best left to themselves. He will turn out a great scholar, and we shall get the credit of making him so, though in point of fact we shall have done nothing for him whatever."

The following ten years of Hamilton's life were outwardly uneventful. In 1814 he took his master's degree at Oxford. Meanwhile he had, for unexplained reasons, dropped medicine, and studied law and been already admitted to the bar at Edinburgh, where he fixed his residence. He never rose to eminence at the bar, lacking fluency as a speaker, being impatient of the petty details of the profession, and more prone to spend his time among the mustiest books in the Advocates' Library; in short, as Lord Jeffrey regarded and termed him, "an unpractical man." Yet he was already becoming known and sought out on account of his reputation for vast learning, and that, too, by foreigners who visited Edinburgh, among others by our countryman, Edward Everett. There he seems, in the phraseology of to-day, to have interviewed, rather than to have allowed himself to be interviewed by them, and so made them tributary to his own avidity for varied information. In this, as in so many other respects during the earlier period of his manhood, and indeed, to a great extent, throughout his whole career, he justified the judgment of a contemporary who styled him "rather a recipient than a creator."

Among other topics on which he spent much research, in the first years after fixing his abode at Edinburgh, was that of his hereditary claim to the baronetcy of Preston. This claim he established to the satisfaction of a competent jury in the year 1816, and was "declared thenceforward entitled to bear the name and style of Baronet of Preston and Fingalton."

In 1817 he visited Germany in the interest of the Advocates' Library, and again in 1820 to collect evidence in a case at law. In neither case was his stay a prolonged one, nor does he appear to have come in contact with German philosophers. But he was led to study the German language and to interest himself in its literature.

In 1820 the chair of Moral Philosophy in the University of Edinburgh became vacant through the death of Dr. Thomas Brown, and the resignation of Dugald Stewart, its titular occupant. Accordingly Hamilton, following Scotch custom, procured testimonials as to character and qualifications, and presented them to the Town Council, in which body, singularly enough, the power of appointment was lodged, with an application for the position. Notwithstanding the incontestable superiority of his credentials and qualifications, the Town Council — a body, for the rest, scarcely competent, as such bodies are generally composed, to judge of the merits of candidates for university appointments — moved by political considerations (Hamilton was a Whig, and the majority of the Council were Tories), elected, by a strict party vote, Hamilton's Tory competitor. It was not till sixteen more years of waiting had passsd, when Hamilton was already forty-eight years of age, that he at last secured a position suited to his tastes and abilities — a position which he honored, and in which he rendered himself illustrious. The student of Kant's biography will be reminded of the similar fate of this renowned German, Hamilton's partial master.

In the following year, however, 1821, Hamilton was elected to a professorship of Civil History, at the attractive salary of one hundred pounds a year, levied by a duty on ale and beer. The attendance upon instruction in this topic was purely voluntary, and had run very low. Hamilton threw himself with zest and energy into the labors required of him, and prepared a course of lectures on the modern history of Europe down to the outbreak of the French Revolution. Shorter courses or occasional lectures upon general literature and political philosophy were added. The attendance upon them was gratifying, and the impression produced deep and lasting. Hamilton appears to have continued to perform the duties of his position for some eight or ten years, when "through the bankruptcy of the city" "the salary ceased to be paid," and the lectures were discontinued.

The learned and recondite researches were meanwhile constantly pursued with energetic avidity, and directed to literature, philology (including Greek grammar), and philosophy. In an interview with that philological prodigy, Dr. Sam. Parr, Hamilton displayed such extraordinary and exact learning in the line of the Doctor's own specialty, that the venerable man at last burst forth in amazement, "Why, who are you, sir?"

The claims of phrenology having been loudly asserted at Edinburgh about this time, Hamilton turned his attention to this subject, not simply in the way of theory, but by numerous experiments, conducted, as he stated, on "above one thousand brains of above fifty species of animals." His medical education had peculiarly qualified him to conduct such experiments with intelligence, and he seems to have been possessed with a strong native bent to inquiries conducted by this method. Later in life we find him indefatigably experimenting with his children and himself, and it is stated that he made "discoveries of very considerable importance both in physiology and anatomy." His conclusions with reference to phrenology were emphatically adverse to the pretensions of that alleged science. In animal magnetism and mesmerism—subjects then discussed with special interest—he found much that seemed to him worthy of attention and belief, but in *clairvoyance* nothing.

In March, 1829, two years after his mother's death, Hamilton married his cousin, Miss Marshall, who had for some time been a member of his mother's family. This union was of the greatest consequence to him, for, as we shall see, it was to the self-sacrificing assistance and constant encouragement of his wife that he owed, in the greatest measure, all he accomplished after his appointment to the position in which the bulk of his labors were performed.

In the year 1829 Prof. Macvey Napier, whose interesting correspondence was published a few months ago, succeeded to the editorship of the Edinburgh Review. With a view to rendering this periodical more a vehicle of philosophical discussion than it had been heretofore, he called upon his friend Hamilton for assistance, and by dint of persistent pressure and encouragement secured his compliance with the request. The subject proposed for the first article was the philosophy of M. Cousin — more especially his doctrine respecting the cognoscibility of the so-called infinite or absolute. Among the reasons which, according to Hamilton's own subsequent statement, made him disinclined to undertake the review of Cousin, was his professed knowledge "that a discussion of the leading doctrine of [Cousin's] book would prove unintelligible, not only to 'the general reader,' but, with few exceptions, to our British metaphysicians at large." (In a letter to M. Cousin, written in 1834, several years after the publication of the article in question, Hamilton indicated his contemptuous sense of British incompetence — at that time — in matters of the profoundest philosophy by saying, "I do not believe there are five readers of the 'Review' who are qualified to comprehend anything above the superficial psychology dignified in this country with the name of metaphysic, far less to understand the merits of your philosophy and that of Schelling.") Whatever we may hold respecting the philosophical positions maintained and criticised in the review of Cousin — a question which we will keep, for the moment, in abeyance — it was, at the time, a singularity in British periodical literature, and commanded immediate attention both at home and abroad. With Kant, European philosophy had fifty years before passed a critical and all-decisive point. Yet Kant's principal work had not yet been translated into English, and except for Coleridge, England had scarcely known that Kant had lived and spoken. But here was an anonymous writer who, with a brilliant mastery of style, an appearance of accurate and easy familiarity with the later developments of continental (and especially German) thought, and an authoritative peremptoriness of dialectical statement, came forward and spoke, under Kantian inspiration, a new, yet intelligible language — delivered a deeply interesting and, if true, important message, touching questions concerning radically the problems of the possible range and the duty of human faith and knowledge. The article was soon translated into French and Italian. M. Cousin (then at the zenith of his — not purely philosophical—popularity), whose doctrine it vigorously attacked, made inquiry concerning its authorship, and entered into the most friendly and encomiastic correspondence with Hamilton, between whom and himself a relation of apparently hearty mutual admiration and esteem continued ever afterward to subsist.

Until the year 1836, when he was appointed to the chair of Logic and Metaphysics at Edinburgh, Hamilton continued his contributions to the Edinburgh Review, on subjects partly pyschological and logical, partly literary, and partly (and numerously) educational. In the latter Hamilton discussed the subjects of university patronage and superintendence (with reference to the universities of Scotland), the "state of the English universities, with more especial reference to Oxford," the "right of dissenters to admission into the English universities," and other topics pertaining to the system of higher education. To say that these discussions abounded in learning and good sense, vigorously applied to throw light on imperfections and abuses, and to restore a proper conception of university functions, and that they bore valuable and acknowledged fruit in legislation and practice, is barely to meet the requirements of truth with respect to them. They furnish an extremely instructive study for any one interested in the theory and practice of higher educational institutions. Prof. Veitch says, with evident justice, that with his "articles on the Universities and University Reform . . . commenced Sir William's practical influence on the machinery for the higher education of the country—an influence hardly less powerful and commanding than that of his speculative writings on the philosophical thought of the times."

In the year 1836, on the occasion of a vacancy occurring in the chair of Logic and Metaphysics in the University of Edinburgh, Sir William Hamilton, by an almost evenly divided vote of the municipality, was elected to the position. The election was forced, in opposition to prejudices and insinuations of the most varied and vulgar kind, by the overwhelming weight of testimony, from foreigners as well as distinguished Britons, to Hamilton's remarkable and preëminent fitness for the post in question. The election took place in July, and Hamilton entered in the following November on the performance of the functions as a professor, which he continued to exercise during the remaining twenty years of his life.

Although, throughout his life, ever an enormous reader and busy thinker, Hamilton was always given to exercise procrastination in the matter of writing. Such work he was always prone to put off till the last moment and then to perform only under the immediate pressure of some sort of necessity. The preparation of his university lectures formed no exception to this rule. This work he delayed till the beginning of the session was close at hand, and he was then fain to defer the opening of his course for a few weeks. From such an impolitic course his friends dissuaded him, and the result is described in the following passage from his biography by Prof. Veitch:

"The first course of lectures was composed during the currency of the session of five months. He gave three lectures a week, and each lecture was, as a rule, written on the night preceding its delivery. The lecture-hour was one o'clock in the afternoon, and the lecturer seldom went to bed before five or six in the morning. He was generally roused about ten or eleven, and then hurried off to the College, portfolio under arm, at a swinging pace. Frequently, notwithstanding the late hour of going to bed, he had to be up before nine o'clock, in time to attend the Teind Court. All through the session Lady Hamilton sat up with her husband each night until near the grey dawn of the winter morning. Sir William wrote the pages of the lecture on rough sheets, and his wife, sitting in an adjoining room, copied them as he got them ready. On some occasions the subject of the lecture would prove less easily managed than on others, and then Sir William would be found writing as late as nine o'clock of a morning, while his faithful but wearied amanuensis had fallen asleep on a sofa. Sometimes the finishing touch to the lecture was left to be given just before the class-hour." (*Memoir of Sir William Hamilton*, pp. 206-7.)

The lectures prepared and delivered by Hamilton during the first year of his incumbency related mostly to psychology and have been since published, and are generally known as the Lectures on Metaphysics. In the following year a course of lectures on logic (since published under that title) were given, and during the remainder of Hamilton's life these two courses were repeated in alternate years. To provide for the needs of more advanced students, Hamilton at one time proposed a special course, to be devoted solely to the discussion of the more abstract questions of metaphysics, and inserted in the draught of the programme of university instruction the announcement of such a course. But the governing body of the university, the town council (or city government) — listen to this absurdity! — in the exercise of their consummate wisdom, expunged this announcement from the programme, because, among other reasons, the proposed new course related (in the language employed by the college committee of the town council) to "an abstruse subject, not generally considered as of any great or paramount utility."

Hamilton's lectures were popular, attracting an increasing number of auditors till the end of his life. It was his expressed and never-forgotten object to teach, *not philosophy*, but *to philosophize*. By special hours devoted to familiar examinations and discussions respecting the topics of his lectures, by special honors and prizes for those who, in the judgment of their fellows, showed marked ability, by indicating courses of reading and subjects for essays, by the formation of a metaphysical society for students, by receiving students at his own house,— by all these and other methods, all of which depended on his own earnest purpose and personal influence for their effectiveness, he made the teaching of his department a powerful factor of university education.

In discussion and controversy — of which latter he had his full share — Hamilton often assumed an authoritative, peremptory, uncompromising tone, founded on strong conviction combined with feeling. From bodies of foreign scholars he received numerous honors. His works include the two volumes of his university lectures — styled "Metaphysics" and "Logic,"— a large volume of "Discussions on Philosophy and Literature," which contains his contributions to the Edinburgh Review, and an edition of Reid's works, accompanied by numerous annotations and by long but unfinished "Notes," which are of decisive importance for the study of his philosophy. He was engaged at the time of his death in editing the works of Dugald Stewart, and had made exhaustive studies for a life of Luther. His attitude with reference to christianity was reverential and sympathetic. His theological learning was unusually extensive, and he lived and died in the communion of the established church of Scotland.

Hamilton can scarcely be said to have left a complete and systematic statement or demonstration of his philosophical views. The very multifariousness and minuteness of his scholarship stood partly in the way of this. Still, his philosophical attitude was clearly marked, and his doctrines exerted a wide influence, in America as well as in Great Britain. Let us attempt to see what this attitude was.

It was determined, we may say, speaking generally, by Reid and Kant, as their attitude was, in turn, determined or elicited by Hume.

Hume (it will be remembered) reasoning, in general, from the point of view of pure, passive experience and observation (which, as we know, attains only the transient and phenomenal), and, in particular, from Locke's theory of ideas, or representative images, and not things, as the direct objects of knowledge, had denied, not only with Berkeley, that we have any knowledge of an external world possessing substantive reality, but also that we have any such knowledge of mind. All that we know is the subjective impressions which the mysterious beings who usurp the use of the personal pronoun *we*, are alleged to experience, along with their actual but arbitrary and inexplicable relations of succession and coëxistence, or "association." Belief and conviction were simply cases of a peculiar vivacity in impressions, or in their fainter residuary copies, to which alone Hume gave the name of ideas.

Reid, still professing to follow only the so-called method

of induction and observation, as the only one authorized by "common sense" and competent to the discovery and cognition of truth, applied this to the question of the constitution of the human mind and the substance of mental experience. Antecedently to all inquiry, "human nature," in the light of Hume's professedly exhaustive account of it, as constituted solely by "three laws of association, joined to a few original feelings," appears to Reid as a ridiculous "puppet," in comparison with man as actually known to himself; a puppet, "contrived by too bold an apprentice of nature, to mimic her work. It shews tolerably by candle light; but brought into clear day, and taken to pieces, it will appear to be a man made with mortar and a trowel."

Now what Reid expects and professes to find by his psychological analysis is only facts, ultimate facts, and not their explanation; the latter lies beyond the range of philosophy, *i.e.* of all knowledge, according to Reid's (which, as he everywhere professes, is the Baconian) conception of it. He examines, then, the facts of mental experience and finds that they include, among others, sensation (or sensible perception), memory, and imagination; that the first is accompanied with the belief of a present existence, memory with belief of a past existence, and imagination with no belief at all; that perceived qualities are immediately referred to an objective, material existence (substance) in which they are united; and that mental operations are with the same immediateness ascribed to a spiritual agent or mind. These are simple, ultimate, indefinable, inexplicable facts of our mental experience. They precede all ratiocination. Our belief in matter and mind is not, as preceding philosophers had maintained, an inference, from the presence of idea-images in the mind. The destruction of this theory of ideas is ostensibly one of the main objects of Reid's argumentation. He professes to find the theory utterly unintelligible and without the slightest warrant in any observable facts, and ascribes to it the "shocking paradoxes" of Berkeley and Hume. No (he maintains), in sensible perception is immediately given the conception of a sensible object and the inexpugnable belief in its existence. In the consciousness of mental operations is immediately given the conception of a mental agent and the belief in its existence. In neither case, as Reid imagines, does any "idea" come between the mind and the object of its conviction. Behind these facts, according to him, it is impossible to go. Reid concludes that they are founded in the constitution of our nature; that they are principles of our nature, or principles of common sense. These principles are not known only through the fact that analysis is unable to resolve them into simpler elements, but also by a practical test. Principles, says Reid, "which the constitution of our nature leads us to believe, and which we are under a necessity to take for granted in the common concerns of life, without being able to give a reason for them — these are what we call the principles of common sense." And finally there is also a rational criterion by which they may be known. For, we are also told, in one of Reid's later works, the "sole province" of common sense is the first office of reason, namely, "to judge of things self-evident." It is the faculty of principles, a general designation for all indemonstrable, but still ineradicable, knowledge or belief.

Reid's reply to Hume, then, was the "philosophy of

common sense." Hume's philosophical scepticism was alleged to be unfounded, because derived from an unwarranted (though generally assumed) theory of knowledge, as immediately conversant with representative ideas, and not with things, and also because it was in absurd contradiction to the actual, inductively ascertained, primary necessities of belief and practice, or to "human nature." The demonstration of this contradiction, however, could not greatly have disturbed Hume, who was fully aware of its existence. Hume knew that he was calling in question the accepted declarations of the "common sense" of the vulgar and of the "reason" of metaphysicians. This was what he meant to do, and he would have laughed at any one who should have attempted to put him to shame by telling him so. And if Reid had succeeded in showing that the so-called "ideal system," on which Hume's scepticism was founded, was a myth, it would still have been open to Hume to persist in a doubt which he had once found it possible to maintain in defiance of self-styled "common sense," believing, or hoping, that if the argument alleged by him were found baseless, yet another might be found which could not be overturned. But Reid did not disprove the doctrine of knowledge through ideas, in any sense in which Hume's scepticism depended on it. On the contrary, Reid maintained the same thing. He could not but distinguish between the subjective and the objective side in every act (or, rather, *state*) of cognition, and the former corresponded perfectly to Hume's "impressions" and "ideas." All that Hume had said was that our knowledge is only of the subjective side. Reid virtually said the same thing. Perception and reflection, as states of mind, are immediately known to us.

Perceived object and mind, he holds, are not. Perception and reflection are, in Reid's own language, only signs which "conjure up, as by a kind of natural magic, a conception and belief of that of which we never before had any notion or conception," namely, of matter and mind. The former were to the latter, not indeed as resemblant images to their originals, but still a *tertium quid*, standing between knowledge and being, and separating the former from the latter. They were inexplicable signs of reality, whose interpretation (*i.e.* the "belief" in which) was inexplicably forced upon us by our "nature," and that was all there was to be said about them. So Reid simply reasserted as facts the phenomena of mental experience, which Hume admitted, but sought to explain, or to explain away; while Reid, on the contrary, simply declared that they were on their very face both inexplicable and inexpugnable.

Reid, then, in the matter of philosophical knowledge, did not get beyond Hume, nor did he profess to do so. For him, as for Hume, the substantive nature of either mind or matter is beyond knowledge. His utmost pretension, in this regard, is to show that through an unfathomable, "magical" necessity of our "nature," we *must* consent, and be content, firmly to believe what we cannot know. The difference between Reid and Hume is found chiefly in their psychological interpretations of belief. Hume makes it to be a phenomenon of panoramic consciousness. It is a case of special intensity in our ideas. Reid makes of it a wholly mysterious factor of our "constitution."

Reid's method (the "Baconian," empirico-psychological method of descriptive analysis) and presupposition (that appearances, *phenomena*, alone are knowable) being the same in nature as Hume's, it is not surprising that, like Hume, he only arrives at the recognition, without insight, of phenomenal facts. The facts can be recognized and described; their meaning and warrant remain shrouded in mystery. The merit of Reid consists in the circumstance that among the facts recognized and emphasized by him are certain ones which really belong to the domain of the dynamic, vital, philosophic consciousness mentioned in the last chapter. The only consciousness expressly known to Reid is the sensible, imaginative, representative, *picturesque* consciousness recognized by Hume. But the facts in question, he sturdily and rightly maintains, do not belong to such consciousness, though, for lack of philosophic insight, he is unable to account for them in any other way than by ascribing them to "natural magic"—which is not to account for them at all. But on the basis of these facts, beliefs, or "principles of common sense," Reid maintains very praiseworthy views in ethics and æsthetics.

Kant, in reply to Hume, makes (like Reid) no attempt to rescue the knowledge of reality. We know, he admits, only phenomena, which are modifications, however determined, of mind, corresponding to Hume's "impressions." But the order of the concatenation of phenomena in our knowledge is not arbitrary, as Hume had asserted, but fixed and necessary. Our knowledge, as to substance, is only from and through sensible experience (external or internal—the "panoramic consciousness"). But a critical analysis of the conditions, upon which alone experience is possible, shows that there are known and predetermined forms which it must assume, or grooves in which it must run. These forms, known or cognizable, *a priori*, as necessary and universal, are the mechanism of mind, independent of experience, but useless and without significance, except as applied to the material of knowledge furnished in experience (*i.e.* phenomena, not real " things in themselves "), while yet determining the form, and so the possibility, of all experience. These forms, "spontaneous functions of the mind," " categories of the understanding," or "ideas of pure reason," now, are, like Reid's "beliefs," works of the dynamic, vital consciousness, which is the real organ of philosophy, as indeed of all real knowledge. In contrast with Reid's uncritical dogmatism, Kant seeks with critical rigor to deduce them in systematic completeness, and in all their necessity and universality, from the very nature of mental experience. In this, it is needless to say, he is infinitely superior to Reid. But, like Reid, he shares in the constitutional intellectual infirmity, or scientific prejudice, of his century, in being unable to see in anything but sensible consciousness a possible type or standard of reality. This, however, at once reveals itself to Kant, as it always does, and must do, to all accurate inquirers, as a scene, not of reality, but only of shadow, appearance, or intrinsic unreality. Since, then,— the argument proceeds — reality is inaccessible to human knowledge, unless sensibly revealed, it follows that it, the true " thing-in-itself," is for us absolutely unknowable. Real being, therefore, which empirical psychology, in spite of its own demonstration that it cannot be an object of sensible perception, still pertinaciously conceives as if it might be an object of such perception if only our senses were superhumanly quickened, becomes merely a mysterious object of unintelligent persuasion or belief, an alleged "*thing*-in-itself" (as though it were a sort of transcendental *stuff*), but, in reality, the purest nonsense, a veritable hodge-podge of contradictions. This is the valuable (?) contribution to his philosophy which Kant derived from his study of British psychology.

In the light of this ontological negativism, Kant's forms of sense, functions of the understanding, ideas of reason — in short, everything which in mental experience is demonstrated to transcend, limit, and determine sensuous consciousness — become just as mysterious as Reid's "beliefs" or "principles of common sense." They seem to demonstrate that mind is more than a *tabula rasa* or "piece of white paper," having an independent nature and reality of its own, and being an independent and vital source of real, ideal activities. But now we are told that mind and all its forms of thought are, without "sensuous filling," empty and insubstantial, a mask, a spectre. They are somewhat mythically described as having only "logical," not real or ontological, value and significance. Mind is something, and it is nothing. It is the all-efficient determining factor with reference to the form of knowledge, but it is a factor whose own substance and reality are reduced to the mere shadow of a "point of view." All this absurdity and jargon result simply from the potent spell of the sensuous prejudice above noted.

But the very fact that Kant in any way recognized these non-sensuous forms and functions of mind, showed that he was also under another spell — the spell of vital, absolute reality. In demonstrating their necessary presence in the commonest phases of sensible experience, he was demonstrating the power and reality of that only true (non-sensuous) type of all *real being*, which is revealed in man as essential life, "energy of intelligence," ideal activity, not a merely passive state of conscious feeling, but self-conscious spiritual *doing*, or *dynamic self-consciousness*. Kant demonstrated that there was an intelligible element in mind and in knowledge, as well as a sensible one. And but a step separated him from the recognition of the truth, which lies, and has always lain, at the core of all affirmative philosophy, that the intelligible element is the commanding one and determines, not only the form of phenomenal knowledge, but also the substance of real knowledge (knowledge of reality). With this unexpressed truth, as with a burden, Kant's philosophy is heavily laden. It prompts him "practically" to regard the reflection, that "*I am thinking*" ("*ich denke*"), as more than a mere substanceless *Vorstellung*, or idea, logically necessary, indeed, to every state of mental experience, but otherwise, or ontologically, insignificant, and as noting the truth, evidenced in the most immediate experience, that there is in man a real and potent *self*, a personally identical, actively conscious spirit. It moves him to substitute for the bastard conception of a "*thing*-in-itself," as the *substrate* of phenomena, the genuine and legitimate one of a "*noumenon*" or an intelligible, *i.e.* ideal, spiritual power and reality, as the *soul* and *life* of phenomena. In short, it dominates all those positive "practical" convictions, in his vigorous defense of which (and not in his "theoretical" negativism) is to be found the true source of Kant's immense power in the history of thought and of moral culture.

For — and this is the final and capital point to be noted with reference to Kant — while Kant (under the influence before indicated) had declared that the real was "theoretically" unknowable, there were certain practical convictions concerning it, of incalculable significance, which Kant regarded as absolutely necessary, though theoretically indemonstrable and inscrutable, for consistent thought. These flow, for Kant, especially and ostensibly, from the nature of man's moral consciousness, and their particular objects are God, and the immortal, rational, free soul of man. But they also flow, by none the less necessary implication, from the dynamic, or really positive, element in Kant's critical theory of knowledge. Accordingly, when Kant's successors laid hold upon the "practical" side of his doctrine, and developed a philosophy, in which supreme reality is ideal, spiritual, divine, and the supremely real in man is of kindred, participant nature, they could justly claim to be the true continuators of Kant. (It is only to be regretted that Berkeley, nearly a century before, had not found similar "continuators" in Great Britain!)

Hamilton, now, with reference to the substance of his views, is the child of Reid and Kant. He is superior to Reid in dialectical agility, but far inferior to Kant in the spirit of critical, patient and systematic thoroughness. Under Kantian inspiration he develops, in forms of sharp outline, the self-confessed, yet comparatively unobtrusive, theoretical agnosticism of Reid. Under the influence of Reid and of British psychological method, he emasculates the element of virile idealism, which was in Kant. Sharing in the moral earnestness of both Reid and Kant, he seeks to render his teaching subservient to the development of moral and religious character.

For Hamilton, as for Reid and Kant, sensible consciousness furnishes the type or standard of substantive, or ontological knowledge. Empirical consciousness is held to be the Bible of philosophy, and in appealing to it for answers to ontological questions, we must remember that "here understanding and imagination coincide." What *is* (for us) is only what appears in (picturesque, imaginative, panoramic) consciousness. But what appears in consciousness, is only phenomena. The ultimately real is therefore, for us, unknowable. "Existence, absolutely and in itself, is to us as zero." All our knowledge is relative, being confined to conditioned existence (*i.e.* existence "in special modes," standing "in a certain relation to our faculties," and "under modifications determined by these faculties themselves") in time and space. (To the "three categories" of "conditioned existence, time and space," Hamilton reduces Kant's "forms of sensibility" and "categories of the understanding," *i.e.* he, in tendency, eliminates the dynamic element from Kant, as an empirical psychologist would be likely to do.)

This is the famous law of the Relativity of Knowledge, which is but a new and unnecessary version of the old story concerning the incompetence of sense to penetrate to, or grasp, reality. It is the law of the "imbecility" of human understanding, and is otherwise stated and defended as the "law of the conditioned," according to which the object of all our possible knowledge is not only contradictorily opposed to the absolutely real or unconditioned, but in a mean between two contradictorily opposed varieties of the unconditioned, of which, though both are inconceivable, one or the other must, by the logical laws of contradiction and excluded middle, of necessity, be held to be real and existent. This alleged logical constraint which we are under, to believe what we cannot conceive, is construed by Hamilton, with some impressiveness, as teaching the "salutary lesson" of faith in the invisible.

The "lesson" is indeed a salutary one, and is the first one to be learned in philosophy, as in religion. But it does not follow from Hamilton's data and arguments. The data are all essentially sensualistic, and the arguments sophistical. And it must be added that the subject of the arguments would never occur to the human mind, and be made a theme of inquiry, if the whole nature of mind were absorbed in sensible, static consciousness. Sense never inquires for any reality transcending that which is immediately presented to it in phenomena. (If all our knowledge were really, as Hamilton avers, but a transcript of conditioned or phenomenal consciousness, it would never occur to us to ask after the unconditioned or real. Such a purely passive, vegetative state of mind would rest quite content with itself, and not even the circumstance that the "knowledge of contraries is one" would furnish a sufficiently powerful lever to lift it out of its drowsy self-sufficiency into a conception of, much less to incite it to active inquiry concerning, the "unconditioned.") The fact that man does raise such an inquiry is direct evidence that he is not wholly sense, that he is not simply a bundle of perceptions or impressions, or a complex series of mere conscious *states*, but that there is a dynamic element in him, an ideal real nature, a spell of potent reason, a spirit, for whose activity sense is but the occasion and subsidiary instrument. The works of this nature appear in the thought of every man. They obtruded themselves upon Hume's notice, who treated them, in consistent agreement with his purely sensational empiricism, as mere illusions. Their power and reality were recognized, as we have seen, by Reid and Kant, who, however, in consequence of their (conscious or unconscious) sensualistic prepossessions, were unable to vindicate for them any other than a "magical" origin or a "practical" significance. Hamilton is clearly aware of them, and recognizes them as (in the Kantian phrase, which he imitates) fruits of an "original spontaneity of intelligence," or functions of the "regulative reason." These are no merely phenomenal states of consciousness, but active, self-illuminating functions of real, living mind. Their theoretical significance is of the highest order, and the questions which they suggest are rational ones, relating to the intelligible, and not to the sensible; to the real and not to the phenomenal. It is in the "real" to which they point, in which, from the point of view of mere sense, we are religiously and practically bound to have "faith," but into which, from the point of view of rational intelligence, we are bound to seek for *insight*. This truth, as old as philosophy, the modern world, blinded and confused by mathematico-scientific prejudice, has had theoretically to learn anew. Hume startled the world into reflection upon the subject, and Reid, Kant and Hamilton are engaged in the unsuccessful throes of the endeavor to unlearn the Humian prejudices of their age with reference to it, and to arrive at a clear apprehension and enunciation of the truth in question. Hamilton struggles and comports himself in them like an intellectual athlete. But the tenacity with which he clings to the old sensualistic prejudice, while yet under the (for him) theoretically inscrutable charm of the old, yet ever new, because ever present, rational inspiration, is the very reason why he, more conspicuously even than Kant, falls into a maze of contradiction and absurdity.

The Unconditioned, Infinite, or Absolute (Hamilton's names for the ultimate and real) is a rational conception. As such it is inconceivable, except as a rational object, or, in other words, as a spirit, as God. Naturally, such an object is not sensibly perceivable, any more than music is visible. The whole burden of his ontology is, that, because not sensibly perceivable or imaginable, it is unknowable. Yet all his arguments concerning the Unconditioned are founded on the supposition that it is and must be thus "conceivable." * The "Infinite" and "Absolute" of Hamilton's discussions are the Pseudo-Infinite and the Pseudo-Absolute of space and time. Space and time are, for Hamilton, as for others, characteristic forms of sense, of phenomenal consciousness, of conditioned existence. Hamilton's arguments would persuade us that they are forms of the "Unconditioned," or of ultimate, supreme reality, and our "faith" in God, so far as they are concerned, is made to depend upon the alleged logical constraint which is laid upon us, to admit that the intrinsically unimaginable would be imaginable, if only *our* imaginations were not so unfortunately "imbecile." It is only on account of the frailty of our "minds" that the inherently non-phenomenal does not become for us a conscious phenomenon. This is, in effect, but the reappearance of the Kantian (or, for that matter, the Lockian, and in general, the psychological) conception of a "*thing*-in-itself," *i.e.* a time-and-space object which is not a time-and-space ob-

---

* It is important to note, in reading authors like Hamilton, Mill, and Spencer, that for them the conceivable means the imaginable, and the inconceivable the unimaginable.

ject, a phenomenal reality which is essentially non-phenomenal. It is the phenomenal trying to be its own double, the shadow seeking to find in itself substance. That, under these circumstances, the "Unconditioned" should appear to Hamilton as "a fasciculus of contradictions," is not astonishing!

I do not stop to show otherwise in detail the inconclusiveness of the arguments by which Hamilton would force us to believe in such a "fasciculus" of absurdities. If the problem is contradictory in terms, if it proposes to find life in death and essential reality in essential phenomenality, it is obvious that the "reasonings" employed, if at all specious, must be correspondingly sophistical. I only remark that, if the "Unconditioned," in the terms proposed by Hamilton, is inconceivable and irrational, this fact has nothing to do with the possibility that the Unconditioned, as living Spirit, may be a clear object of rational intelligence.

The same dominance of sensualistic or "scientific" prejudice, in treating of rational or philosophical problems, is illustrated in Hamilton's views concerning causation. The kind of causation which he has in mind in his discussions is that secondary or quasi-causality which is contemplated in the physical science of phenomena, where *life* and *efficiency* are systematically kept out of view, and attention is directed only to the order of succession among phenomena or to the mathematical equivalence of successive states or aspects of phenomena. Naturally, when with this conception Hamilton approaches the problem of divine, *i.e.* real, spiritual, efficient causation, he reaches conclusions, for the necessity of accepting which agnosticism furnishes a welcome substitute.

The same prejudice, finally, leads him to look upon the problem of sensible perception (the perception of "external objects") as the cardinal problem of philosophy (!), and to propound concerning it opinions full of contradiction and confusion.

But enough on this point, my only object here being to indicate in general outline the intellectual attitude of Hamilton with reference to philosophical problems. The real source of Hamilton's strength and of his widely diffused and quickening influence is to be found, as in the case of Kant, in his practical, urgent recognition of that dynamic, ideal side of mind and life, which, as an instrument of literal, theoretical cognition, he was unable to turn to any account. To this should be added the contagion of his dialectical ardor and the example of his immense erudition. His defect is, that he does not raise philosophy out of that quagmire of psychology in which (under Kantian inspiration?) he recognized that it was sunk. He complained of the substitution of "superficial psychology" for "metaphysics," and the complaint holds good against himself. In this respect his friend and younger contemporary, James Ferrier, builded better than he.

Twelve years before his death Hamilton was afflicted with a stroke of paralysis, from the effects of which he never recovered. His mind remained, however, to the last unimpaired. At times his lectures had to be read by another, standing in his place. At other times he would be assisted to his chair and read half of the lecture. At home various literary tasks were on his hands, and under the gentle pressure of his wife's monitions, or the more weighty stress of some practical necessity, were carried fitfully forward. At last the brain, unnaturally tasked for so many years, gave way. Congestion of the brain set in, and the strong man was laid low in death, May 6, 1856.

In the last hour of his conscious life he gave utterance to the trust on which his heart was stayed, in those words of the Hebrew psalmist, grand in their simple beauty and inexhaustible significance, "Thy rod and thy staff, they comfort me." The best spirit of his life and work is expressed in the following words, inscribed upon his tombstone:

"His aim was, by a pure philosophy, to teach that now we see through a glass darkly, now we know in part; his hope that, in the life to come, he should see face to face, and know even as also he is known."

CHAPTER XI.

JOHN STUART MILL.

JOHN STUART MILL was preëminently his father's son. Doubtless, in the thoughts and feelings of every man, regarded purely as a scientific phenomenon, or in what may be termed the visible, historic or natural, as distinguished from the invisible or spiritual character of every one, there will be found a more or less complete correlation with his intellectual and moral environment. To this extent he is said to be the product of his circumstances. Education, as it is perhaps oftenest understood, namely, in the sense of *training*, consists precisely in the adjustment of circumstances, the shaping of environment, in the hope of bringing forth the type of empirical character which corresponds, by natural or habitual correlation, to the means employed; and this in distinction from, and to the exclusion of, that other, more profound, more essential and, indeed, indispensable part of true education, which lies in the awakening and stimulating of free, vital powers, through the enkindling communication of the sparks of a genuine ideal life from the educator. The former, or drill, method is the one which is peculiarly adapted for application in the case of brutes — creatures mostly susceptible only of a purely mechanical culture — and if one would witness its results in their purest, most unmixed form, the best course is to visit a menagerie, or any other place where trained animals are exhibited. Very admirable, we willingly exclaim on witnessing these results — very curious, and reflecting great credit on the ingenuity of the trainer. But it will hardly occur to us to confound the process to which the brute beasts have been subjected with what is termed *education*, and to speak of *educated* birds, horses, monkeys, etc. Only human beings are capable of *education*, and that because, in their case alone, in order to *educe*, and in its full measure to call forth into actuality, the truly human element within, with all its wealth of diviner possibilities, something more is necessary than simply to catch your subjects, and then to tame and drill them. Hence the pedagogue whose excellences are exclusively those of the disciplinarian is no true educator, and I do not wonder that he is cordially hated of all youth; at the most, he only supplies the negative condition of education — a condition, indeed, whose urgent necessity is not only freely to be admitted, but most earnestly to be insisted upon; yet, after all, only a condition, or background, not the essence of education. The latter is only accomplished, in the highest sense, when the soul is awakened to the consciousness of an ideal purpose, as that which constitutes the radicle of its own nature — of a possibility or possibilities of character and life, the realization of which is incumbent upon itself and must be its own essentially free work, and, in general, when acquisition (knowledge, whether theoretical or practical, obtained by the way of direct literal communication) has, through the force of active, re-creative mental labor, turned to insight and acquired the virtual quality of an original, living and lasting possession (according to the phrase of Goethe,

> "Was du ererbt von deinen Vätern hast,
> Erwirb es, um es zu besitzen").

Education, in any proper sense, is thus essentially the pupil's own work. "Horse-taming Hector" must also be his own tamer, would he be effectually and to best purpose tamed. (The true educator, accordingly, is restricted to the employment of indirect means.) Or rather, as I believe, he accomplishes his best, really educating work without the conscious or intentional employment of any means, but rather through the spontaneous, enkindling flashings of his own life — his own "energy of reason," his own "energy of love."

It follows, from all that has been said, that any attempt to apply to a human being the drill method, pure and simple, must always be attended with an element of uncertainty in its results, since it leaves out of the reckoning that most important of all factors, the moral freedom, the free, creative intelligence, of the pupil, which is liable at any moment to take matters into its own hands, and thus to upset the most confident calculations of the would-be *trainer*. Still the method is sometimes used with fearful success, the consequence then being that the free soul of the pupil is blinded and dazed — effectually held captive — and that the man becomes a machine, or, at most, a parrot. John Stuart Mill spoke out of an abundant experience when he said, "The power of education [training] is almost boundless" (Essays on Religion, p. 82).

For, in a very peculiar sense, John Stuart Mill was the result of a deliberate course of training, and that at the hands of one — his father — whose philosophy wholly excluded from recognition the human soul and human freedom, and who, accordingly, regarded education wholly as an affair of drill. We shall thus find the younger Mill bearing very conspicuously the marks of a machine-made, in distinction from a self-made, man. At the same time we shall find that the independent, personal, vital factor in him, though permanently obfuscated, was (naturally) not annihilated, and that its rather blind, but most earnest and most persistent, attempts to assert itself are the source of all that is most interesting in his life, and most significant (though also most confusing, because apparently most contradictory) in his philosophy. We must first, now, consider what sort of a man his trainer was.

The father of John Stuart Mill was a Scotchman. His grandfather was a master shoemaker, doing at one time a prosperous business at Northwater Bridge, a small hamlet, where his children were born. The eldest of these, James Mill (the name seems to have been spelt, indifferently, Mill or Milne), born in 1773, showing excellent capacities, it was determined that he should receive more than a common education. It seems to have been his mother — described as a "proud woman," descended from an historic, but latterly unfortunate, family — who especially insisted upon this, and did everything in her power to smooth the way for her son. Doubtless, too, the father, a man of rigorous Scotch piety, would enter sympathetically into the project, in the hope that his son, provided with due learning, might become a pillar of the kirk in its public ministry. At all events, through the efforts of his parents (principally, if not exclusively) he was provided with a sufficient preliminary education, and subsequently through the favor of Lady Jane Stuart (whose husband's name reappears in the name of the principal subject of this chapter), he was enabled to go through a course of study at the University of Edinburgh, with a view to entering the ministry. In due time he was licensed to preach, but, not obtaining an appointment to his liking, repaired, in the year 1802, in the company of Sir John Stuart, to London, there to begin the career of an unusually energetic literary Bohemian. For a period of seventeen years he maintained an incessant activity as newspaper editor, review writer, translator and author; earning, a part of the time, a rather precarious subsistence, as is shown by the following query, addressed by him to a friend in Scotland, in a letter written five years after his coming to London (Feb. 7, 1807), and which I cite for the additional reason that it shows that the writer was not yet conscious of any insuperable moral or intellectual difficulty, separating him from the christian ministry. The query runs, "Have you no good kirk yet in your neighbourhood, which you could give me, and free me from this life of toil and anxiety which I lead here?" Meanwhile he bore witness to the fact of his participation in our common human nature by falling (presumably) in love, getting married (at any rate), and proceeding to rear a large family, "conduct than which," says his son in his autobiography—in view of the circumstance that he had "no resource but the precarious one of writing in periodicals"—"nothing could be more opposed, both as a matter of good sense and of duty, to the opinions which, at least at a later period of life, he strenuously upheld." This marriage took place in the year 1805, and on the 20th of May in the following year John Stuart, the first of eight children, was born.

Two years later James Mill formed an acquaintance through which a decisive influence was exerted upon the subsequent turn of his mind and character. This was the acquaintance of Jeremy Bentham, the noted projector of law reforms (concerning which, it is interesting and characteristic to note, he put himself, somewhat quixotically, in direct personal communication not only with the crowned heads of Europe, but also with the President and the several Governors of the United States), and famous as the defender of utilitarianism in ethics. Bentham was an eighteenth-century type of character, lasting way over into the nineteenth. Him the spirit of the self-styled era of enlightenment possessed, the spirit which prided itself on its freedom from illusions, and whose greatest illusion was just this pride. He was a Philistine *à outrance*, who thought that all that mankind needed to know, and, duly viewed, all that they were really able to know, was on what side their bread was buttered, and that if renouncing all pretense of any other, more exalted knowledge, and trampling on the abuses directly or indirectly sheltered under such pretense, they would keep to what they had, namely, to sensible matter of fact, and make the most of it, human life would acquire the priceless advantage of assuming a scientific form and become one uniform mass of sensible felicity. Bentham belongs preëminently to the class of intellectual cave-dwellers who deny the light which fails to reach them. I speak now, naturally, of Bentham, having reference primarily to his universal or, if you please, philosophical point of view, to the metaphysical assumptions (or denials) which fix the limits of his conception of the world and of human life. And this I do, not without reason, surely: for has not J. S. Mill told us, in his essay on Bentham, that the "first question in regard to any man of speculation is, What is his theory of human life?" I am not, therefore, concerned to discuss

— far less still to deny — the value of any services which Bentham may have rendered in the correction of practical abuses in law and judicial practice, or in the suggestion of better forms of law and procedure. Nor would I have Bentham deprived of any credit due him for his political liberalism and practical philanthropy. I say only that Bentham, first through the reading of Helvétius (according to his own confession), and then of Hume, Hartley, Priestley, and Paley, was led to the adoption of principles which he thus unequivocally expresses at the beginning of his introduction to the Principles of Morals and Legislation: "Nature has placed mankind under the governance of two sovereign masters, *pain* and *pleasure*. It is for them alone to point out what we ought to do, as well as to determine what we shall do. On the one hand, the standard of right and wrong, on the other the chain of causes and effects, are fastened to their throne." This is the metaphysical — or quasi-metaphysical — kernel of Benthamism.

James Mill, being introduced to Bentham and to the small circle of Bentham's intimate friends, soon became one of his most ardent and uncompromising disciples. — indeed, by general admission, the foremost and ablest of them. On the other hand, Bentham was equally attracted by Mill, desiring much of his company, and being able, through his pecuniary independence, to secure it by means which, in addition to their adaptation to this immediate end, were also well fitted (whether thus intended or not) to foster in Mill a sense of material obligation, if not even of dependence. At his invitation, Mill, with his family, for a number of successive summers, resided with Bentham several months as his guests, in the country. Besides, Bentham bought a valuable house near his own city residence and rented it to Mill for the same price that he had been paying for inferior quarters elsewhere. In the society of Bentham and his friends Mill soon fell into practical atheism, and, in philosophy, into unqualified sensationalism. God, religion, ideal obligations, love, privilege, were obsolete ideas, pernicious myths, prejudices. Nothing was known, or knowable, or certain, but sensations. As a student at Edinburgh, James Mill had already shown a marked interest in philosophical subjects. The lectures of Dugald Stewart on psychology and moral science had fascinated him. Prof. Bain has been able, by consulting old registers of the University Library, to ascertain what books he drew from the library while a student. Among these are many books on philosophical topics, and it is especially curious to notice that the record of books drawn and studied by Mill contains evidence that, in Prof. Bain's phrase, he made at this time a "dead set at Plato." The form which his matured views finally assumed was anything but Platonic; it was, indeed, absolutely anti-Platonic; yet it affords touching evidence of the fascination exerted over him by the golden-tongued ancient master, that in directing the education of his eldest son special stress was laid by him on the study of Plato, and apparently of Plato alone among the ancient philosophers, and that in the final exposition of his own views (in the work entitled Analysis of the Phenomena of the Human Mind) he defends Plato against the alleged mysticism of his expositors, in the conviction that the real, original Plato agreed with him — with Mill, the direct intellectual descendant of Hume and Hartley, and their continuator — the uncompromisingly idealistic realist with the no less uncompromisingly sensationalistic nominalist! (J. S. Mill expresses a somewhat similar view in his Autobiography, p. 22.)

Before finishing with James Mill, it will be necessary, for the sake of properly characterizing both himself and the intellectual heritage to which he was determined that his son should succeed, to say a word concerning his work just mentioned, and concerning the important, but, till lately (and then principally through the filial labors of J. S. Mill) insufficiently recognized place occupied by James Mill in the history of British speculation. Hume, it will be remembered, had reduced mind to a series of impressions and ideas, themselves so many distinct existences, which were variously combined under the operation of certain recognizable, but otherwise inexplicable, principles of association. After him, though still in Hume's lifetime, but without any acknowledged reference to the particular suggestions of Hume, David Hartley, a pious but somewhat heretical physician, applied himself to show, in detail, how the mental nature of man could be fully explained — sensations only being given — according to purely mechanical laws of association, themselves founded on alleged laws of vibration in the "white medullary substance of the brain, medullary substance, and nerves which proceed from them." Curiously enough, the application which Hartley made of this doctrine was — not to demonstrate that nothing but sensations and their laws of association can be known, — but that nothing is either really known or exists but God: man, as an independent or quasi-independent being, is an illusion; he is, in Spinozistic phrase, but a mode of God, who, in fact, is strictly "all in all." Hartley's doctrine respecting association was adopted and, against the Scotch common-sense school, vigorously defended by Dr. Jos. Priestley, the Unitarian divine, who occupies so honorable a place as a discoverer and experimenter in chemical science. It is this doctrine, reëngrafted — obviously without difficulty — upon Hume's metaphysical negativism, which James Mill took up and further developed, and to which he gave classic expression in his Phenomena of the Human Mind — written in the summer holidays of the years 1823 to 1829, when J. S. Mill was seventeen to twenty-three years of age, and published in 1829. There is in the book an affectation of simplicity, amounting sometimes almost to positive puerility, and suggesting distinctly the tone of a father addressing children whom it is especially necessary to guard against any possible danger of illusion. We have here unquestionably the reflex of some of the instructions previously dinned by the father into the son's young ears, the substance of fundamental opinions which it was meant — and not in vain — that the son should accept as common-places not to be questioned. The book adds nothing to what had been previously said by Hume and Hartley (and Bentham), except a peculiar ingenuity of development, a more complete systematic form, and a delusive appearance of perspicuity, along with a resolute consistency, which fears no consequences. Our knowledge, it is held, is only of sensations and the mechanical laws of their coexistence and sequence. Such conceptions as *substantial existence* and *power* are names, at most, for our ignorance. Science, for the most part, consists only of skillful contrivances for naming our sensations. We shall see how faithful the son remained, or sought to remain, to these instructions.

I will only add, concerning James Mill, that he possessed, in addition to an ample fund of native Scotch probity and thrift, indomitable mental energy and industry, and was resolved to exact the same, with interest, from his children. His manner with them was stern, and even repellent. "After John," says Prof. Bain, "the next elder children seem to have disappointed him, and he never looked upon them with any complacency." "His entering the room where the family was assembled was observed by strangers to operate as an immediate damper. This was not the worst. The one really disagreeable trait in [James] Mill's character, and the thing that has left the most painful memories, was the way that he allowed himself to speak and behave to his wife and children before visitors" (Mind, No. VIII, Oct. 1877).

This was the man, and such as above described were the principles and attachments of the man, who, a son being given him, was resolved so to educate him — so to *make his mind* (to adapt the language employed by the elder Mill) — that he might be "a worthy successor" of both himself and Bentham (letter to Bentham in 1812). "It was a bold hope, but one destined to be fully realized," says Fox Bourne (in a sketch of J. S. Mill's life), who also remarks upon the "jealous interest" with which Bentham appears to have watched the boy's education. The father, in addition to labors of the most engrossing kind, took his son's training into his own hand, and gave him a hot-bed education, the like of which has, I fancy, rarely been known. With the details of it, as given in J. S. Mill's autobiography, many are already acquainted. New information respecting it has lately been presented to the world by Prof. Bain (in recent numbers of "Mind").

The whole is simply amazing. At the age of three years (so people told him; at all events when he was so young that in after years he could not recall the time) he began to learn Greek, by means of "lists of common Greek words, with their signification in English," written out for him on cards by his father. By the time he was eight years old he had read Æsop's Fables, the whole or a part of Xenophon's Anabasis, the whole of Herodotus and of Xenophon's Cyropædia and Memorials of Socrates, some of the lives of the philosophers by Diogenes Laertius, part of Lucian, two orations of Isocrates, and six dialogues of Plato. Of these latter, Mill remarks that one of them, at least, might better, in his judgment, have been omitted, as it was totally impossible that he should understand it. But, he continues, "my father, in all his teaching, demanded of me not only the utmost that I could do, but much that I could by no possibility have done." It is only fair to add that the father was himself ready to perform what would have seemed for him — an exceedingly impatient man — next to impossible, namely, in the absence, at that date, of Greek-English lexicons, to serve patiently, himself, as a lexicon for his son, who, sitting at the same table where his father was engaged in the long and serious labor of writing his history of British India, and in other literary occupations, was permitted at any moment to interrupt him for the purpose of asking the meaning of a new Greek word. In addition to this Greek reading, evening lessons in arithmetic were given him by his father. Further, he was left free a considerable time, and encouraged to read English books according to his taste. These were mostly histories, including Robertson, Hume, Gibbon, Watson's Philip the Second and Third,

14

Hooke's History of Rome, a portion of Rollin's Ancient History, Plutarch (translated), Burnett's History of his Own Time, the historical part of the Annual Register down to 1788; all this on his own account; then, further, by his father's direction, Millar's Historical View of the English Government, Mosheim's Ecclesiastical History, McCrie's Life of John Knox, and Sewell's and Rutty's Histories of the Quakers. As he read he made notes of the subject-matter on slips of paper, which served as memoranda for the report his father required him daily to give of his reading, while they were taking their morning walk before breakfast. At the same time his father would discuss with him the subjects of his reading, and in particular he used, says Mill, "as opportunity offered, to give me explanations and ideas respecting civilization, government, morality, mental cultivation, which he required me afterwards to restate to him in my own words." Thus at an age when most boys are rolling hoops, flying kites, learning their letters. or, at most, reading story-books, with words of one or two syllables, Mill was deeply immersed in ancient history and philosophy, as well as in modern history and the rudiments of his father's philosophy. A few works of travel, it is true, were placed in his hands by his father, and read by him with great satisfaction. Of playthings he had none; of children's books only one, Robinson Crusoe, in which we may imagine that he took a doubly intense delight, after all that had practically been done to wean and starve whatever boyish fancy he may have had. He was also permitted to read, from borrowed copies, Arabian Nights. Cazotte's Arabian Tales, Don Quixote, Miss Edgeworth's Popular Tales, and Brooke's Fool of Quality. It will be admitted that all this was a great deal to have been done by one scarcely more than a prattling infant. Mill's youthful brain was a docile and effective engine, which wrought mechanical wonders under the direction of so untiring and exacting an engineer as his father. It was a case of high pressure *training*, if not of soul-emancipating and soul-enlarging *education*. That, of which the absence is most painfully felt, is the encouragement of filial love, and of reverence for a divine ideal and a divine reality, whose light and life are the true light and life of men.

According to this beginning, mainly, Mill's education went forward to the end. In his eighth year he begins to learn Latin, and at the same time to assist his father in the instruction of the younger children of the family — a work which he was compelled to continue until he reached his maturity; the whole family appear to have been exclusively home-taught. At the same time he reads, for his first Greek poetry, the Iliad. Pope's translation of the Iliad he declares that he subsequently read through as many as twenty or thirty times. But it is unnecessary to run through all the details of his work and reading in the following years. The materials for an account of them may be found in his autobiography, and still more in Prof. Bain's articles (especially Mind, No. XIV). I add only that as early as his seventh year he made his *début* in authorship, through the composition of a brief Roman history, founded on Hooke. This was followed up by other attempts in the following years, some of them in verse, *e.g.* one book in continuation of Homer's Iliad; some, too, in the form of tragedies. It is worthy of notice that his father required of him, as a task, the writing of English verse, after he had once begun it of his own accord; and this, not because he possessed, or his philosophy allowed, any conception of poetry as a spontaneous, irresistible, organically creative inspiration, but because, looking at the matter with purely utilitarian eyes, the poetic form seemed to be indeed a better contrivance than prose for expressing some things, and also because (in Mill's words) "people in general attached more value to verse than it deserved, and the power of writing it was, on this account, worth acquiring." (Autobiography, p. 15.) One would have supposed that this should have been a sufficient reason for seeking, by example as well as precept, to bring "people in general" to better knowledge! It cannot occasion surprise that James Mill, as (like Bentham) a genuine son of the eighteenth century, and determined adherent of an utilitarian, mechanical "philosophy," agreed with Hume and Voltaire in depreciating the prince of poets, Shakespeare, and used, as we are told, severely to attack the English idolatry of him. J. S. Mill freely admits that this course of training did not make him a poet! Mill mentions that he used to sing Dryden's Alexander's Feast, and some of Walter Scott's songs, "internally," to music of his own; some of the airs which he thus composed he remembered late in his life. Music remained, to the end of Mill's life, his favorite art.

In his twelfth year, Mill's father began with him a careful course of logical training. In the same year, as his father's History of India was going through the press, he read the manuscript aloud while his father corrected the proofs. This practice seems to have contributed admirably toward the father's purpose of "making" his son's mind according to his own notions, for Stuart Mill vaunts the "number of new ideas which [he] received from this remarkable book, and the impulse and stimulus, as well as guidance, given to [his] thoughts by its criticisms and disquisitions on society and civilization"; and he was, and till the end of his life remained, impressed with it as "one of the books from which most benefit may be derived by a *mind in the course of making up its opinions.*" In the next year he was taken by his father "through a complete course of political economy."

I pass lightly over the account of his year's residence in France, in the family of Sir Samuel Bentham, brother of Jeremy Bentham. During this period a journal of his doings was kept by Mill and forwarded to his father, along with disquisitions on all sorts of grave topics. Portions of this journal are communicated by Prof. Bain. The evidence of work done is, as Bain well remarks, simply stupendous. The boy kept almost constantly at his books from long before breakfast till the afternoon dinner, and then again in the evening. To this were added lessons in music and dancing. At Montpellier he attended courses of lectures at the *Faculté des Sciences*, on chemistry, zoology, and logic — the latter by M. Gergonne, whom Mill terms "a very accomplished representative of the eighteenth century metaphysics," substantially his father's and his own. Of the distinguished Frenchmen whom he met, Laplace is mentioned, and M. Say, the political economist, at whose house he was for a short time entertained as a guest, and where he met, among others, Saint-Simon, Auguste Comte's master, and subsequently notorious on account of his socialistic theories.

In Mill's own view, the greatest advantage which he derived from his residence in France was "that of having breathed for a whole year the free and genial atmosphere of continental life." He felt, he declares, although without stating it clearly to himself, the "contrast between the frank sociability and amiability of French personal intercourse, and the English mode of existence in which everybody acts as if everybody else (with few or no exceptions) was either an enemy or a bore." He professes subsequently to have perceived that this state of things, "among the ordinary English," arises from "the absence of interest in things of an unselfish kind . . . reducing them, considered as spiritual beings, to a kind of negative existence." Are we to see in this a reflection on the circumstances which surrounded Mill's own youth? Was it that he was already obscurely conscious of the disharmony between the purely intellectual, ungenial, chilling, mechanical training which was intended to render him the inheritor and continuator of others' (namely, his father's and Bentham's) modes of thought, and a possibility of his own nature, which only needed the quickening warmth, the *educating* influence, of a sympathetic moral atmosphere to cause it to blossom out in rich forms of genuine life, far grander than anything of which his teachers practically had, or admitted, any conception?

For, were I to pause here and state beforehand — as the occasion tempts me to do — the conception of John Stuart Mill, which I have derived from a careful study of his life and works, I should say that he was utterly inexplicable, except on the theory of such a disharmony existing as matter of fact, whether he was more, or less, or not at all, clearly conscious of it and of its meaning. The training which he received, I may premise, was thoroughly successful. Of the correctness of the "views" held by his father, and by the school to which he belonged, he was perfectly convinced. Other, clear, theoretical convictions he had, in the main, none. But these convictions, though professedly covering exhaustively the whole realm of knowable *existence*, really touched only the merest surface of the realm of truth and *being*. So far as they anyway related to the inner substance of this realm, to its life, its power, its vital reality, they consisted simply in negations and denials. But the foundations of Mill's nature — as of every man's nature — were laid deeper than this. That by which man takes hold on — participates in — being, lies deeper than the surface. It is ideal and vital, not only phenomenal. It is organic, not simply atomic. It is power, energy of intelligence and will and love, and not merely blind force and fate. And I have yet to be convinced that that man exists — for *real existence* is nothing but incarnate truth — who does not, at least at some epochs in his life, betray by sympathetic, even if unconfessed, vibrations of the inmost, truest nature, the harmony in which that nature would fain place itself with essential truth and essential being. Some men succeed more completely than others in concealing from themselves and the world the practical, visible, or, rather, to change the figure, audible evidence of this undertone, which betokens an essential nature, upon which all that is termed phenomenal — the empirical consciousness, "*states* of consciousness," "facts" of mental coëxistence and sequence — is but a superficial incrustation, and which wholly eludes the grasp, or, better, overflows the limits of those mathematical or inductive formulæ which express the utmost attainable results of phenomenal science. James Mill possessed the power to do this to a far greater degree than his son. True, the latter remained to the end, in profession and intention, faithful to the letter and spirit of his father's method. But his vital experience was constantly wresting from him admissions, the full theoretical significance of which was lost for him, through his persistent attempt to make them appear consistent with the method in question, or, that failing, to put them off as ultimate, impenetrable, though indefeasible, facts, incapable of being comprehended by any method. In other words, the man Mill was infinitely broader than his — for the most part negative — philosophy. And when Prof. Jevons says, with truth, that "there is hardly one of his more important and peculiar doctrines which he has not himself amply refuted," I interpret this as due to the practical conflict in Mill between a narrow philosophy, which he was successfully trained to wear through life, as a kind of intellectual straight-jacket, and a native richness and grandeur of essential humanity — *i.e.* of essential *being* — which could be hampered and distorted, but not suppressed. This conflict always appears in the case of natures, not essentially frivolous and frothy, whose lines of thought and intellectual conviction, being essentially physical, and exterior, are utterly incommensurate with the felt depths of interior, spiritual being. Spinoza is an illustrious case in point. It is the ideal nature overflowing the boundaries vainly set for it, that constitutes the peculiar moral attractiveness of such men for all serious minds. It is this that, in spite of Mill's provokingly hard-headed obstinacy in bandaging his own eyes — perhaps, rather, in consequence of it — contributes an element of grave, quiet, sadness to the impression derived from the contemplation of his character, which to noble minds is really touching and winning. In support of this general judgment upon Mill, I shall presently adduce particular proofs. But first, I shall recall, in brief summary, the remaining incidents of his life.

Returning from France in the middle of 1821, the remainder of the year and the larger portion of the following one were given to psychological studies. Condillac, Locke, Helvétius, Hartley, Berkeley, Hume, Reid, Dugald Stewart, Brown on Cause and Effect (it is in this order that they are mentioned by Mill), were the authors studied. It is expressly mentioned, that of Locke and Helvétius his father required him to make abstracts, accompanied by comments of his own, which were afterward read by or to his father, and thoroughly discussed. At the same time he made a beginning of reading law with John Austin, in connection with which his father put into his hands Dumont's redaction of Bentham's Principles of Morals and Legislation. His previous education, he admits, "had been, in a certain sense, already a course of Benthamism." But the reading of this book was like a new and original revelation of what he had already been told. It was, he says, one of the turning-points in his mental history. It made him "a different being." The principle of utility, of which the book was an extended application, took such hold of him that, through its influence, he who had been "brought up from the first without any religious belief," now had (says he) "in one of the best senses of the term, a religion." It lighted up his life, and gave a definite shape to his aspirations.

Here again, then, we find Mill giving visible evidence of a nature which demanded the food — craved the education and encouragement — which his teacher did not give. There was the felt want of a religion of some kind, and Mill, throwing himself with an unusually noble ardor into the first thing that seemed able to supply the deficiency — into a system which, he then thought, opened up an indefinite "vista of improvement" for the human race, and for the practical realization of which he could labor with all his heart — thought that he had at last a religion, but only to be quickly undeceived. At the same time the reading of another work, founded on Bentham's manuscripts, and entitled "Analysis of the Influence of Natural Religion on the Temporal Happiness of Mankind," convinced him of the impossibility (revelation being of course out of the question) that an intelligent being (naturally in the Benthamic sense of this expression) should hold any other than such a quasi-religion as he had adopted. Burning as with the ardor of a young convert, he founded a utilitarian society, composed of a few members, among whom he was the leading spirit, and who held their meetings in Bentham's house. This society continued in existence for two or three years. In the year 1824, only eighteen years of age, he wrote three articles for the newly founded organ of liberalism, the Westminster Review. From this time on, throughout his life, he continued a prolific contributor to newspapers and other periodicals. In the next year, 1825, he was largely occupied with editing Bentham's treatise on evidence, learnt German, and founded a speculative debating society, which met at the house of Mr. Grote, the historian. The meetings of this society were continued three or four years, during which such works as his father's Political Economy and Analysis of the Phenomena of the Human Mind, and also logical topics, were taken up.

In 1826, at the age of twenty years, occurred that remarkable crisis in his mental history, the account of which constitutes the most suggestive chapter in his autobiography. It was, after all allowance has been made for the depressing influence of nerves overstrained by constant intellectual training, simply a fresh bursting by his own spirit of the bonds which had been laid upon it. From Bentham he had learnt that the greatest sensible, or immediate, happiness of the greatest number of individuals was the true end of life and labor, and to this he had ardently assented. He now realized that, if this end were attained, he, for one, should still be unsatisfied. He accordingly sunk into a state of dejection, which only ended when, at the expiration of a protracted period of mental distress and self-questioning, he perceived that, however true the happiness-doctrine might be in theory, it would not hold in individual practice. While, with that peculiar doggedness of intellect which would not permit him to deny the theoretical convictions in which he had been drilled, he still continued, and that to the end of his life, to maintain that "happiness is the test of all rules of conduct and the end of life," he perceived that it was to be attained only by treating it as if it were not the end. It was only to be secured as an incident to the prosecution of some other "ideal end." "Aiming thus at something else, [men] find happiness by the way." This is precisely the doctrine of the moralists whom Mill, as an abstract reasoner, professedly opposed, from Plato and Aristotle down to the present day. It were easy to indicate the source and the precise nature of Mill's confusion. I content myself now with pointing out this new instance of the fact that Mill's vital practical experience carried him far beyond the terms of the theory which he had learned, and to which he clung; nay, more, into admissions in flat contradiction with it. It was only because the presuppositions of his theory allowed no place for the larger truth which he felt, and on which he proceeded in no small measure to act, and because he would not revise those presuppositions so as to make them square with facts of vital experience, that he was obliged in theorizing either to ignore these facts, or else, at a loss of consistency, which no words avail to conceal, to gloss them over and seek to make them appear as an obvious corollary from premises in which these very facts were denied beforehand. It is interesting to note that it was precisely from Wordsworth, the poet-philosopher of mind directly opposite to that in which he had been brought up, that in the next-following years Mill derived greatest comfort and spiritual furtherance, and that through personal intercourse with men so far removed in spirit from his earlier utilitarian associates as John Sterling, Frederick Maurice, and Carlyle, he received further spiritual invigoration. Those who have assented to the views set forth in the beginning of the fourth chapter of this volume (on Shakespeare) will not think it strange that Mill, possessing some of that which may be called the vital philosophic susceptibility, should have found it ministered to by the poet, the seer, and the divine. Yet all this, of so great practical significance to him, he sought to put off or conceal under such phrases as "culture of the feelings," "internal culture," "the reaction of the nineteenth century against the eighteenth,"— interesting phenomena, indeed, which it were highly unjust and uncandid to ignore, but which have no deeper ascertainable ontological significance than mere matter-of-fact associated sensations, or "states of consciousness," which are the atomic ultimates of the whole experiential and sceptical philosophy.

In the year 1836 Mill was obliged, on account of an illness in the head, to ask for three months' leave of absence from the place in the India House, where his father, who died in this year, had served since 1819 or 1820, and he himself since 1823. Three years later he was obliged to absent himself still longer. Nothing but his excellent physical constitution had made him hold out so long under the constant mental strain, without vacations, to which since his infancy he had been, first perforce, and then voluntarily, subjected. In the same year his brother Henry died from just such an overstrain.

In 1843 was published his system of logic, which had been on the stocks for several years. The unusual attention which it attracted, and the marked influence exerted by it for a quarter of a century, have now become a matter of history. Mill's object was to counterwork the theory that there is in the human mind any source of certitude, or any universality or necessity inherent *a priori* in the forms of knowledge, independently of individual "experience." (One of Mill's abundant contradictions is the profession of this purpose, and the disavowal, almost in the same breath, of any intention to prejudice the decision of metaphysical questions!) But the observant student notices that in the most important portions of his discussion he is ever and anon introducing, with a naïve innocency of bearing, at once refreshing and irritating, under the names of "belief," "persuasion," "natural prompting," and the like, the very *a priori*, universal, organic, rational, and recreative element, which he would exclude, and which he then seeks to make it appear that he has deduced, either strictly, or, in his phrase — a strange phrase for a logician to employ—"as far as any human purpose requires," from pure observation and "objective," physico-psychological "experience." If it were possible to have a double logic, of which one part, under the name of *phenomenal logic*, and appropriated to the scientific treatment of *phenomena* (sensible appearances) as objects of knowledge, could be wholly severed from the other, which should be called real logic, and should formulate the methods of real, substantive, or philosophical knowledge, we might say that Mill's work was an attempt to supply the former; but an attempt fatally unsuccessful, if judged by the puzzlingly uncertain statement of its data, and the abundant *non-sequiturs* found in all its polemical part. Through repeated and extended references in his logic Mill did much to call the attention of Englishmen to Auguste Comte, the founder of the French school of Positivists.

In 1848 followed the work on Political Economy.

In the year 1851 occurred Mill's marriage to Mrs. Taylor, the "almost infallible counsellor," whose friendship and assistance he had previously enjoyed for many years, and whose memory, after their brief married life of seven and a half years, had been terminated by her death, remained to him a "religion." More remarkable and touching devotion to the memory of a woman has rarely been shown than that paid by Mill to the memory of his wife, in his Autobiography, and in the introductory page of his (or, as he says, their joint) work, "On

Liberty." It is not only in most marked contrast with his father's unchivalrous, not to say brutally unkind, treatment of his own wife (J. S. Mill, too, has nothing to say, in his Autobiography, of his mother), but is also another passionate manifestation of that potentiality of essential human life which was wholly ignored in his training.

I scarcely need to mention his other works, his Representative Government, Subjection of Women, Examination of the Philosophy of Sir William Hamilton, Utilitarianism (contained in his Dissertations and Discussions), or the honorable circumstances of his entrance into parliament, to procure which he manfully refused to conciliate voters by the utterance of the half truths or downright falsehoods of the demagogue, or make any direct or indirect use of pecuniary "arguments," or his creditable, though brief, career in parliament. A large part of every year after his wife's death, or as much as was practicable, he passed near her grave in the south of France, in "communion with her memory." There his death ensued on the 8th of May, 1873.

To recapitulate, now, what has already been foreshadowed, or perhaps, even, with sufficient distinctness stated, respecting Mill's philosophical and human attitude and quality, and to furnish the "particular proofs" promised, a short space may suffice. I have said, virtually, that Mill possessed a considerable degree of heat, with little or no light. By virtue of his very existence he participated through the roots of his being in the universal being, which all truly positive philosophy (it is a curious illustration of the topsyturviness of ideas in certain quarters, including those frequented by Mill, that what is now-a-days popularly known as "*the* Positive

Philosophy" is a body of doctrines which, on their philosophical side, are wholly negative) declares, and ever has declared, as it ever must, to be life and action, power, spirit, and the power of this participation wrought in him as a sort of dim instinct, a hidden flame, ever and anon bursting the shell of negations in which it was enveloped, disturbing and confusing the computations in which it was an unacknowledged factor; but, for the rest, ignored, or explained away as only a (substanceless) phenomenon like any other, or, if it forced more explicit recognition, put, in a highly unphilosophical manner, into the basket reserved for nuts too hard to crack, and to which, therefore, it were frivolous and useless to pay further attention. This was the heat-element, which bore more fruit, as may, from the foregoing, well be imagined, in Mill's life than in his doctrine. Of the light-element, in the sense of *speculative insight*, few persons to whom the term philosopher has been popularly applied ever possessed less of it than Mill. It was a fundamental tenet of the philosophy which he inherited and adopted, that such insight was impossible, and the very notion of it preposterous. Almost the whole of that which in Great Britain had for two hundred years passed for philosophy, had consisted, essentially, in a laborious attempt to prove the non-existence, or non-attainability, of the very conditions of philosophy. The effect of this upon the English mind Mill recognized and deplored; its cause wholly escaped him. With a touch, let us hope, of exaggeration, he complained of the absence among the English youth of his time "of the ardor of research, the eagerness for large and comprehensive inquiry, [characteristic] of the educated part of the

French and German youth. . . . Out of the narrow bounds of mathematical and physical science" he professed to find "not a vestige of a reading and thinking public engaged in the investigation of truth *as* truth, in the prosecution of thought for the sake of thought." Here it is the "heat" in Mill that speaks. But with a provoking deficiency of philosophical light (*insight, knowledge,*) he proceeded to do all in his power to cultivate further those intellectual conditions from which the intellectual apathy, of which he complained, had in the largest measure sprung. For of what did he complain? Of the confinement of intellectual interest within "the narrow bounds of mathematical and physical science." But the whole stress of English philosophy, taking its cue from Bacon, had been laid on the pretended proof (in reality only the dogmatic assertion) that outside of the boundaries of mathematical and physical science, and apart from the method employed and the presuppositions adopted in such science, nothing further was to be known, except the "negative truth" (in Mill's phrase) that further knowledge was impossible. This tendency reached its extreme logical outcome in David Hume and James Mill, J. S. Mill's particular guiding-stars. All that which, according to them, can be known, whether of nature or mind, is reduced to the merest surface-facts of consciousness, pure mental phenomena, "impressions," "feelings," opaque facts of mental experience, superficially visible, numerically distinguishable, but otherwise incomprehensible and inexplicable. Mill's logic is intended as one long and elaborate (though partly indirect) enforcement of this view. Being and power, the two fundamental conceptions of philosophy, the polar stars of speculative insight, are summarily put out of court, or, if admitted in name, it is only as a professedly necessary accommodation to popular phraseology and, for the rest, as mere names for our ignorance, *i.e.* for nothing. Being and power are, indeed, not physical conceptions. They lie behind and explain the physical realm of knowledge, but are not contained in it as such. The attempt to realize them as physical conceptions, or to discover them by physical methods of sensible observation and experiment, necessarily fails. Hence they are, by the school which —with what would have to be termed unparalleled effrontery, did it not proceed from pure blindness — terms itself "experiential," declared *non avenus*. Causation, the law and substantive manifestation of power, is reduced to matter-of-fact succession and nothing else, and being, to less than its own shadow, namely, only to a "permanent possibility" (whatever that may mean) of its shadow, projected in the form of feeling. Mill complains, further, of the lack of a disposition to investigate "truth *as* truth," or to prosecute "thought for the sake of thought." But the pillars of "truth *as* truth" are universal and commanding, and the "prosecution of thought for the sake of thought" presupposes that there is something to be prosecuted under the name of "thought," and a power or faculty with which to prosecute it. But Mill's philosophy—which is nothing but empirical psychology, arbitrarily universalized and put, to its own injury, in the place of philosophy — has no eye for such truth. It expressly denies its attainability, or that there is evidence of its existence. All knowledge is made intensely subjective, individual, being confined to particular states of consciousness, and to the actually observed, but, by express declaration, not necessary, and otherwise unfathomable, order which exists among them. Accordingly, also, no provision is made for thought, as something which, if it, and an organ appropriate to it, exist, is necessarily something other than mere atomic or complex *states* of consciousness. No provision is made for the recognition of any mental *activity* whatsoever, and, such activity being nevertheless presupposed, nothing is left for it to do but to stare at and analyze its own "states." We must say that Mill had a dull sense of the proper ideal of philosophy, but that the method and presuppositions which training had caused to be to him as a second nature, led him at every step by which he sought to approach it, not toward, but away from it.

The predecessors of Mill—Hume and James Mill—with a systematic consistency which necessitated a sublimely reckless disregard of, or appearance of blindness to, the fundamental facts of vital, intellectual experience, had reduced everything, without exception, of which man has a conception, to associated sensations. Memory, expectation, belief, personal identity, mind,—and matter as well,—all were identical with sensations, not functions or entities apart. That J. S. Mill should have perceived and frankly admitted that they were in error, does not prove that he was possessed of any specially profound philosophical insight; it is difficult to imagine how, having any insight at all and any honesty in relating what he perceived, he should have done otherwise: but it does prove that he had forced upon him some consciousness of a number of the elements or data of philosophical speculation, of which indeed he confessed his inability to make any constructive use, but to which he would not, therefore, absolutely shut his eyes. For him they are "ultimate facts," inexplicable by any theory, because not explicable by the theory or method which he had been taught and which he obstinately continued to consider as the only one appropriate to "philosophical" inquiries. Of these ultimate facts recognized by Mill, the fundamental one, on which all the others depend, is personal identity — self. In accordance with the letter and spirit of his inherited method, he defines Mind (that to which selfhood, or personal identity, should pertain, or, rather, of which it is the substantive essence) abstractly as a "permanent possibility of feeling," and concretely as a "series of feelings." But, he adds, this series of feelings is "conscious of itself as past and future." How this can be, Mill naturally finds incomprehensible, for it is absurd. It seems to point to a true "Mind, or Ego," as "something different from any series of feelings." In his Examination of the Philosophy of Sir William Hamilton, Mill is content to leave the matter as a "final inexplicability," an "ultimate" or "inexplicable fact," of such nature that when "mind" is defined as above (as a "series of feelings conscious of itself," etc.), it must be understood that the terms are used "with a reservation as to their meaning." This last phrase has a curious and dubious sound, coming from a reputed metaphysician and logician. A definition with a "reservation." And how much of a reservation? This much, namely, that the definition is to be regarded as no definition; that it omits, or describes in terms which confessedly reduce to the absurd, the nominal subject of the definition; that it is a description of *appearances*, as they present themselves to the empirical psychologist, abstracting from the *noumenon,* or essential reality, by reference to which alone they are explicable. The world did not have to wait till Mill's day to discover that in appearances as such there is contradiction. Plato knew it, and perceived that therefore it was only in a secondary sense that they could be said to be the subject of knowledge; it was the characteristic of essential or philosophical knowledge that it penetrated beneath appearances and was satisfied with nothing less than being. But the whole wisdom of sensational psychology, vainly attempting to supplant and appropriate the name of philosophy, ends where Plato's began. Superficial description takes the place of essential definition, surface-sight of insight. I hasten to add, that in his notes to the second edition of his father's Analysis of the Phenomena of the Human Mind, the assumption of a "Mind, or Ego, different from any series of feelings," no longer appears to be regarded by Stuart Mill merely as a conceivable or possibly necessary one, but as really necessary, and such mind is there described as that "impenetrable," "inner covering," that "inexplicable tie" or "bond of some sort," which, "to me, constitutes my Ego." This is equivalent to a complete confession, on the part of Mill, of the radical inability of the "experiential psychology" (arbitrarily so-called) to meet the requirements of a philosophy of mind, or of a philosophy of matter; for Mill's account of matter depends directly (notwithstanding his apparent unconsciousness of the fact) on his account of mind (see, on this latter point, the capital book by W. L. Courtney, *The Metaphysics of J. S. Mill,* London, 1879, p. 69); in other words, this psychology leads to no philosophical results at all. But we have here another illustration — and a fundamental one, since it lies at the very root of Mill's doctrine, and indeed of all philosophy — of the truth of my main thesis, namely, of the disparateness between Mill's inherited theory and method and the depths (to him, it is true, utterly obscure) of his vital experience.

Further illustrations of this conflict between the purest, most resolute externalism, and consequent superficiality, in theory, and an internal, though ever confused consciousness, or better practical knowledge, which tended to overshoot the theory on all sides, are not wanting, though, perhaps, not now needed. I will simply allude to Mill's doctrine of the will. The will he declares to be "wholly a phenomenon." This, for him, is the same as to say that it is not a power. It, and the actions said to result from it, follow the same laws of so-called physical causation, or "invariable sequence," with all other natural phenomena. This is the doctrine of necessity, as it is usually termed, in fancied opposition to the doctrine of the freedom of the human will. But the word necessity, and the doctrine called by that name, produced in Mill a feeling of unendurable oppression and dejection. It seemed synonymous with fatalism, and his own vital experience told him that it must be false. He recalled the fact that, according to the empirical doctrine of causation supported by him and his predecessors, there is no necessary connection between cause and effect, but only matter-of-fact sequence. Hence he declared triumphantly that the phrase "doctrine of necessity" was misleading, *i.e.* expressed a falsehood, and he proceeded in effect, and even in terms, to maintain a very rational doctrine of freedom, while professing only to uphold a corrected doctrine of necessity, and not freedom. (For that matter, he need not have feared to call it a doctrine of freedom, for the only intelligent defenders of freedom perceive that between necessity and freedom, properly understood, there is not opposition, but intimate alliance, the true necessity being not the enemy but the instrument, and even the essence, of the true freedom.) But, in this matter, Mill's moral nature carries him far away from the terms of his theory, and renders his exposition extremely contradictory and confused, causing him constantly to posit will as virtually far more than a powerless, mechanical phenomenon, moved only by impulsion, and to make of it a rational, and, in its measure, self-directing power.

The like could be shown concerning Mill's practical attitude with reference to other fundamental doctrines of ethical philosophy, where, while adhering as closely as possible to the terms of the theory of the natural, mechanical man, he discloses a powerful, though confused and fettered, sense of the spiritual man and its law of love and liberty, as the true ideal and end. Here he is deceived by his doctrine of inseparable association. Happiness being, by general admission, inseparably associated in idea with the realization by man of his true humanity,— *i.e.* with the attainment by him of his true end,— Mill confounds happiness, the passive state, with this end, which is essentially a condition of *active being*. But we have already seen that Mill early found that his theory (founded on such a confusion) would not hold good in practice.

Finally, a mournful instance of the moral hurt done to Mill by his thoroughly externalistic philosophy, in separating him from a clear and happy recognition of a profound ethical idealism to which his inmost nature was inclined, is furnished in the first of the posthumous essays on Religion, the essay on Nature. Here, looking at nature wholly from the outside, he finds it replete with horror and cruelty, an incarnate demon. What good, he concludes, nature brings to human beings, "is mostly the result of their own exertions." Precisely. Here only a narrow boundary separates Mill from the profound doctrine of that noblest of modern ethical philosophers, the elder Fichte, for whom the world ("nature") was simply the "material of duty," the necessary foil and instrument of human, *i.e.* moral, endeavor, the condition of the success of such endeavor, viewed apart from which, and from its laws, it was, in a radical sense, viewed in a false light and must appear full of absurdity and darkness.

It will have been observed that, in the progress of this discussion, I have looked aside, in the main, from Mill's part in discussions and agitations, which are comparatively independent of philosophical speculation, and this, both because my plan required this course, and because Mill, in these other relations, has been sufficiently appreciated by others.

I conclude that J. S. Mill's greatest personal misfortune was that he was born the son of James Mill, and not of Johann Gottlieb Fichte. He presents the appearance of a noble nature confined in intellectual fetters, which, forged for him, he himself did his best to rivet upon himself, without wholly succeeding. He attracts a sympathy at once regretful and affectionate. Perhaps his speculative failures, engraved already so conspicuously upon the tablets of the intellectual history of his race, may contribute more for the world's final instruction than the inconspicuous successes of many another less renowned.

CHAPTER XII.

HERBERT SPENCER.

HERBERT SPENCER is the leading living representative of that type of thought which we have found prevailing in British climes all along from Bacon to Mill. The sceptre so long and effectively wielded by Mill was transferred, without difficulty, into the hands of Mr. Spencer. As in the death of the former, one of his admirers, with pardonable enthusiasm of affection, but unpardonable insularity of view, deplored the loss of "not only the great philosopher, but also the great prophet, of our time," so Mr. Spencer, living, is to his followers (in the language employed by one of them) "the greatest of living philosophers," and the undoubted prophet of a new dispensation. Is the dispensation indeed a new one, or only a continuation of the old? What, too, are the prophet's credentials, and of what worth are they? These are the points which we must presently consider.

When Herbert Spencer's biography shall be written, the world may surely expect to find in it a story of peculiar interest. As yet, naturally, only a meagre outline of the facts on which it would be founded has been given to the world. Mr. Spencer was born in Derby, April 27, 1820. His father and grandfather were teachers. Owing to his imperfect health, his early education was superintended at home by his father. Much of the time he was left free to amuse and instruct himself in his own way.

Under these circumstances he developed a marked fondness for entomology, and busied himself in finding, rearing, and making drawings of various members of the insect world. He assisted his father in physical and chemical experiments, and began to indicate a peculiar aptitude (says Prof. Youmans) for "manipulation and invention." At the age of thirteen he was sent to study with his uncle, the Rev. Thomas Spencer, rector of Hinton, with whom he remained three years. Here his attention appears to have been specially directed to mathematics. On returning to Derby, it is reported that he studied perspective with his father, on the principle of independent discovery. The problems were given to him in such form that he had himself to discover, and not simply learn by rote, their solution. His father is said to have published an "Inventional Geometry," prepared on this plan. At the age of sixteen a "new and ingenious theorem in descriptive geometry" was published by Herbert Spencer in the "Civil Engineers' and Architects' Journal." In the following year he began work as a civil engineer under Charles Fox, on the London and Birmingham railway. After four years of such employment he devoted two more to mathematical and miscellaneous studies. "All the time," says a writer in the New American Encyclopædia, "he had in progress some scheme of invention, improvements in watch-making, machinery for the manufacture of type by compression of the metal instead of casting, a new form of printing-press, and the application of electrotype to engraving, afterward known as the glyptograph."

It will thus be seen that the whole stress of Spencer's early education, as well as the general bent of his mind, were preëminently mechanical and physical. The liberal training of the university was denied to him, as to Mill, and it does not appear that the lack of it was supplied for him by any such thorough course of home training in classical and historical literature as was provided for his predecessor. Indeed, such a course as Mill was put through would have been almost certainly fatal in its consequences for one of Spencer's delicate constitution.

But the taste for literary work was also early developed in Mr. Spencer. As a comparative youth he became a frequent contributor to various (mostly scientific) journals. In the year 1842 he began to publish in the "Nonconformist" a series of papers on "The Proper Sphere of Government." These papers were collected together and published in pamphlet form in the following year. In the same year he visited London in search of literary employment, but not succeeding, returned again to the practice of engineering. From 1848 to 1852 he assisted in editing the "Economist." Henceforth his life and work were those of a writer. In numerous review articles on the most varied subjects he began to set forth the applications of the conception subsequently developed by him in more systematic form — the conception of physical evolution as a universal law. His first book, which, like all his other later ones, is pervaded by the same conception, was published when he was thirty years old, in 1850, under the name of "Social Statics." In 1855 followed "The Principles of Psychology." In 1860 the prospectus of a "system of philosophy," founded on the idea of physical evolution, was announced, and to the production of it the author, amid many oppositions of infirm health and (at the first) of deficient means, has steadily devoted himself. There have appeared, in accordance with this plan, the "First Principles," "Biology," "Psychology," "Sociology" (in part), and "The Data of Ethics"; not to mention other writings which, if not a systematic part of the general scheme, are all subservient to its main purpose.

Mr. Spencer's strength lies in his familiarity with the conceptions of physical science. He astonishes his readers through the apparently encyclopedic comprehensiveness of his scientific information. This qualifies him to take up and repeat with an effect of imposing authority the parable of his British predecessors, to the general effect that such conceptions and such information constitute the impassable limit of all possible human knowledge. His weakness is in his deficient knowledge and grasp of philosophic ideas. I find no evidence that the history of philosophic thought is much better than a sealed book for Mr. Spencer. He is familiar with the ideas and methods of British psychology and psychological pseudo-philosophy, and he knows something, at least, of that negative side of Kant's doctrine which we have above (Chapter X) recognized as akin to, and due to the influence of, British thought. But this, if the views maintained in this volume are correct, must be regarded as an accomplishment of doubtful philosophic value. At most, it can only encourage an insular Philistinism, and not speculative or spiritual insight. But when, therefore, I note in Mr. Spencer the conspicuous absence of such insight, or of specifically philosophical intelligence, I am simply noting that which was also true of his intellectual forerunners, and which the very exclusiveness of his scientific training was naturally calculated to intensify, rather than to correct.

The unwelcome verdict which the student of the history of philosophy finds himself compelled to pass upon that line of British thought which we have contemplated in these chapters is, that it remains essentially at that stage which is illustrated by the pre-Socratic "philosophers" of ancient Greece. The earliest of these thinkers directed their attention to the contemplation of the physical universe, and sought to invent and, more or less, to demonstrate by experimental proof some descriptive theory concerning the process of the universe. For the notion that the physical world had resulted, historically, through some evolutionary process suggested itself from the outset. However heterogeneous and varied the world, in its contents, might at present appear, yet it was held that all things were but diverse modifications of one elementary material nature. Hence the earliest "philosophers" (aptly termed in the history of philosophy, the rather, "physiologists," or physicists, men who theorized about sensible nature) applied themselves to discover what was the original state of matter, whether water, air, fire, or some "indefinite" element (just as, now-a-days, theorizers of the same class, armed with a better knowledge of physical phenomena, conclude that it was gaseous, or "nebular"), and to define, or at least *name*, the law (order or process) of the subsequent evolution of the universe. Thus it was common with them to hold that the universe was subject to periodic evolution and dissolution (like Spencer to-day), and Heraclitus went so far as to estimate the number of years included in one such period. One can but admire the divining instinct which enabled these children in science to anticipate conclusions which the more comprehensive knowledge of our days is deemed (in general) but to confirm. Then followed other, more reflective, philosophers (or incipient philosophers), who perceived that these physical inquiries concerning the processes of phenomena led to no conclusions concerning the nature of being, but the rather, that if the sensible conceptions on which they were founded were to be regarded as ultimate, human reason was landed in an inextricable maze of contradictions. (Compare, in modern times, Kant's "Antinomies of Pure Reason," echoed by Hamilton, and reëchoed by Spencer.) Then arose sophists like Protagoras, who affirmed that nevertheless sensible conceptions — *appearances* — were indeed ultimate and final for man, that beyond them knowledge could not pass, and that consequently the absolutely real and true was unknowable. Reviewing the ground, we may say that the mental attitude of the earliest thinkers corresponds roughly to that of the men of pure (physical) science to-day. Such men, while engaged in their peculiar, and honorable, and useful work, are unconscious of philosophical questions, and make no more pretension of answering them than the optician (for example) does of answering questions relative to the theory and charm of music. Those who come after are conscious of philosophical questions, but unconscious, or only dimly conscious, of the method by which the answers to them are to be sought. They are dialecticians and rude psychologists, but have not yet entered the portals of real, positive philosophy. These are first opened wide, after Socrates, by Plato and Aristotle, who find power and being, the reason, life and reality of "things," in imperial, knowable mind. The parallelism with British philosophy, which breaks off where Plato begins, may be instructively extended by including certain phases of post-Aristotelian philosophy, which are mainly but a reversion to, and amplification of, the ruder pre-Platonic types of thought. I single out, for mention, the stoic renewal of a purely physical conception of the universe, with the accompanying bastard conception of an all-determining fate, which, in theory, plays such confusing havoc with the stoic's ineradicable sense of moral freedom. Thus, it is only when the philosophic spirit, in the spring-time of occidental thought, was either unfledged or had already lost its virile power, that its fruits furnish a prototype of what has too generally been regarded at home as the most "advanced" type of British thought in the last two centuries.

As for Mr. Spencer, his preliminary (negative or dialectical) contention is that the ultra-phenomenal, the real, or absolute, mind, matter, God, in short, "our own and all other existence, is a mystery absolutely and forever beyond our comprehension"; then, positively, he maintains that whatever is knowable, *i.e.* the phenomenal, sensible, has received its final explanation for us when it is recognized as illustrating a law of universal evolution from homogeneity to heterogeneity, or of dissolution, proceeding in the contrary direction.

I am not now concerned to examine whether Mr. Spencer's formula of evolution is correct and in exact agreement with facts, or not. It has been vehemently questioned, but whether with reason or not, it is wholly beside my present purpose to inquire. The conception of evolution is, as such, neither philosophical nor anti-philosophical, neither religious nor irreligious. If true, it is true for the same reason for which the conception of gravitation is a true one, namely, because it is agreeable to sensible fact. It is a physical conception, and the "Law of Evolution," if correctly stated and duly established, is but an accurate statement of the observed or observable order of sensible phenomena. The conception of evolution differs from other physical conceptions only in its claim to greatest generality. It seeks to sum up in one phrase, or in one scientific law, all the cases of law or order which are visible in the phenomenal universe. If defective in statement, and, by reason of its very generality, difficult to be completely demonstrated, it is certainly correct in idea. The phenomenal universe is everywhere the illustration of law. It is only in virtue of this fact that it is in any sense rationally apprehensible or intelligible, for it is only in virtue of this fact that it presents a tangible surface or "handle" to knowing mind. Nothing in the universe but order is, strictly speaking, knowable, since mind can know nothing that is not in some way cognate to itself, and nothing in the phenomenal universe but order, which is the direct proclamation and manifestation of mind, is thus cognate. Moreover, all the cases of order in the universe (all the particular, special "laws," which science discovers) would conspire to produce chaos, and so destroy their own intelligibility, if they did not (in Leibnitz's phrase) "consent together," *i.e.* if they were not harmoniously united as parts in one organic, universal order. There can be no doubt of the directive and almost inspiring influence of such a general conception as this on the labor of scientific specialists in all the subordinate departments of physical inquiry. And when Mr. Spencer, therefore, taking up an idea which is as old as human thought, but which, in the peculiar form in which it is adopted by Mr. Spencer, had been specially hovering over the scientific world for the past fifty years, gave it a definite shape, made it the central object of his vigorous teaching, and illustrated its applicability most plausibly and variously, it is not surprising that he exerted a quickening and captivating influence upon a vast number of scientific minds. This, thus far, is as it should be. It is the scientific workers who will have finally to establish or disprove the correctness of Mr. Spencer's special formula. That is not a question of pure thought. Meanwhile the conception involved serves its legitimate and valuable scientific purpose, just so far as it keeps before the minds of scientific men the ideal, above noted, of an universal, all-inclusive organic order in the whole realm of phenomena. I may go farther, and add that it serves a philosophic and religious purpose, so far as, by being in accordance with the aforesaid ideal and confirmed by observation, it illustrates comprehensively, in its application to the realm of phenomenal existence, the central truth of philosophy and religion — the truth that existence, considered absolutely, is spiritual and rational, and hence that derivative or phenomenal existence must, by its *order*, proclaim its own spiritual and rational origin. Every scientific law illustrates this; and, of course, a law comprehensive enough to include in itself and so sum up all other, minor scientific laws, would do so in the highest degree.

But it must not be forgotten that this philosophical significance of scientific law is a thing with which science, as such, has nothing to do. It has simply to ascertain and record the order of phenomena. It has to do only with sensible matter of fact, not with ideal truth. It determines what are the experimentally observable rules concerning the coexistence and sequence of phenomena. Its laws (as we have seen elsewhere) are not philosophical principles. The establishment of a new scientific law, no matter how comprehensive, is not the establishment of a new philosophic principle. (It is at most only — as hinted just above — the confirmation of an old one.) The fact of its comprehensiveness does not in the slightest degree modify its nature as a mere rule of order concerning phenomena, or clothe it with the vital, dynamic, ontological attributes of a philosophical principle. Strictly speaking, therefore, the phrase "Philosophy of Evolution" is an egregious misnomer. Evolution is no more philosophy than gravitation is. It has no other *kind* of philosophical significance than that which may be indirectly connected with any other scientific law. Conceding that the law of evolution has been established, the nature and the wording of philosophical problems have not been changed one whit. Mr. Spencer and his followers may affect to think otherwise, and beginners in philosophy, whose first intellectual nourishment is derived from the perusal of their works, will almost certainly be persuaded of the absolutely revolutionary and finally decisive character of the "new" conception, in its relations to philosophic thought. In reality, all that is discernible in the "philosophy" of evolution, is a recurrence of the old scientific prejudice which has rested like a pall on British thought since Francis Bacon's time. The so-called "*philosophy* of evolution" is an extra-scientific accretion of philosophical convictions, for the most part negative, wholly dogmatic, amusingly oracular, and thoroughly irrelevant, about a scientific law of phenomena, which is held to sum up all that is positively knowable. The convictions are not new, nor do they follow from the "new" (?) scientific law in question. They rest on the same general grounds from which the doubts, denials, and agnosticisms of earlier British thinkers were derived; on the same arbitrary substitution of sensible for rational conceptions, of static appearance for dynamic substance, of death for life, of empirical psychology for philosophy. For Spencer, as for his forerunners, "conception implies imagination." The exclusive source and highest, and indeed only, type of knowledge is sensible, static, imaginative, panoramic consciousness. Knowledge is confined to felt phenomena. It is the accurate recognition of the historic or matter-of-fact order of phenomena. In other words, knowledge is essentially identical in nature with physical science; this is with Spencer, as with his forerunners, at once premise and conclusion.

Mr. Spencer holds that the real is unknowable. This does not follow from the law of evolution, but from the assumptions above noted. That it follows necessarily from such assumptions, has been so often demonstrated, from the time of the ancient Eleatics and Sophists down to Kant, and is a truth so obvious to the simplest inspection, that it has become a commonplace of philosophic thought. In an especial manner, as we have seen, had it become a commonplace of British thought, in which it also figured as a piece of profound and decisive wisdom. It is not wonderful, therefore, that Mr. Spencer deems it necessary to devote but a comparatively small space to the demonstration of this thesis, or that he makes this (from his arbitrary premises) easy task still easier for himself by citing bodily from his predecessors.

As an argument addressed to those who, not dogmatically, but on good grounds of history and of self-conscious, rationally vitalized experience, claim to know better, or, in other words, to those who appreciate the nature of philosophic truth and of the data on which and the method by which it is theoretically established, it has not the slightest weight. What is proved is, that if sensible or phenomenal conceptions, such as time, space, physical "substance," and scientific causation (regular, temporal sequence merely, or scientific law,) be taken as ultimate, we involve ourselves in contradictions, the recognition of which is, *pro tanto*, the recognition of our nescience. Ultimate reality cannot by their aid become an object of thought. The argument, thus considered, is good, and the conclusion is universally accepted in all but popular, unreflective, and uncultured thought. The argument becomes sophistical and easily imposes on an immature learner, through the unconcealed postulate which accompanies it, that these conceptions, if any, must indeed be regarded as ultimate in human knowledge; which being conceded, the argument of course suffices to establish the "imbecility" of our understandings and the necessity and legitimacy of taking refuge from the burdensome labor of real, vital cognition in the asylum of our enforced ignorance. This postulate none but a tyro in speculation, or *insight* into living truth (a thing generally different from scientific information concerning the phenomena of the universe) will ever grant or has ever granted. Philosophy has never had a positive content except when it has called the ultimate (not the relative) validity of the conceptions referred to in question. But philosophy with a positive content has long existed historically, and its living well-spring has an ever-present existence in the self-conscious, spiritual personality of man. The validity of the former is not examined, still less is it disproved, by Mr. Spencer, whose mind, for the rest, on the side of philosophical or speculative intelligence appears to be a complete blank. And from the latter, notwithstanding that it exists in him, as in every living man, he neglects to draw, because his inherited and long-nourished scientific prejudices prevent him from recognizing it in its effective and rationally illuminating reality. In the philosophy of the Unknowable the dogmatic sensational negativism of the eighteenth century simply lives again.

But Spencer, like all of Hume's successors in the employment of the purely sensational method in philosophy, is less consistent than Hume, in that he positively affirms the existence of the unknowable. From the point of view of this method the most that can be said is, that the real, if existent, is invisible; it does not come within the range of sensitive consciousness. Were man as a knowing being confined to such consciousness (a contradiction in terms, which Spencer, in common with his predecessors, holds as an axiomatic truth), it were psycologically impossible that the conception of the sensibly unknowable should enter his mind. The fact that it does thus enter is immediate proof that man is more than a physically sensitive organism, and that knowledge is something more than merely mechanical, analytical dissection and registry of passively felt experiences, or of "phenomena." It indicates that his is an actively living, rational nature, capable of organic insight, of rational conceptions — capable of forming, for example, the non-sensible conception of *being*, and of finding it realized, not in the pictures of panoramic consciousness, not in a *thing* of sense, but in a vitalized object of rational intelligence, or in the effective light and power of spirit. A conception which is peculiarly of this order is the conception of power. Hume, as we know, discovered that for sensational psychology this was an illegitimate conception, and in making declaration to this effect he but anticipated the now universal voice of physical science. Hume's attitude was, like Spencer's, the attitude (psychologically considered) of physical science, which but honestly and honorably confesses the limitations of its true province, when it restricts this province to the field of sensible phenomena, and which now universally and naturally professes to find no reality of power or "force," but only phenomena of motion. For it force is an "abstraction," a convenient, and perhaps practically necessary "auxiliary," or working "idea," but not an object of scientific knowledge, not a scientific reality. It is not an object of sensible observation, it is not a "phenomenon," and if it makes its way into the armory of scientific ideas, it is (as regards its origin) an interloper there, a stranger come from the invisible, ultra-phenomenal, but ever-present, ultimately real, and hence all-controlling land of man's non-sensible, rational, spiritual *being*. If Mr. Spencer (as is the case) makes use of this conception, he does not derive it from the scientific law of evolution, which is but the law of the matter-of-fact "redistribution of matter and motion"; it does not legitimately follow from his (professedly) purely scientific (*i.e.* empirico-psychological) attitude and presuppositions. It is, from his point of view, an arbitrary, extra-scientific, though in its real implications, genuinely philosophical idea, which it is indeed highly natural (since all men, Spencer included, are more than mere physico-scientific beings) to employ, but for which Mr. Spencer has and furnishes no scientific justification. Just so far as he employs this conception he contradicts himself, on good (though unacknowledged) grounds, it is true, but in a manner which demonstrates the inadequacy and falseness of the presuppositions, and of the method, which he persistently advocates.

It is significant, now, that in seeking (singularly enough) to name the unknowable (which, if absolutely such, as we are assured it is, must be unnameable), Mr. Spencer hits upon the words "power," and "persistent force." The sensibly unknowable (which is the only and final object of Mr. Spencer's demonstrations) is indeed power, which, however, because sensibly unknowable, is none the less an extremely distinct object of rational intelligence. It is a vital conception and a vital reality, given in living, *i.e.* rational, spiritual experience. (Compare above, pp. 96, 97.) It is an active attribute of intelligent spirit, and hence cannot be a mere "*state* of consciousness," the only (quasi) reality which sensational psychology recognizes. When, therefore, the unknowable, absolute, ultimately real is termed by Mr. Spencer power, definite recognition is implicitly given to that realm of ultra-phenomenal, intelligible, non-sensible reality, which in self-conscious intelligence is *known* (not simply named) as spirit, as living, actively synthetic mind, as person, or (taken absolutely) as God; the real is indeed power, because it is spirit. But this implication of his phraseology is not explicitly recognized by Mr. Spencer. The rather it is wholly obfuscated, if not absolutely denied. Having no conception of personality otherwise than as a mysteriously necessary, but unfathomable adjunct (given only in the form of "belief") of sensitive, conscious states (*à la* Reid and Mill), he yet argues against the personality of the "unknowable," as though this conception were quite intelligible to him, and denoted nothing else than these conscious states themselves. In other words, just as soon as he seeks to define a rational conception, he clothes it in sensuous integuments, and then substitutes the latter for the reality which they do but conceal. (This procedure is also illustrated by Spencer, and by the predecessors whose arguments he imitates or borrows, in what he has to say of the "infinite" and "absolute.") Mr. Spencer's favorite phrase for the "unknowable" is "persistent force." "Force" is the scientific name for "power," and, as such, has that peculiar emptiness of positive signification (as above noted), that imposing darkness, and inscrutableness, that (to sense) mysterious connotation of inevitableness, which fit it admirably for anthropomorphic investiture with the habiliments of mechanical fate. With these habiliments Mr. Spencer practically — and persistently — invests his "unknowable."

But Mr. Spencer withdraws himself still further from recognition in the "Unknowable" of *absolute being* in the form of *spiritual reality*, by seeking to show that it is something, and what it is, in sensible, physically conditioned consciousness. Here he lapses completely into the order of views which his general theory of knowledge requires. For this theory the notion of power is a pure assumption. What is known, is what is given in the shape of sensitively-conscious states. Mr. Spencer doubtless perceives the absurdity of asserting, from this point of view, the existence and reality of the unknowable, unless it be somehow thus given, and so, after all, in a measure "known." Accordingly the unknowable "Unconditioned," the "Absolute," the finally Real, is declared to be given us in the form of "indefinite consciousness," the "raw material of thought," which remains when all the conditions and limits of definite consciousness are withdrawn. True, these conditions and limits cannot be removed, and the "indefinite" or "unconditioned" consciousness does not exist for us, except in the form of a suppositious imagination. Real imagination (which, for sensational psychology, means *definitely imaging in consciousness*, or *having a conscious state*) or "thought" (which for Mr. Spencer and his predecessors means the same thing) is definite, because conditioned and limited. It is in this sense that Mr. Spencer declares, "thinking is relationing." The "conditioned" (under which we are always to understand something which can be definitely figured or imaged in sensitive consciousness) is said to be alone "thinkable." But the "momentum of thought inevitably carries us beyond conditioned existence to unconditioned existence," *i.e.* from the imaginable to the unimaginable, from the "thinkable" to the "unthinkable." Thought seeks by its own "momentum" to escape from itself, to annihilate itself! A singular reversal of the law of self-preservation, or "struggle for existence," indeed! And a singularly "raw" conception, indeed, is this of an absolutely "indefinite consciousness," which is a contradiction in terms, which can consequently be "given" in no sensitive experience, but which is nevertheless asserted by "scientific," "experimental" psychology as the basis of "an ever-present sense of real existence" and of all "our intelligence"! What all this signifies, on Mr. Spencer's part, is, that he is seeking anew to realize, psychologically, the spurious conception of a "*thing*-in-itself," noted in a previous chapter. After all the demonstrations, in which Mr. Spencer has assisted, that the ultimately real cannot be an object of sense, that to attempt to think it with the aid of sensible conceptions is to land one's self in insoluble contradictions, sensational psychology wearies of its "imbecility," waxes valiant in dogmatism, and, after reducing the "unknowable," the absolute reality, the "king of being," to an invisible minimum (a mere name) of sensible affection, declares it to be not a rational truth, but a psychophysical fact ("state") of sensitive experience.* But in the thing-in-itself there lurks a glimmer of rational connotation, which rescues it from absolute nonsense. The important thing about it is, not that we have an (impossible) *sense* of it, but that it is rationally (Mr. Spencer, in common with all sensational psychologists, says, in effect, *irrationally*, "*mysteriously*") believed to be a *power* capable of *affecting* us; and so, by this element, it leads back, in consistent thought, to the recognition of Spirit, which is the only absolute depositary of power.

One of the most striking illustrations of the utter fatuity of eighteenth century psychological "philoso-

---

* One may fairly infer that the "Unconditioned" comes nearest to being given, in the form of a sensitive state, to those creatures which have reached the first and lowest stage of evolution referred to in Mr. Spencer's Psychology, Part V, Chap. VI, and whose "unorganized consciousness" is said to constitute the "raw material of mind."

phy" was its quixotic devotion to the discussion of the alleged problem concerning the "reality" of the external world. The belated descendants of the masters of this philosophy still speak of it (in the words of Prof. Bain) as the "GREAT metaphysical problem of the eighteenth century," and indeed of all centuries. Mr. Spencer is obviously of the same mind, and in his Psychology marches bravely and confidently up to meet the question, having his feet shod with the elastic sandals of an accomplished verbal dialectician, and bearing on his tongue the whole gospel and wisdom of descriptive psychology. Is it our exalted and exalting privilege, as rational beings, to believe "that there exists an outer object"? This is the weighty question, and he who believes he may answer it in the affirmative, is described to us as a "realist," while he who denies it is an "idealist." The former, with the "rustic," believes in "matter," the latter, only in "sensations." The latter is *sceptical* concerning the existence of outer reality; hence the common phrase with Spencer, "Idealism, or Scepticism," intimating that the two terms denote the same thing. "Idealism," as thus defined, is one of the vain "words of metaphysicians" and is fairly synonymous with "metaphysics." (It must be confessed that in this use of terms Mr. Spencer scarcely offends either the literary or common usage of the English language; the peculiar poverty, or, rather, flabbiness, of significance, too commonly attached to terms of such virile import as "realism," "idealism," "philosophy," and "metaphysics," is the hollow bequest made to the currency of English thought by physical science, and by sensational psychology, its child and ally, masquerading for two hundred years and more in the name of philosophy.) Mr. Spencer, true to the method of Locke, the common master of Spencer and of his other most illustrious predecessors and contemporaries, looks to solve the problem in question by "inspecting the phenomena of consciousness in their order of genesis; using," he continues, "for our 'erecting-glass,' the mental biography of a child, or the developed conception of things held in common by the savage and the rustic." In addition to this powerful means of insight, he betakes himself to "mutual exploration" of his "limbs;" he notices that the vivid and faint states of consciousness (corresponding respectively to "matter" and "mind," or to "object" and "subject") are distinguished by circumstances which confirm our ineradicable persuasion of their absolute distinction, and that each class of states is held together by a "nexus" or "principle of continuity," which cannot, indeed, be observed, but is an article of inexpugnable belief, an object of "transcendent" (*i.e.* for sensational psychology, of *no real*) consciousness, founded, however, above all — this clinches the demonstration — in a nervous structure, which has been organizing and consolidating itself through a gradual process of evolution, through countless ages. "Realism" is triumphant. But, hold! not the realism of the rustic, but the "transfigured realism" of agnosticism. There is a reality, and this reality is doubtless a thing of sense, but it is not for *our* senses. Time and space are (*i.e.* have become through physical evolution) necessary forms of our thought (sensation), and in some way they doubtless correspond to attributes of real existence. But how, we know not. This real existence is for us only a brute "power" to compel us to have the subjective but (absolutely considered) wholly illusory ideas (pictures in sensitive consciousness) of which we are consciously aware; in all other respects it is wholly unknown and unknowable. Realism is triumphant! There "exists an outer object," though not in any sense of the word "outer" that we can comprehend! In reality, as is obvious, this is only a practical, not a consistent, theoretical triumph. Hume, too, held practically, under the mysterious inspiration of "nature," to "realism." All that Spencer theoretically accomplishes, on the basis of sensational psychology, is a revindication of "idealism." The only things of which we know in the form of conscious states, are for him these states themselves; all else is mere matter of "transcendent" consciousness, *i.e.* not of sensitive consciousness at all, hence no object of knowledge; hence, as to its positive contents for us, pure naught! This "transcendent," "indefinable," "indefinite consciousness," is nothing but Hume's "nature." Its content may be summed up in the phrase "unknowable, but constraining power." This content, being confessedly extra-conscious (for sensational psychology), is not evolved through any development of nervous structure. Nervous structure, like everything else which has a physical, evolutionary history, is itself (from the point of view of psychology) only a part of the sensitive consciousness itself, and if, as is claimed, the history of the development of such structure is the obverse of the history of sensitive consciousness, the former is no *explanation* — it is at most only a phenomenal, scientific *description* — of the latter, and still less does it explain that which "transcends" the latter, namely, the notion of power. The fact is, Spencer illustrates anew what we found illustrated in the case of J. S. Mill, and what must be illustrated in the case of every sensational psychologist who has not accomplished the impossible feat of divesting himself of his vital, spiritual humanity (*i.e.* of his true reality) — he illustrates the inability of pure (physical) "science," or of so-called empirical, sensitively observational psychology, to proceed a step beyond the purely analytical description of phenomena, and to enter into the path of real explanation (to substitute comprehension for simple apprehension), without assuming that which is not given among its data, and which it can, therefore, only recognize upon brute psychological compulsion, as "transcendent," inexplicable fact, and, for the rest, must declare "unknowable." Doubtless we ought to be thankful to the self-appointed interpreters of science for allowing us so much, but when they give out their forced, and mostly negative, concessions as marking the farthest attainable limit of human wisdom, we are surely entitled, in the name of self-conscious, vital reason, of living ideal truth, incorporated in man, and the vitalizing and self-illuminating essence of all *reality*, to enter an energetic protest.

With regard, now, to the above-mentioned alleged problem of "realism" or "idealism," the discussion of it shows (as Mr. Spencer's own discussion illustrates anew) that it is no problem. The phenomenal world, the familiar world of time and space, possesses all that "reality," and just that kind of reality, which it is "seen" to possess. Do we "see" what we "see"? Is our involuntary experience what it is? The question is wholly nugatory, and the answer which results from long-winded and pompous discussion is the one which the questions bear upon their face. But it is quite another thing to ask, whether what we "see" and experience, *i.e.* whether the states of conscious, sensitive, physically organic feeling which are vouchsafed to us correspond to the (intrinsically rational) conception of being. And here again the question bears on its face its own answer. Being is (psychologically considered) a rational, intelligible notion, not a state or image of sensitive consciousness, *i.e.* not a "phenomenon." The phenomenal is, in knowledge, essentially surface-state, inert appearance, but possessing all the "truth" which appearance can possess; it is not deceptive; it serves its normal use. Being, on the other hand, is dynamic, life, soul, spirit. In examining the attributes of phenomena as such, we do not find these attributes of being. We say, therefore, not that phenomena are not what they are (they are what they appear, their existence is identical with their appearance), but that they do not fulfill the requirements of the notion of absolute or independent being. They are only functions, functional results, products, of that which truly is, namely, of potent spirit. Their "being" is not essential, independent, absolute, but dependent and derivative. Positive, philosophical idealism, the idealism taught by all affirmative philosophy since the beginning of the world (not by its illegitimate psychological and "scientific" substitutes), proclaims this (which is, after all, only the first and relatively negative portion of its message, the portion on which Berkeley's youthful mind principally rested), and goes on to deserve its name by demonstrating, positively, that being is such as above described. When it declares that being is ideal, it does not (like the "idealism" of pure sensational psychology) mean that being partakes of the nature of sensible "ideas" or images, conscious functions of nervous structure; this were to stultify itself, to make unjust and unmeaning game of thought, and to treat being as identical with appearance. For it the ideal is rational, and because rational, living, and because living, spiritual. The rock of being is absolute spirit. "Mind is the king of the universe." The physical universe, the world of appearance, subsists by the power of Mind. To the outer portals of this conception we find Spencer coming in his verbal recognition of brute, but, as we have seen, from his point of view, necessarily unintelligible Power. Further than this the limitations of his non-philosophical method and data, and his consequent utter lack of insight into the nature of genuinely philosophical conceptions, do not permit him to proceed. But it is too bad that he (like Mill and others of the same class) should be permitted to travesty the thought of thinkers like Berkeley and Kant, by attributing to their inquiries absolutely the same contractedness of purport which belongs to his own. These men, heaven knows, suffered enough from psychological prejudice, but they were not such utter strangers to philosophical intelligence as is implied in ascribing to them the negative "idealism" of sensational psychology, pure and simple, without further qualification. Let us defend the dead, who cannot defend themselves!

I fancy it is sufficiently evident that the scientific law of physical evolution has little enough to do with the determination of problems such as we have been considering. A process which goes on, if at all, only within the sphere of phenomena, a law which in its confessed intention is but a descriptive summing up of the historical process of phenomena, has obviously nothing to do with their ontological explanation, or with the solution of any other specifically philosophical problem, *i.e.* of any problem of ultimate truth or reality. I repeat that it is not the "philosophy of evolution" (in which there is no philosophy), but the old sensational theory of knowledge which has prevailed in British thought since Bacon's time, which determines Mr. Spencer's "philosophical" conclusions (negations). The conclusions are such, in quality, as have always followed, in ancient as well as modern times, from that exclusive premise. But some of them, relating to human mind and morals, he attempts, as we shall presently see, to affiliate in a peculiarly intimate, though illusory, manner upon the law of evolution. His procedure here, however, is but part and parcel of the common procedure of sensational psychology foisted into the alleged place of philosophy. The essential is confounded, as far as possible, with the apparent, the active cause with the condition and law of order, the agent and the end of action with the means, and the former is assumed in each case to be explained when the scientific history of the latter has been made experimentally, or with hypothetical probability, complete. The result is peculiarly exasperating, unsatisfying and confusing, especially to a learner unschooled in philosophic thought, when this method is employed to "account for" man and morality. For in man the essential and the phenomenal, cause and law of action, agent and instrument exist in closest relationship, and yet in most obvious distinction. Man knows that he *has* an animal (phenomenal) side to his nature, but that he *is* spiritual, that he wears a dress of involuntary habit ("association"), but that his inward and essential substance (if he have any) is self-determined, ideal character, that law and mechanical condition are instruments in his possession, but that he himself is a potent agent, in short, that what *appears* about him is but a faint and deceptive indication, and is no part at all, of what he, as *man*, characteristically and essentially is. Now, when he is treated to an analytic account of the former, as though that were the essential thing, while the latter is either not recognized, or, if recognized, is reduced to such an imperceptible minimum that the attempt may be plausibly made to persuade him that it is of no practical importance, or else, finally, while recognized is declared to be so absolutely unknowable that (however important *in se*) he cannot permit himself to shape his notions concerning human life and duty and privilege with any reference to it, it is no wonder that man is puzzled, and cries out in answer to the inquiry after his own identity, with the amazed "little market-woman," celebrated in nursery rhyme, "Lawk-a-mercy on me! this is none of I!" If the "highest truth" (so much "in advance of the time"!) be that essential manhood is essentially unknowable, and hence practically to be left out of the account, while we accept in its place, and devote ourselves to the cultivation of, an apparent man of straw, we will submit, "like little men," to be told this, to be disabused of our unscientific error, and may perhaps even be induced to imitate our advanced leaders in posturing before our fellow-men as noble, devoutly resigned, spiritual martyrs to that letter of "truth" which kills our spirits. But we shall hold convicted of error that saying, not less of all affirmative philosophy than of religion, "The truth shall make you free."

I am not caricaturing Mr. Spencer's doctrine. I am

simply stating what he holds as matter of positive theoretic knowledge, however much he may, to his honor and to the honor of living truth and reality, as embodied in man, by repeated inadvertences, or even by verbal admissions and assertions, convict himself of inability faithfully to restrict himself to it.

Mr. Spencer holds that man is known to himself and can scientifically, and hence, in agreement with the presupposed theory of knowledge, legitimately, regard and study himself only as a congeries of sensuous, physiologically determined states of consciousness. His Psychology is a hypothetical history of the evolution of such consciousness, in terms of the redistribution of matter and motion — more especially of the matter and motion of the nervous system. That he, Mr. Spencer, has, individually, a nervous system, is referred to as a "conclusion" which he has reached (through his demonstration of "Transfigured Realism"?) and which, it is "congruous with facts" to assume, holds good concerning other similar beings, whom, again, it is also congruous with facts to suppose as existing. Nervous affections are molecular changes resulting from the tendency of motion to follow the line of least resistance. Of these affections, states of consciousness are believed to be the obverse, or "inner face." (This belief is indeed stated to be of "remotely inferential character," but on its validity [which, as we shall see, need not be questioned] the whole fabric of Mr. Spencer's psychology depends. It marks the whole scope and the proper ontological limit of his, and of all other "physiological" psychology.) The fundamental law of nervous action is declared to be the fundamental law of intelligence. The physical evolution of the nervous system is, by virtue of the "double face" of the latter, at once also the evolution of "mind," or "what we call knowing." Mind has indeed a "nature," but this nature is "nervous organization." And, this last allegation being admitted, it follows that "if the doctrine of evolution is true, the inevitable implication is that Mind can be understood only by observing how Mind is evolved." So here we are landed upon the alleged rock of principle, upon which Mr. Spencer's psychology, or explanation of "mind," is founded, and this rock is evolution.

But we are not brought face to face with a new principle *in kind*, as compared with the "principles" of explanation employed in the earlier sensational or "associational" psychologies of Hartley, the two Mills, Bain, *et al.* In the one case, as in the others, it is only the sensible or *felt phenomena* of mind which there is any pretension of "explaining," for only such phenomena are admitted to be accessible to knowledge. In either case, by a strict construction, it is not the *nature* of mind, as a dynamic principle which effectuates or is active underneath phenomena, which is clad in them as in a transparent garment, and to the rational, vital nature of whose activities they point and bear both direct and indirect witness — it is not this which is investigated. The whole object of endeavor (so far as this endeavor is strictly *scientific*, and it claims to be nothing else) is accurately to recognize the phenomena as given matters-of-sensible-fact, and to demonstrate the "law" or rule of order which is observed to hold good concerning their varied coexistences and sequences. "Explanation," in this order of inquiry, means ascertaining and naming the rule of coexistence or sequence, which a given phenomenon or class of phenomena observably illustrates. The subordinate "laws" of mental phenomena, which are recognized and thus employed in "explanation" by Mr. Spencer, are of the same kind, and are the same in substance, as those employed by his British predecessors and contemporaries (laws of "association"). His peculiarity is that he seeks, in the true scientific spirit, to make them all appear as subordinate cases or modifications of the comprehensive phenomenal law of evolution.

This is a thoroughly legitimate work, in which Mr. Spencer has accomplished much. There *is* such a thing as mental *science*, just as there is also (though Mr. Spencer, in common with the school from which he springs, denies this) a mental *philosophy*. As above intimated, in mind the phenomenal and the real, state and activity, motion and power, the shadow and the substance of soul, coexist, and that, too, in the closest apparent relationship. The former is the subject of historical, descriptive, analytical science; the latter is at once a subject and the universal organ of philosophy, or of substantive cognition, and not merely of phenomenal recognition. The only danger is that the two orders and subjects of inquiry may be confounded — that either science or philosophy may, uncritically, take its own peculiar explanations to be, in the one case, final, or, in the other, exhaustive. This danger is illustrated in the case of all the members of the British school of psychology, and by none more signally than by Mr. Spencer.

Mr. Spencer does indeed issue, in his Psychology, his usual *caveat* against the pretense that the investigations in progress are to reach the "substance of Mind." And the grounds on which he does this are peculiar, and of a piece with those which are employed by him to establish the universal incognoscibility of absolute or true reality. He does not place himself on the common-sense, obvious ground that one thing is not another; that the scientific ascertainment of the order of static appearances is not identical with the philosophical investigation and cognition of the dynamic principle of reality, and that the presuppositions and method of science are not necessarily those which are legitimately peculiar to philosophy. Whatever is not cognizable through the investigation of phenomena by the peculiar method and with the peculiar and generally recognized limitations of physical science, is arbitrarily held to be, for this reason, absolutely unknowable. All arguments founded on such a basis of pure assumption are necessarily sophistical. They may perplex a learner, or induce the valueless assent of the thoughtless, but cannot convince the thoughtful. The important thing to notice is, that arguments thus founded assimilate in imagination that, whose incognoscibility is to be demonstrated, to those sensible conceptions which confessedly are insufficient to express it, being indeed wholly disparate to it. In order to disprove substance, we endeavor to think of it as shadow! The natural result of accustoming one's self to such an irrational endeavor, is a constant tendency to repeat it and finally to imagine or practically to proceed as if the endeavor were both legitimate and successful. This result I find illustrated in the case of Mr. Spencer (in common with so many other philosophically uninstructed or ungifted men of pure science). Its crowning and commanding illustration is found in those deliverances of his which relate, either professedly or by implication (as in his psychology of the "Will"), to ethical topics. This is natural, for it is peculiar to ethical philosophy that we are concerned in it with the true and characteristic, or *ultimate*, nature of man as man. We shall contemplate this presently.

Mind, I have said, is a reality, as well as a bundle of phenomena, though only the latter are presented in static, sensitive, imaginative, consciousness, and so scientifically "known." As a reality it is dynamic, synthetic, vital, and knows itself in active self-consciousness. And thus it is implicitly or explicitly known to every man. We have seen how the knowledge of it forced itself, as an ineradicable "belief," upon John Stuart Mill, although, since it found no place in scientific (static, sensitive) consciousness, it was for him, not a thing of light, but of darkness, not of "knowledge," but of ignorance, described (in the use of words which, nevertheless, well implied its active, synthetic, and hence its really, vitally, substantively knowable nature) as an "inexplicable *tie*," or "*bond* of some sort." Mr. Spencer—notwithstanding his prevalent tendency to think of mind as a "substance," of which "we cannot think . . . save in terms that imply material properties," and as being such a "cause" as can be "thought of" (sensibly imaged) only in the form, not of power, but of sensible succession — has also a clear enough notion of mind as of some thing "which holds impressions and ideas together," a "principle of continuity," or, in other words of personal identity, a "self." This is an intelligible notion, corresponding to experienced, vital reality, but it is not an image of sensible consciousness, not a pure, physically conditioned "feeling" or "state of consciousness," and hence, according to the arbitrary assumption of sensational psychology, not an object of "reason" (!) or "knowledge." This is (incompletely stated) what the "ego" *is*, and it is a very clear object of self-conscious knowledge; otherwise how should we have a conception of it, how should we know that we "believed" in it? And yet, although, in Mr. Spencer's words, "belief in the reality of self is, indeed, a belief which no hypothesis enables us to escape," when we have this belief we do not know in what we are believing. The "reality of self" is unknowable (because not a sensible phenomenon, not pictured in sensitive consciousness, like a tree or a stone), and belief in it is a "belief admitting of no justification by reason" (and so, then, the belief in the "Unknowable" universally admits of no such justification! all that which we hold as most vitally and absolutely true, because necessary in consistent thought, and founded in the most *vital, ever-present experience,* we hold, in spite of "reason," by practical, impenetrable, brute and irrational, necessity! Surely this is not "free thought," but "free thoughtlessness," not the empire of reason, but the self-confessed "imbecility" of irrationality!). This "belief," which would furnish (as far as it goes) an admirable working hypothesis for the construction of a rational, *real* (ultra-phenomenal) psychology, because so necessarily and immediately "given" in practical, vital experience, that "no hypothesis enables us to escape" it, should, if Mr. Spencer's purpose were purely scientific, simply be ignored, but not, on irrelevant grounds, declared unjustifiable; and then he might, in the spirit of a purely "scientific" descriptive psychologist, go on to show that the sensible phenomena of consciousness, in their historic succession, occur in an order, or according to a complex system of "laws" or rules of order, which may be summed up under the word, or "law" of, Evolution. But, no! the phenomenal must become, to all intents and purposes, the real, and the scientific account (phenomenal description) of the former must be (arbitrarily) held to exclude the possibility of a true cognition of the latter. All deductions from the "necessary" belief in self, all other "beliefs" (in reality, *cognitions*) which are inextricably bound up with it, must be held to be illusory; among others, the "illusion" respecting the "freedom of the Will," which "consists in supposing [agreeably to 'a belief which no hypothesis enables us to escape'!] that at each moment the *ego* is something more than the aggregate of feelings and ideas, actual and nascent, which then exists," namely, that it is a self, a principle of continuity or identity, possessing at least *power* enough to "hold together impressions and ideas." All this is gratuitous, extra-scientific absurdity, contradiction and dogmatism.

Mr. Spencer's method, then, is verbally to recognize the real along with the phenomenal, and then either to declare the former unknowable, or the belief in it deceptive, and then (again) to persuade himself that after all, in ascertaining (or hypothetically constructing) the law or order of the phenomenal, he has practically accounted (as it regards mind and morals) for the real. This confusion of a mind bred in the prejudices and assumptions of a sensational psychology seeking to overleap itself— this, and not the nature of the subject-matter of discussion itself, is the source of all Mr. Spencer's conspicuous ineptitudes and failures in psychology. These have been so often pointed out that, even did our space permit, it were needless to catalogue and demonstrate them in detail anew. The list would be as long as the number of mental functions which are verbally treated of in his psychology. I limit myself to the following observations.

What real or rational psychology has to treat of is what I have just termed, deliberately, *mental functions*. The names of these functions are many, as, consciousness, memory, intelligence, reason, will. All these, and others, are *active functions* of mind. They are all nominally discussed by Mr. Spencer, but only nominally; for he puts in the place of mental *functions* "mental states," which latter are for him not functions of mind, but of the nervous system.

Concerning the facts of consciousness, as such, Mr. Spencer declares that they are "absolutely without any perceptible or conceivable community of nature with the facts" of the nervous system. They are "truths of which the very elements are unknown to physical science." A "unit of feeling has nothing in common with a unit of motion" (which is the unit of all physical, and so, in particular, of all nervous processes), and "no effort enables us to assimilate them." And if such assimilation were possible, we should be warranted, by occasional reflections of our author, in supposing that it is the physical which must be assimilated to the psychical, rather than the contrary, since physical phenomena (we are reminded) are known only in and through, or as modes of, consciousness. While we are led "by a very indirect series of inferences to the belief that mind and nervous action are the subjective and objective faces of the same thing, we remain utterly incapable of seeing, and even of imagining, how the two are related. Mind still continues to us a something without any kinship to other things," etc.

And yet the case is not altogether so desperate; for "we have good reason to conclude that at the particular place in a superior nervous center where, in some mysterious way, an objective change or nervous action *causes* a subjective change or feeling, there exists a quantitative equivalence between the two." So that, instead of the absence of "any perceptible or conceivable community of nature" between "mind" and nervous action, there is evidence, sufficient to compel rational assent, that they are both subject to quantitative measurement, and that nervous action "causes" (*i.e.* of course, is the *physical cause* of) mental states.

I need not stop to comment at length upon the confusion in the use of the terms "objective" and "subjective," which is obvious everywhere in Mr. Spencer's "philosophy," and is implied, in particular, in the foregoing extracts. The objective, speaking absolutely, is for Mr. Spencer the unknowable; all that is known to us, be this physical or psychical, motion or conscious feeling, is subjective and, as such, purely phenomenal. From this point of view there is absolute community, and not contrast, between the physical and the psychical. But within the sphere of the subjective or phenomenal itself, Mr. Spencer makes (in accordance with popular phraseology) a new distinction of subject and object, which may have its measure of practical, scientific convenience, but which has no ontological significance. (It is the confusion of this phenomenal distinction with the before-mentioned absolute one, which lends to the so-called problem concerning the existence of the external world its transcendent importance and *ignis fatuus* brilliancy for the subjective "idealists" mentioned by Spencer, as well as for

Spencer himself.) According to this second distinction, the objective is the physical, or "matter and motion," while the subjective is consciousness. To this distinction, now, having only a relative validity, Mr. Spencer practically attributes an absolute character. He does this, namely, in as far as he surreptitiously invests the objective in this second sense (matter, motion, nervous system) with the causative, determining *power* which he elsewhere more accurately restricts to the region of the unknowable. The argument is, in effect, this: The subjective in the second sense is the constant concomitant of the objective in the second sense (this premise is unquestionably correct); hence, the objective in the second sense (more especially nervous system) is to the subjective in the second sense (conscious states) what the objective in the first sense (or, considered absolutely, the unknowable, but alone powerful, real) is to the subjective in the second sense (the powerless phenomenal, which includes *both nervous system and conscious states*). This confusion is the result of Mr. Spencer's failure to keep in mind the distinction between real and phenomenal (or scientific) causation. The latter is not, strictly speaking, causation at all, but only regular coexistence or sequence. In this non-literal sense of the term it is perfectly correct to say that nervous action is the "cause" of sensibly conscious states. But all that this means is that one set of phenomena (popularly, but not absolutely, termed objective) occurs in regular correspondence with another set of phenomena (which, absolutely considered, are just as objective, or, rather, just as little objective, as the former). Mr. Spencer, then, technically,—*i.e.* restricting the meaning of the term "cause" to its scientific significance,—is in the right as far as he really (not ostensibly) goes. But he is in the right only because all that which he explains of consciousness (*i.e.* brings under descriptive "law") is its phenomenal, non-characteristic side (not that side by virtue of which it is real mind, dynamic, synthetic, penetrative, comprehensive, "looking before and after"). And such explanation, again, he is enabled to offer only because nervous action and phenomenal conscious state are *not* without "conceivable community of nature," but, on the contrary, of identical nature, being both, while coordinate, and so distinct, within the sphere of the true "subjective" or phenomenal realm, yet identical, inasmuch as they are nothing but coördinate parts of *the same* realm. That which is antithetically opposed, not only to nervous action, but also to sensitive or affectional consciousness (on its passive, purely phenomenal side), as the real to the apparent, is mind in its intelligible, active functions, or, in other words, *mind as such*. This, I repeat, Mr. Spencer only verbally recognizes; in his reputed "explanations" of it, he eviscerates it, and contemplates only its phenomenal hull. Not content with the perfectly scientific endeavor to exhibit this hull, as subsisting in analogues or incidents of the processes summed up under the phrase "redistribution of matter and motion," he proceeds, practically, as if the hull were the kernel, and as if the statement of the "law" of the former were an exhibition of the vital substance or reality of the latter. Of course he thus contradicts in tendency his (false) demonstration of the unknowableness of reality, and illustrates its strict theoretic truth as regards himself (or any other purely sensational psychologist). The real is known to him in name, and he seeks to explain it by reducing it under the law and nature of the phenomenal.

Consciousness, we are told, is impossible without change of conscious state, and the concomitant analogue of such change is found in the molecular oscillations and the transmissions of motion which go on in the nervous system. "In the lowest conceivable type of consciousness—that produced by the alternation of two [psychical] states—there are involved the relations constituting the forms of all thought. And such an alternation of two [physical] states is just that which occurs in the ganglion connected with one of these rhythmically-moving organs." But the "relations constituting the forms of all thought," as Mr. Spencer tires not of remarking, are summed up in the terms "likeness and unlikeness." Let us admit this. But likeness and unlikeness are intelligible, not sensible, relations, the apprehension of which implies a characteristic *mental function*. This is a synthetic activity, which implies the bringing together of more than one "state" under the focus of a single view, or, in other words, comparison and identification or, as the case may be, discrimination. The "alternation of two states" of sensible consciousness may illustrate and serve to keep before the mind the terms of comparison, and the alternation of two states of "rhythmical" nervous motion may serve "in some mysterious way" to "cause" the conscious states, but the *recognition* of the likeness or unlikeness of the latter is an ideal, synthetic act, which, by Mr. Spencer's confession, is not identical with either of the "states" ("no consciousness without *change* of state," hence no consciousness of or in a single state), and hence not identical with both. But Mr. Spencer proceeds as if the contrary were true, and seeks by a thoroughly confusing and self-contradictory analysis to reduce likeness and unlikeness (which are qualitative relations), through a passing identification of them with the quantitative relations of "equality" and "inequality," to mere varieties of alternate, local change, or modes of motion. The terms of comparison are to be identified with the act of comparison, the analytic condition with the synthetic cause. This is precisely the method of the elder and younger Mill, and of all other purely sensational psychologists. But it does not recognize or explain, it simply explains away, the first or most elementary characteristic of *real* consciousness.

Now, it is just such a reduction of synthetic, real act, to analytic, phenomenal state, which Mr. Spencer attempts throughout his psychology. Knowledge, we are told, is of relations, the discernment of which is the peculiar function of intellect. The "immediate terms, or the ultimate components of the terms, between which relations are established in every cognition," are "epi-peripheral feelings, real or ideal." But now, as before, in the particular case of the relations of likeness and unlikeness, so in the case of relations universally, Mr. Spencer (yielding to the like blinding prepossession with his forerunners,—the elder Mill, for special example,) seeks to identify relation, in nature, with its terms. These terms are alleged "feelings." The establishment or recognition of a relation between them is an ideal, synthetic act, which contemplates both terms, and is identical in nature with neither. Not so says Mr. Spencer. A feeling is "any portion of consciousness which occupies a place [sic] sufficiently large to give it a perceivable individuality," etc. A relation is "characterized by occupying no appreciable part of consciousness." A feeling is "suspected" and "scientifically" held to be a compound of nervous shocks. A single nervous shock is imperceptible and hence "constitutes" no feeling. "Each relational feeling may in fact be regarded as one of those nervous shocks which we suspect to be the units of composition of feeling." So then "intellectual" relation is in reality "relational feeling," but not perceptible. It occupies "no appreciable part of consciousness." It is one of those nervous shocks which are singly imperceptible and must be compounded in order to give true feeling. And so, then, the "relational element" of knowledge, which is rightly held by Mr. Spencer to be the fundamental and characteristic one and the true object of intelligence, is not "appreciable in consciousness," is not "given" for recognition, and so is not known at all; and so there is no knowledge! — It is true, the "relational element," as such, is not given in sensible, static consciousness, but in rational, dynamic self-consciousness, for it is a characteristically ideal *function*; it is intelligible, and not sensible. But Mr. Spencer, having an eye to recognize only the *fact* of the intelligible, but not its substance, seeks to reduce it to the sensible, and ends by making it psychologically less than that, namely, nothing. (Spencer's account of the "relational element" in knowledge might be turned about and its absurdity exhibited from other points of view, did space permit or the occasion require it.)

It is in a similar manner that memory, prevision, inference, reason and volition are "explained." The something "which holds together impressions and ideas" (the synthetic power), which Mr. Spencer had recognized, through a necessary but (for him) inscrutable "belief," as the reality of mind, disappears here, as well as elsewhere, under a dissolving analysis which we are practically required to regard as exhaustive. The whole result is to set before us, in the way partly of true and partly of hypothetical description, what mind is *felt* to be (in the sensuous sense of this term as it is employed in sensational psychology), and not what it is intelligibly *known* to be. We have, according to the originally professed intention, an account of certain appearances only. This is the perfectly scientific work which pure physiological psychology is still prosecuting with success, and were, on Spencer's part, all very well, if a lack of clear philosophical insight did not lead him to palm off his work upon himself, and to seek to palm it off upon others, as a complete account of man in his practical and true reality. We are treated to a "*psychologie sans âme*"—to a mass of real or hypothetical statistics concerning the phenomena, in connection with which mind reveals its activity, and are vainly invited to contemplate in this ourselves, according to our final reality. To ask for more is to yield to an "ancient or mediæval bias," and to be guilty of anthropomorphism! One would say that our conception of man cannot well be too anthropomorphic.

This account of Mr. Spencer's doctrine is not exaggerated, for, in addition to the evidence of its correctness furnished on nearly every page of the "Principles of Psychology," the crowning proof is furnished in the nature of Mr. Spencer's ethical conceptions. These (which I must not now discuss in exhaustive detail) rest on a basis specially prepared in the "Psychology," though (professedly) generally founded, like the views expressed in all of Mr. Spencer's works, on the doctrine or law of evolution.

That which characteristically marks Mr. Spencer's attitude in treating of man as a moral being is the same thing which we have observed in regarding his treatment of man as "mind"; it is the pertinacious determination to put the "outward appearance" in the place of the "heart," to substitute the scientific history of the changing phenomenal for the philosophic recognition and demonstration of the real, in its eternal and unchanging power and truth, to install the natural man in the place of the spiritual man, the apparent self in the place of the true self. Ideal truth is to be assimilated to sensible "fact"—with the same result, in kind, of which we have caught a broad glimpse in the "Psychology," namely, that the real, synthetic, vital, while nominally "explained" (*i.e.* hypothetically described) in terms of the sensible, in reality is analyzed away, and becomes less than nought. The specifically human is interpreted (?) in terms of the sub-human. The instrument and concomitant condition becomes the agent. The limitation becomes, not "wings and means," but the thing limited. The law of nervous action is identified with the law of all morality (as, previously, with the law of all intelligence). Pleasure and pain, the sensitive concomitants and more or less remote signs of essential good and evil, are substituted for good and evil themselves. Thus apparent good and evil alone are recognized, and these are measured by reference to apparent pleasure and pain, not true pleasure and pain by reference to absolute good and evil. The perfect man is the man whose nervous organization is perfectly adapted to surrounding physical conditions. He is sensitive flesh and blood alone, and not spirit. Morality is the irresponsible result of physico-organic evolution, not the self-sustaining work, as it is the self-imposed requirement, of the ideal, true man. To the true, spiritual man, endowed with conscience (*i.e.* with substantive self-consciousness, the consciousness of the true nature of the real, vital, but for Spencer "unknowable" and practically illusory, self, and of the law which must be followed in order to be true to it) and an energetic will thoroughly under the control of conscience, and living at any incomplete stage in the general history of evolution (now, for example), life would be "wearisome" (*i.e.* painful), and "in so far wrong." Nay, it must speedily result in "death of self, or posterity, or both." But what? Of the true self, or only of the present physical integument of self? Of the latter only, which, with the physiologically determined, sensitive consciousness connected with it, is the only self that Mr. Spencer's ethics contemplates. The man whose morality is in advance of his time (*i.e.* in advance of the general stage of evolution reached in his time) is to be held, for the reasons just mentioned, to live to no purpose. Jesus of Nazareth was such a man. Indeed the christian centuries have held that — irrespective of any theories respecting the comparative evolution of his nervous organization — he lived a life of such absolute truth to the real, living, super-physical self as to become the sole historic illustration of the perfect man. The result was that "death of self" of which Mr. Spencer speaks. Yet he lived to greater purpose than any other before or since his time, and he furnishes the most typical instance of the reality of the ("unknowable") ideal as—not an inscrutable "force"—but a true, intelligible, spiritual power to shape and mould a world's destinies.

I have said that in Mr. Spencer's ethics, as in his psychology, the "real, synthetic, vital," which for him is professedly the unknowable, is recognized in terms and then really explained away by identification with the phenomenal. The real in mind we found exhibited in synthetic, ideal functions. The real in morality involves just such functions. They are all well summed up (by implication) in the word "purpose." A strictly moral act is purposed, intended. Moral energy manifests itself in the realization of definite purposes. Moral purpose implies a "looking before" to an ideal end, the accomplishment of which is recognized as a duty (or, in perfected morality, as a privilege). This ideal anticipation and recognition is a synthetic intellectual function; the practical realization of the conceived purpose is an active moral function. All this is more or less explicitly recognized by Mr. Spencer in terms, but in the practical development of his views completely disappears from sight, being merged in something other than itself. The ethical is held not to be intrinsically differentiated from the non-ethical. The transition from the latter to the former is "gradual"—the same thing which, in the "Psychology," was affirmed of the transition from the simple nervous shock to the "most transcendent" functions of intelligence. In other words, the transition is no transition. The higher is at most but a compound or complex repetition of the lower. It is *substantially* identical with the lower—just as, for example, relation was identical with the elementary unit of feeling; and the result, with reference to ethical ideas, is the same in kind which we witnessed in connection with Mr. Spencer's treatment of the "relational," they are not explained, but explained away. Ethics is defined as a part of the theory of conduct in general, and conduct "excludes purposeless actions." Conduct is "either acts adjusted to ends, or the adjustment of acts to ends; according as we contemplate the formed body of acts, or think of the form alone." Here ideal purpose becomes at once identical with mechanical, matter-of-fact adjustment, and Mr. Spencer's allegation, that "Conduct in general" is "thus distinguished from the somewhat larger whole constituted by actions in general," is left, necessarily, without proof. The notion of *purpose*, as pointing to the effective and independent agency of an ideal, self-centered, personal and spiritual power, is wholly eliminated. ("Conduct" is a mechanical process, the compulsory outcome of past, evolutionary conduct.) Ethics has a "physical, biological, psychological, and sociological" aspect, and all these aspects are phenomenological incidents in the progress of physical evolution. But it has no peculiar or specific aspect of its own, and "can find its ultimate [*sic*] interpretations only in those fundamental truths [? *facts* of *appearance*] which are common to all of" the aspects named. This is equivalent to saying that ethics has, in common with all other topics of inquiry concerning things or beings in the physical universe, a physico-scientific side (which is perfectly true), and that while, abstractly considered, it must be admitted to have a philosophic, or real and vital and commanding, side, this is unknowable for us, and must be left out of the account, while we pay our exclusive attention and allow our final convictions to be determined by exclusive reference to the scientific side (which is gratuitously false — being an extra-scientific, negatively "philosophic," dogmatic assumption. It is interesting to note that philosophic truth, as truth grounded in the most profoundly real, rational, vital experience, is so "unknowable" to Mr. Spencer, that, just as, in psychology, conceptions other than his own must be held due, not to reasoned and experimental conviction, but to "ancient or mediæval bias," so, in ethics, whatever is not of physical or scientific "knowledge" [or pseudo-philosophical assertion] is a matter of unreasoned "creeds," of inscrutable and arbitary "revelation," or of unbridled fancy, and is "bequeathed" to us from a "past" epoch, within and since which, it is true, many fundamental ideas are admitted to have undergone no historic evolution or change, but which is nevertheless for some indefinable reason worthy only of distrust, if not of contempt. As though ethical philosophy had never existed, and had never had a rational justification! As though Kant, for example, had never lived and spoken! And as though *man* were not — not only an historic, but also — a present *reality*, possessing in his own living spirit an unchanging and inexhaustible source of ultra-phenomenal truth — at least, concerning himself!)

What is insufficient and false about Mr. Spencer's ethics is, therefore, not any genuinely scientific, or, if you please, evolutionary element which may be in it, but the treatment of this element as though it concealed, instead of, in its real and due measure, revealing the super-phenomenal (or super-scientific), philosophic element, the element of vital, self-luminous (because rational and spiritual) reality, the object of living and hence spiritual self-consciousness. The consequence of this error is the contemplation of man, in common with the whole universe, as the subject and scene only of purely mechanical, automatic, irresponsible and unreasoned processes. The special source of the error, as it regards the treatment of ethics, is found in Mr. Spencer's psychology, where personality is eliminated as inscrutable and, therefore, practically unreal (and in its place is substituted, as before noted, the "aggregate of feelings and ideas, actual and nascent," which exists at each moment), and where freedom, the immediate, conscious attribute of personality, is consequently denied. Such elimination, substitution and denial are purely arbitrary. They are neither required nor justified by pure science, and are in direct contradiction with experimental truth. They are part and parcel of a pure prejudice, of a gratuitous predetermination to regard the knowable universe of being under the one category of mechanism.

This category presents itself in thought at once upon looking at the whole field, or at any portion of the field, of *phenomena,* as such, and exclusively. What is there viewed is simply isolable, opaque, surface *facts* of "motion and configuration" (in the language of Professor Clerk Maxwell), together with their matter-of-fact order of co-existence and sequence. The *truth* which explains them is not identical with the facts themselves, nor with the laws of their order (which "laws" are nothing more than a convenient summing up of the facts themselves). Mr. Spencer finds this "truth" in an impenetrable "Force" or (as he alleges) *contradictory* "First Cause." It is not contained in the laws of these facts that they are automatic, blindly self-determining, and withdrawn from the control (or better, not instancing the present activity) of rational power. This may be the first appearance *to us;* this may be the first interpretation which we place upon the facts. But in thus interpreting them according to first appearance we are going behind the facts themselves, and this, too, not with the aid of reasoned, philosophical insight, nor with the authority of science, but on the untrustworthy wings of a rude imagination. This is not science, but anthropomorphism, and anthropomorphism in the most superficial sense of this term. It is of this that Mr. Spencer is unquestionably guilty. And this fault coheres with his definition of true causation, whether in "mind" or in "matter," as the operation of inscrutable, hence non-rational, non-spiritual, wholly unintelligible power or "force"—an efficient Naught, as empty of significance or of reality as its anthropomorphic synonym, Fate.

Positive, affirmative, reasoned philosophy, resting on the only true substantive *experience* (= etymologically, *trial, proving*) possible for man, is also guilty (?) of anthropomorphism, but in a higher, nay, the highest sense of this expression. Of this it is neither ashamed nor vain. It is impelled to it by the logic of (not phenomena alone, but) reality. It, too, looks upon all causation as the operation of power — but not simply of power in name (whence termed unknowable), but of real, known, intelligible, and hence rational, spiritual, power. It, too, admits necessity; not, however, the necessity of fate, but the necessity of the Best. It not only recognizes, but glories in, scientific law (be this properly termed Evolution, or something else), because it sees in this the finger of intelligence working toward an intelligible, rational, "divine event," the manifestation of the Good. It believes in "invariable and universal law," in every sense in which this expression is capable of rational or really scientific significance, because it recognizes, in the power which sustains it, unvarying (because perfect) and universal reason and goodness. But it does not believe that descriptive law (the only sort known to exact science), because observable in the phenomenal results of all activities, whether divine or human, is a fatalistic, iron power to determine, as by constraint, the order of those activities. It believes in mechanism, first, because it witnesses mechanism as a phenomenal fact; and, secondly, because it sees in it the necessary *means*, or instrument, through which the unchanging *ends* of perfect reason, perfect spirit, perfect good must be reached. But it does not commit the absurdity of supposing that the instrument practically creates itself and is subservient to the ends which are accomplished through it, simply by accident. As the characteristic essence of man it recognizes a true, self-centred, spiritual, potential personality — at once self-illumining, because rational, and also illumined through its kinship and vitally dependent relation to the divine source of all *true*, and hence *spiritual*, being. Through his vital self-consciousness (which, on the moral side, is conscience) philosophy insists that man is placed in immediate — not sensible, but intelligible — relation to the root of his real being and, *pro tanto*, to the ultimate nature of universal being. In this dynamic, essentially living (not "biological") consciousness are given immutable norms of thought and of moral judgment, whose vital power is exhibited in all men (and even, *mutatis mutan-*

dis, in the whole physical universe without restriction), but of which many may not be explicitly conscious, and which many may deny in terms, though never wholly in practice. The history of human morals discloses a series of variously successful, or unsuccessful, attempts to determine how these norms are in practice to be applied, or how men *ought* to act. No system of morals will ever be able to dictate beforehand for every man how he shall, in each case, solve this practical question, for the special cases are infinitely numerous, and the determination how one shall act often permits only an instant's deliberation. And here lies the place of each man's own responsibility, the place where his freedom is to be realized and to be used as a sacred trust, and the place where his dignity, his worth, his real, ultra-phenomenal, human substance are to be manifested and vindicated. And here, too, is the place where man finds his own perfect freedom in *self-imposed* necessity, in conscious, energetic maintenance, on the one hand, of the law of his own ideal being, and, on the other, of the ideal law of the universal Power, or of God, which, as Providence, coöperates with him (whether according to a "law of evolution," or otherwise) to sustain his well-directed efforts, or to thwart them if ill-directed, and to bring forth the fruits of universal good. This "anthropomorphism" is of the true kind. It gives to man the true "form of man," as he is immediately *known* (not *sensibly felt*), as he is in his ever-present reality, and not simply as a phenomenon. And in interpreting reality universally, or absolutely, after the same type; in other words, in proclaiming divine Spirit, God, as the king and fount of being, it proceeds according to the rational necessities of thought, or according to the rational necessities of the problem itself. The Absolute Reality, which is in the first instance the Unknown, it conceives in terms of known reality, and finds that no other procedure is "congruous" with all the facts of man's nature and the nature of things. This procedure, whereby not only man, but the whole universe, is placed in intelligible continuity, though not identity, with the Absolute Reality, or Supreme Cause, is surely more rational than to term the latter unknowable, and then to invest it with irrational attributes of mechanistic fate, of which, strictly speaking, the whole universe furnishes no scientific example, and for which the only warrant is the confessed "imbecility" (or *atony*) of thought and the undisciplined flights of sensuous imagination.

True philosophy is catholic. It welcomes science as in truth its handmaid. It reveres religion, which is but the faithful love and service of the supreme object of philosophy's demonstrations. But it insists that things distinct shall not be identified with each other, nor adulterated by admixture of elements foreign to themselves.

From this point of view we are certainly justified in insisting, in special behalf of British philosophy, that the *coup de grâce* be at last administered to the idea which has so long had all the power of a superstition, that so-called empirical, phenomenally descriptive, sensational, or physiological psychology, or that physical science, be its highest law evolution or gravitation, is, *as such*, either philosophy or any specific part of philosophy, or has any competence whatever to answer, even negatively, philosophical questions. Its only proper attitude with reference to such questions is that of the pure geologist, for example, with reference to problems (we will say) in political economy. Questioned with regard to these, he will, speaking as a geologist, simply say, "I know nothing about them." British promoters of physiological psychology, æsthetics, ethics, etc., whom the nature of the case does not instruct to this effect, may, let us hope, be led to pause and reflect, when the greatest living leader in their line of scientific inquiry, Prof. Wundt, enforces (in his *Logik*, 1880) this view in language too forcible to be mistaken or, one would suppose, unheeded, and, more, urges, as the conception of the universe to which the philosophical interpretation of science inclines with the force of overwhelming probability, a conception generically identical with the one which has just been set forth.

Let science grow, by all means, conquering the realm of changing phenomena, and ensuring to man the empire of physical nature. But let not this kind of knowledge obscure for us — what it can never change — the immutable pillars of vital reality and everlasting truth.

www.ingramcontent.com/pod-product-compliance
Lightning Source LLC
Chambersburg PA
CBHW032027220426
43664CB00006B/390